Seeking a Lasting City

*The Church's Journey
in the Story of God*

D0107212

Other titles in the Heart of the Restoration series:

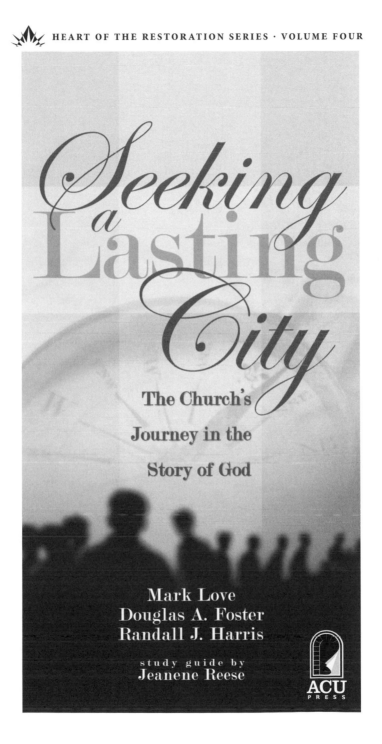

Seeking a Lasting City

The Church's Journey in the Story of God

Mark Love
Douglas A. Foster
Randall J. Harris

study guide by
Jeanene Reese

ACU
PRESS

SEEKING A LASTING CITY:
The Church's Journey in the Story of God

The Heart of the Restoration, Volume 4
Douglas A. Foster, Series Editor

ACU Box 29138
Abilene, TX 79699
www.acu.edu/acupress

Volume Editors · Sherry Rankin & William Rankin
Study Guide · Jeanene Reese
Cover · Sarah Bales
Author Photo · Steve Butman Photography
Book design & typesetting · William Rankin

This book is set in Adobe® Minion Pro 11 / 13, a font drawn by Robert Slimbach that was originally issued in 1990 and issued as an OpenType® font in 2000. This book was composed in Adobe® InDesign™ on an Apple® Macintosh®.

ISBN 0-89112-039-4

LCCN 2005922320

¶ 10 9 8 7 6 5 4 3 2 1

Dedication

The authors wish to acknowledge the following churches that have shaped them spiritually and supported them through the years. Here, they have learned and are learning what it truly means to be the church of Christ.

Mark wishes to thank

Eastland Church of Christ · Eastland, Texas
Springfield Church of Christ · Springfield, Oregon
Eastside Church of Christ · Portland, Oregon
University Church of Christ · Abilene, Texas
Park Row Church of Christ · Arlington, Texas
East County Church of Christ · Gresham, Oregon
Highland Church of Christ · Abilene, Texas

Doug wishes to thank

Fourth Street Church of Christ · Tuscumbia, Alabama
Highland Park Church of Christ · Muscle Shoals, Alabama
West End Church of Christ · Nashville, Tennessee
Bellevue Church of Christ · Nashville, Tennessee
Jackson Park Church of Christ · Nashville, Tennessee
Minter Lane Church of Christ · Abilene, Texas

Randy wishes to thank

Bentonville Church of Christ · Bentonville, Arkansas
White Station Church of Christ · Memphis, Tennessee
Donelson Church of Christ · Nashville, Tennessee
South 11th and Willis Church of Christ · Abilene, Texas
Highland Church of Christ · Abilene, Texas

Contents

Acknowledgments

We wish to thank a number of colleagues who have read and commented on this manuscript at various stages of its production. These people contributed immensely to the thinking and writing that went into the book, though we wish to acknowledge that we alone are responsible for its final content. We're thankful for the guidance and support of the *Heart of the Restoration* series directors and of our Salado Group colleagues. In particular, we want to thank Jack and Jeanene Reese, Jeff Childers, Bill and Sherry Rankin, and Mark Hamilton for their assistance.

In her work on the study guide, Jeanene Reese wishes to thank the authors, the editors, and her colleagues at ACU who provided assistance and support. She's especially grateful for assistance from Mark Hamilton, who suggested an investigation of David Lipscomb and the Nashville cholera outbreak of 1873 for the case study, and Wimon Walker, who wrote the "Special Announcement" in the scenario "Politically Correct or Not?" and who collaborated with her in the development of this scenario. She also wishes to thank her husband, Jack, for his support and help.

The writing of a book is always a painful activity, the literary equivalent to giving birth. And working with several authors makes the process even more complex. Yet in the end, the difficulties of working collaboratively are overwhelmed by the joys of bringing forth something that—while by no means perfect—is, we pray, a positive

v

contribution to the current discussions in Churches of Christ and elsewhere about the identity of Christ's church.

Mark Love
Douglas A. Foster
Randall J. Harris

Abilene, Texas
July 2005

Preface to the Series

From its beginning in 1906, Abilene Christian University has existed as an institution of higher education to serve the fellowship of the Churches of Christ. While we welcome students and supporters from a variety of Christian traditions who are sympathetic with our Christ-centered focus, we know who our primary constituents are. ACU's Bible Department, now the College of Biblical Studies, has for almost a century been a guiding light for our fellowship through its contributions in Christian scholarship and ministry. Thousands of missionaries, ministers, elders, teachers, and Christian servants have come under the positive influence of these godly professors. They have steadfastly upheld the lordship of Christ, the authority of Scripture, and the necessity of living a life of Christian service through the church.

Abilene Christian University, in conjunction with its ACU Press, launched the *Heart of the Restoration* series with *The Crux of the Matter* in 2001 and now continues it with the fourth volume, *Seeking a Lasting City*. This volume deals with ecclesiology—the way the church continues to shape and transform God's people. It follows volumes on the heritage of Churches of Christ, the reading of Scripture, and the identity and nature of Christ. The next volume—the final one in this series—will address worship.

We pray that this series will help stimulate discussion and make a meaningful contribution to the fellowship of Churches of Christ and beyond. The authors of these volumes are all faculty members in ACU's College of Biblical Studies. In these books, they have sought to model a biblical spirit of unity in Christ, with individual perspectives on the details of the gospel message. Above all, the writers of these books are all committed to the lordship of Jesus Christ and to his church, and they are committed to restoring the spirit of the Christian faith "once for all delivered to the saints."

My special thanks go to Dr. Jack Reese who shared the dream of this series with me from the beginning. Dr. Doug Foster, as the editor of the series, has made the dream into a reality. My thanks go also to our benefactors, who believed that the project would result in a clearer articulation of our faith and identity in Churches of Christ at the dawning of a new century.

> Now to him who is able to do immeasurably more than all we ask or imagine, according to his power that is at work within us, to him be glory in the church and in Christ Jesus throughout all generations, for ever and ever! Amen.
>
> *Ephesians 3:20–21*

Royce Money, President
Abilene Christian University

1

In the Beginning...

Family Stories

Stories. They get in your bloodstream and define who you are. When you sit around a dinner table with your family, you tell stories about your past. Some stories produce laughter, like the time Grandpa drove the pickup into a ditch when a bee got trapped inside. Some we tell with wonder, like the day a child was born, or baptized, or married. Still others we hear again with pain, like the tragic car accident that claimed family members. These tales, taken together, are the glue that holds people together, a kind of shared language that means you're connected. All you have to say is a word or phrase, and your family members nod knowingly. Knowing the stories means you're a part of each other's lives, a member of the family. When you meet someone you care about, you almost immediately begin telling your stories. Why? Because you want that person to be connected with you as well.

Knowing stories doesn't just connect people in the here-and-now, though. Knowing stories links us to the past as well as to the future. Some of us have no idea who our great-great-grandparents were: where they worked, what foods they liked, their political opinions, whether they had blue eyes or brown. Except for an old photograph with a name scrawled on the back, they're strangers to us. But if stories about them have been handed down to us, we remember. Through those stories, even people long gone are still a part of our families. When we tell the stories to our children, the connections will continue.

It may seem strange to start a book about the church by talking about stories, but as with all families, stories play an important part in the church's life. The Bible starts with "in the beginning." It's a story, too. Not a fiction, to be sure, but a narrative. Something deep inside us responds; we want to know about those who have gone before us, to know what started "once upon a time." What happens next? Who are the characters? As indispensable as the epistles are, we don't start toddlers off in Bible classes by reading them Ephesians or 1 Peter: we start them with stories—Noah and the flood, David and Goliath, Lazarus's resurrection, the feeding of the five thousand. Why? Because children love stories; it's in their DNA.

God understands this; in fact, he made us this way. As he explained his covenant requirements to the Israelites after their escape from Egypt, he told them:

> "When your children ask you in time to come, "What is the meaning of the decrees and the statutes and the ordinances that the Lord our God has commanded you?" then you shall say to your children, "We were Pharaoh's slaves in Egypt, but the Lord brought us out of Egypt with a mighty hand. The Lord displayed before our eyes great and awesome signs and wonders against Egypt, against Pharaoh and all his household. He brought us out from there to bring us in, to give us the land he promised on oath to our ancestors. Then the Lord commanded us to obey all these statutes, to fear the Lord our God, for our lasting good, so as to keep us alive, as is now the case. If we diligently observe this entire commandment before the Lord our God, as he has commanded us, we will be in the right." (Deuteronomy 6:20–25)

2   When the children ask the meaning of God's commands, they are to be given a story, for the story gives the commands their meaning.

Like the Israelites, we Christians are the chosen people of God, and knowing our own story is equally essential—not in a dry, academic kind of way, but for building vital, spirit-filled churches that are empowered to carry on the tale.

A Different Kind of Family Conversation

The nature of the church seems to be one of our favorite family topics. Overall, this is a good thing. After all, the church is one of the Bible's favorite topics, as well. Due to the influence of individualism in the larger culture, many religious groups hardly talk about the church, or community, at all. In contrast, many of our most passionate conversations in Churches of Christ tend to be about matters related to the church. For example, we spend a lot of time discussing what is allowable in worship. Who can do what and when? Can we use praise teams? What music is best? What role, if any, can women and children have in worship? We also spend a lot of time talking about leadership. Who can be a leader? What does a leader do? What does it mean for an elder to be the husband of one wife? What in the world do deacons do? Can leaders be called things other than elders or deacons? These are all concerns related to our understandings of the church. While these conversations occupy a lot of our energy, they are not always very productive. Too often, they produce more heat than light.

This is not just a recent problem. If what a family divides over is any indication about what they deem important, then the nature of the church has certainly been important to Churches of Christ. We divided over music in the church and how the church organized for world missions. We divided over whether or not the church could have Sunday schools, kitchens, or support orphanages from a congregation's budget. The church has always occupied our attention, but not always in the most productive ways.

Not surprisingly, our family story in Churches of Christ includes an impressive number of writings about the church. From Alexander Campbell's essays on "The

3

Ancient Order of Things" in his journal the *Christian Baptist*, to G. C. Brewer's *The Model Church* (1957), to the impressive spate of recent books, much ink has been spilled exploring the nature of the church. So, why are we adding our voices to this already well-established conversation? Is there anything left to say? Do we really need to say more?

> For other recent discussions of the church, see these titles:
>
> C. Leonard Allen, Richard T. Hughes, and Michael R. Weed's *The Worldly Church: A Call for Biblical Renewal* (1991);
>
> Everett Ferguson's *The Church of Christ: A Biblical Ecclesiology for Today* (1996);
>
> F. LaGard Smith's *The Cultural Church* (1992); and
>
> Tim Woodroof's *A Church that Flies: A New Call to Restoration in the Churches of Christ* (2000).

These are questions worth asking. Some readers will be concerned about the appearance of yet another book on ecclesiology (this is the established term for the doctrine of the church) because they fear our family conversations have placed too much emphasis on the church and not enough on Jesus. We share this concern. It is possible to make the church the end in itself and more important than the gospel that gave rise to it.

But on the other side of the coin, large numbers of young people in Churches of Christ do not think a person must be involved in any kind of church to be a good Christian as long as he or she has a personal relationship with Jesus. In this belief, they reflect the excessive individualism of much of early 21st century American religion. One of our students recently captured this perspective nicely. She related that she used to think of going to church the way she thought about going to a gym. A person who goes to a gym is more likely to stay in shape than a person who doesn't. Still, it is not essential to go to the gym to stay in shape. Nor, so she thought, is it essential to be a part of a church to be spiritual. Like this student, many dismiss the church as a nice, but non-essential, addition to personal salvation in Jesus Christ.

The church, however, is far too important in the purposes of God for it to be thought of as a personal, spiritual gym. The gospel has never just been about saving individuals but about creating a community where walls are broken down and humans are reconciled not only to God but to one another as well. Given the perspectives revealed by many of our students (and other church members we know), the topic of the church deserves more attention.

How can we give the church the attention it deserves without contributing to our sometimes excessive and divisive emphasis on it? Our understandings of the church need to be deepened without overwhelming the gospel itself. More to the point, we need to find ways to talk about the church that do not predictably result in a family feud. We want to bring attention to the topic of the church, but attention of a different sort. We want to understand the church in relation to the story of God.

We have written a "narrative ecclesiology." To do narrative ecclesiology is to place the doctrine of the church in the context of an unfolding story. We understand the church to be a story-formed, story-living community. By story, we do not mean "fiction," but a series of meaningful events that have a beginning, middle, and end. Efforts to understand the church are not best served by dividing it into categories or classifications. Rather, we understand the church best when we tell its story, paying particular attention to matters of plot, character, and meaning. The church is faithful when it lives within the story of God.

However, in Churches of Christ, we've often understood the church's faithfulness not primarily in terms of its story, but of its structures. We ask: what is the organization of the church? The name of the church? The worship of the church? The work of the church? This approach has an impressive legacy in our history. With these structures as our starting point, our efforts to reform inevitably focus on returning to the Bible and getting these things right. This approach, however, creates nagging questions. Is getting these structures right God's mission in the world? What happens when the structures are right, but there is no seri-

5

ous engagement of the gospel with the world? Moreover, the kind of precision in detail necessary to duplicate structures from one time and place to another is often difficult to find in the Bible. Does the Bible adequately support this kind of endeavor?

Church structures are important. But we believe those structures find their meaning and relevance by virtue of their connection to a story. It is possible to separate our understandings of the church from the story that gives the church its life. And when this separation occurs, the church loses the perspective necessary to participate faithfully in God's mission in the world.

Nothing provides perspective like a story. One congregation we know fought and fought over whether or not to replace their dilapidated old folding chairs that they used weekly in worship. At one level, the choice for new seating was a no-brainer. Not only were the chairs old and unsightly, they were dangerous. A few actually collapsed under unsuspecting worshippers. Still, the congregation fought over whether to replace them, as if the kingdom of God itself were at stake. Only when they saw the issue in light of their congregational story did they understand why they were fighting. For the original members of the congregation, the chairs symbolized the founding vision of their group to be radically non-institutional. That original vision had been subject to several little compromises along the way—the building of a traditional church building and the hiring of a full-time preaching minister, to name a few. The chairs were an emotional last straw. But to others who had joined the congregation's story later, the chairs were an embarrassing symbol of the disorganized way things were done in other aspects of the church's life. These more recent members were drawn to the congregation because of the theological freedom they found but were embarrassed because services never started on time and because decisions seemed to be made haphazardly. For them, the chairs were a symbol of what was wrong with their community. The telling of the church's story allowed the perspective necessary to see the chairs in a

6

proper light. Once the story was remembered, the chairs became chairs again and the congregation was able to talk with reduced rancor about its mission and vision.

In some ways, Churches of Christ have been like this congregation, arguing about structures without the perspective provided by the church's journey in the story of God. By gaining a narrative perspective, we hope to impact the kind of conversations we have about the church. We harbor no illusions that this book will cause all conflict over the church to cease. We do hope, however, that it will be a different kind of conflict. Passionate disagreement, after all, can be a vital sign of health. Still, we would rather the passionate conversation focus more on mission and vision than on chairs.

In fact, we think this is precisely the advantage of a narrative approach to understanding the church. Story and mission go together. The biblical record reminds us that when story becomes secondary to form, mission is lost. When the story is forgotten, doing worship correctly displaces living justly, loving mercy, and walking humbly with God. And when the church becomes more a set of structures and less a way of life in the world, its focus becomes obsessively inward, and it thinks of its life as an end in itself rather than a life lived for others. When this happens—when the church's focus moves excessively inward—quarreling and controversy rear their ugly heads. The family discussion becomes passionate in divisive ways, and we generate more heat than light. In fact, the church devours itself.

When narrative frames the church's self-understanding, though, God remains the primary actor in the story. Story allows plot to clarify mission, and it also allows characters to find their proper role in relation to one another. So a narrative approach allows the church to find its proper place in relation to the coming of Jesus, the sending of the Spirit, and the gospel of the Kingdom of God. In light of this, a narrative approach reminds congregations that their primary point of reference is not another congregation, but God himself. Consequently, conversations about the church that begin with God produce less judgment and more mercy. They may be passionate, even produce significant disagreement, but

7

they proceed within the nature and character of God himself. They bear the possibility not only of heat but of light as well.

Seeing the Church as God's Story

So how does narrative help us talk about the church? If we don't define it by its structures, forms, and boundary markers, how do we look at it? What will it mean to understand the church through its story? Just like a family, the church has a story that connects each generation to the others. We are linked not through human DNA but by the blood of Christ, our elder brother and spiritual forebear. Instead of talking about the problems and needs of the church exclusively in the here-and-now, divorced from other chapters of the story, we want to look at today's church through the lens of a narrative that is larger, stretching back through Pentecost and beyond and forward to the great feast in the New Jerusalem. Viewing the church this way has many advantages.

First, looking at the church narratively reflects the truth of our experience. People don't live in a theory or a concept. If someone were to ask you about your church experience, you'd most likely tell stories. Some would be wonderful and some dreadful, but all of them would reflect what it means to be the church. This lived reality, both glorious and terrible, in fact is the church. We can't try to make it some romanticized ideal; the church is the living, enfleshed people of God—warts and all.

Second, narrative prevents us from over-identification with external characteristics. When these characteristics become more important than the story that gives them meaning, powerful ritual devolves into mere ritualism. For example, in Churches of Christ we have been blessed with the great legacy of weekly participation in the Lord's Supper. But most of us have had the experience somewhere along the way of engaging in Communion with a group that was so divided and antagonistic to one another that the Supper of the Lord became an ugly parody of its true meaning: unity in Christ. Or if we're not careful, the Lord's Supper may become so routine that we do it with little or no thought and meaning attached. The actions may be "cor-rect," but the true significance is obscured because the story isn't made the focus. Many passages in the Old Testament show the peril of religious activities that have gotten separated from their deep meanings in God's ongoing story (Amos 5:21–24, Micah 6:6–8, Jeremiah 7:1–15, Isaiah 58:1–5 for exam-ple). The solution, of course, is not to dismiss such actions and characteristics as meaningless or unimportant but to keep them vital and alive by constantly filling them with the power of God's unfolding story.

> God wants the hearts of his people, not empty ceremonies:
>
> I hate, I despise your festivals, and I take no delight in your solemn assem-blies.... Take away from me the noise of your songs; I will not listen to the melody of your harps, but let justice roll down like waters, and righteous-ness like an ever flowing stream.
>
> *Amos 5:21–24*

Third, viewing the church in terms of a narrative reminds us of the importance of every moment—includ-ing ours. The story is always at stake. Many of us are weary of "crisis" language when it comes to the present situation in Churches of Christ, and it may well be a bit alarmist (we are often prone to see our particular moment in history as the most crucial). But in a good story, every chapter is important and advances the story in some way. Throughout church history, pivotal moments have gener-ated actions and decisions that sent the church in certain directions—sometimes for centuries. Whether we are at such a moment now will only be certain from the vantage of the future, when consequences are more fully played out and the implications of decisions made now are seen in their fullness. Still, seeing the church not as a static thing but as an unfolding story means every generation of Christians must take responsibility for its chapter. We are all with God, even now, writing this story. To receive and pass it on faithfully is an awesome responsibility.

Fourth, narrative points to the "unfolding" nature of God's mission, especially its "already" but "not yet" aspects.

As Christians, we live between the times—between God's ultimate revelation of his plan in the life, death, and resurrection of Jesus Christ and the consummation of this plan when "every knee will bow and every tongue will confess that Jesus is Lord" (Romans 14:11).

Despite physical, emotional, and mental anguish, we are "already" living out the story of God's triumph over sin, sorrow, disease, death, and the devil himself in the resurrection of Jesus Christ. As Paul says,

> We do not want you to be unaware, brothers and sisters, of the affliction we experienced in Asia; for we were so utterly, unbearably crushed that we despaired of life itself. Indeed we felt that we had received the sentence of death. He who rescues us from so deadly a peril will continue to rescue us; on him we have set our hope that he will rescue us again. (2 Corinthians 1:8–10)

But this story is "not yet" finished. We continue to live in a world attacked by Satan and the powers of darkness "because he knows his time is short" (Revelation 12:12). We do not experience the total triumph of God in this world at present, nor do we expect to until God in his time turns the last page. We live out the story of God's ultimate victory in the resurrection of Jesus Christ while awaiting the final triumph.

Fifth, viewing the church as a story shows that the church is not the end in itself. The church is not only the result of God's work in Christ to create new community but the instrument whereby that reconciling work continues. Coming out of a couple of centuries of what can only be described as denominational competition, we sometimes slip into thinking that the whole point of evangelism is to get a person into our church rather than some other. Add to this the peculiar American notions of success, and the goal becomes seeing how big our particular congregation can get. Church growth becomes the point.

That's not to imply that dying congregations are preferable to those that are growing. However, when we see the church as a chapter in the story of the unfolding mission of God, the size of a congregation at any particular time, whether it is growing or declining, or even whether it survives or disappears, is less important than how it plays its role in the ministry of reconciliation entrusted to it by God in this time and place.

Sixth, looking at the church narratively is better than a more static view at reminding us that the church must include both continuity and change. If we focus primarily on the church's form and function, we are likely to think about the church only in our own particular context, which can produce serious distortions in our perceptions of what a church should be and do. Continuity comes from an awareness that we are just one part of God's story of relentless love and reconciliation brought fully to light in Jesus Christ. Losing sight of this story is a constant threat to the church. There are some sorry chapters in the church's history in which ego, power, ambition, and prestige have threatened to eclipse the story of redemption. But even in those dark moments, God has been at work and the story continues, new life emerging from the ashes.

Our claim in this book is that we are part of a story that goes back beyond the 18th century and the beginnings of the American Restoration Movement; back beyond the Protestant Reformation; back beyond the birth of the church on Pentecost; back even beyond Moses, Abraham, and the story of God's chosen people in the Old Testament. Our story goes back to the dawn of creation itself, when a loving God entered into relationship with his creatures. God's eternal faithfulness to this loving relationship is the source of the continuity of our story. There is just one story.

Yet there is more than continuity; there is also change, for this is a living story. Without change, we don't have a story but a statue. The relationship between God and humanity is real and thus constantly changing—sometimes in good ways and at other times in ways that are not so positive. As in any real life story, things are happening. Our lives aren't like static photographs; they're dynamic. Our family relationships constantly change, for instance. We don't relate to the three-year-old, thirteen-year-old, or twenty-three-year-old child in the same way, and the child relates differently to us as she grows, as well.

11

The church's relationship to God and the world is likewise in constant development. If it weren't, the church would be dead. So while we would expect to recognize certain aspects of the church in every time and place, we do not expect it to look exactly the same in each context. This notion of continuity and change is central to the whole idea of a story. If we don't have continuity, we may have sentences, but we don't have a story; on the other hand, if there's no movement, development, change, or action, there's no story, either.

Another problem with a static view of the church is that it leads Christians to misunderstand the gospel in a fundamental way—to see it as a set of propositions to be believed or a set of forms to be erected rather than a call to action in the world. Notice the striking ending to the Sermon on the Mount:

> Everyone then who hears these words of mine and acts on them will be like a wise man who built his house on rock.... And everyone who hears these words of mine and does not act on them will be like a foolish man who built his house on sand.... (Matthew 7:24–27)

The emphasis here is not on understanding, but doing. In the final analysis, the faithfulness of the church is determined not by what we claim to believe, but how we embody God's mission in the world. After all, even the demons have the right theology, according to James 2:19.

Seventh and finally, a narrative view replaces a defensive mentality with a sense of adventure and engagement—and in so doing reflects a deep understanding of what it means to be a restoration movement. Of course the story must be preserved and protected, but that's done precisely by living it out in the world.

If we do not see ourselves as part of God's ongoing story, the church's posture becomes totally defensive. There's nothing to do but protect the gains of the past, because once the structures are right and in place, the journey is over. God has ceased to inhabit the present and propel us to the future. Scripture, however, shows God as the one who does new and surprising things. The biblical narratives are full of God's unexpected reversals of the way the story should go. For instance, while Esau should be the child of promise, Jacob turns out to be. Shockingly, the Messiah of God is born in an animal barn, and the triumph of God is displayed on the cross—a symbol of shame. Churches must be open to God's creative re-direction of the story. Too often, they are more involved in protecting their legacy than in participating in God's unfolding and often surprising tale.

A defensive conception of church also prevents needed reform. The church's story as it unfolds in history is one of both faithfulness and failure. If there's no movement, the church cannot be led by God in directions that more fully embody God's kingdom agenda at each point along the way. For instance, while there is still much room for improvement, there's little doubt God has led us into deeper understanding of his mind on issues of race and diversity in the last half century in North America. On this issue, all of us are grateful that there has been movement. But it wasn't necessarily a movement that came from within. In surprising ways, God used the world to teach the church what our story really means in this area of life.

Conclusion: The Narrative Journey

So, in our discussion of what it means to be a church that pleases God, we don't start in the present, or even in the immediate past. In fact, our story begins long before the church had even been established. After all, God's loving plan to form a holy community did not begin in our time or even in the first century. He planned to have community with people from the moment he created them, and he sought out a chosen people when he selected Abraham. The Old Testament is thus not mere background but a crucial part of God's story. It's where we begin to learn about our spiritual family. The narrative journey continues through the New Testament as God moves us through his story's most dramatic and central episode—the life, death, and resurrection of Jesus Christ and the calling together of disciples to continue his mission in the world.

13

But even then we can't skip ahead to the 21st century. We must see how the story has unfolded in the time between Scripture and today because it's part of our family heritage—it's the story being lived out by our forebears. As such, it's fundamental to understanding our place in the narrative. Only after examining God's work in the past will we be able to turn to our own time and setting to discuss ways Christians can authentically live out this glorious story today.

Even as we write this, we are fully aware that there are competing visions of church out there and a certain amount of turmoil goes with that. The purpose and function of the church is an extremely sensitive issue because it's so vitally important to us all, and we certainly have no wish merely to be controversial. However, we live in a dark and wounded world that's in desperate need of a new story. We believe the church of Jesus Christ is the bearer of that story and that it can have a greater impact on a hurting world than it currently does.

Because we believe God continues to work in the world through the flawed vessel of his people, we write this book in the hope that it may, in some small way, help move our churches even closer to their goal of being "the fullness of Christ" in the world. Even so, we acknowledge that the church is always a pilgrim community, and although on this earth we strive constantly to grow more fully into God's eternal purpose, we know that we seek here no enduring city, but the city that is to come.…

2
The Old Testament & the People of God

"You have seen what I did to the Egyptians, and how I bore you on eagles' wings and brought you to myself. Now, therefore, if you obey my voice and keep my covenant, you shall be my treasured possession out of all the peoples. Indeed, the whole earth is mine, but you shall be for me a priestly kingdom and a holy nation…." The people all answered as one: "Everything the Lord has spoken we will do."

Exodus 19:4–8

My two roommates and I stumbled down the dark hallway to find our "hotel" room in the small village of Independence, Belize. In the course of one day we had traveled with fifteen others from a well-lit "civilization" complete with electricity, indoor plumbing, paved roads, and refrigerated rooms, to a darkened, sweltering land we did not know. We found that night that our accommodations included kerosene lamps, hard, dusty beds, chickens and all other manner of liberated animals with free run of the place, and even a drunk who, not having quite reached his bed, lay sprawled into the hallway. As I groped for my room in the dark that night, I felt like Dorothy in The Wizard of Oz *when she informed her dog, "We're not in Kansas anymore, Toto."*

What many of us found that week in this unfamiliar land was a clarified sense of what it means to be the people of God. Away from the usual props of our comfortable lives, we tasted the anxious joy of trusting God for our bearings. As a sent people with a mission, we discovered a clarity about our faith and witness in the world that we lacked in the confines of our settled worlds. We learned that the gospel did not belong only to us, but to the Belizeans as well. We found that some of the ways we talked about God were distant to their lives. So we learned from our new friends new ways of expressing the gospel as we served them and listened to them. Our strange environs and taxing mission required a rich community life built on prayer and a radical openness to one another. We shared everything we had with each other—wet-wipes, Jolly Ranchers®, water-soaked bandanas, Advil®, sunscreen, and mosquito repellent. Our evening meals at the end of a hot, exhausting day were banquets of thankfulness. I will never forget the rich worship we experienced one evening as we washed the dust of the day off each other's feet and shared together the Lord's Supper. I can still see the tear-streaked faces of my brothers and sisters as we confessed our sins to one another and spoke of the new perspectives we had gained on our life before God.

—Mark

We experienced something in that week common to the people of God throughout the Old Testament—that God often calls his people out of the familiar in order to form in them a distinct community that participates in his life for the sake of others. Sometimes this leaving is a deliverance from oppression. Sometimes the leaving is by the gracious invitation of God. Sometimes this leaving is in the seeming failure of exile. But in each case, leaving the land that is known is an occasion for God to form a people for his mission in the world.

Leaving is not the only movement of God's people we see in the Old Testament. They also *enter* a promised land. And they *settle* in the land with the hope of providing a contrasting way of life to the nations surrounding them. Still, as we will see, even in the "settledness" of the promised land, they are to live out of the formative memory of being God's pilgrim people: even in the promised land, they are to live as an Exodus people.

16

The Exodus & the People of God

The people of God are best understood as a story-formed, story-living people. It is striking how often Israel pauses to recite its story. Regardless of particular circumstances, Israel can always find their bearings by summarizing where they've been. However, they don't always recite all parts of their story. Some are more important than others—some give meaning to the rest. The list of stories that show up in these recitals is fairly predictable: the Creation, Abraham, Moses (the Exodus), David, and exile, but they don't appear with the same frequency. While some recitals begin with creation, most leave it out altogether. Abraham appears in many recitals, but not all. Some talk about David, while others do not. The only story found in all the recitals is that of the Exodus. In fact, several of the recitals begin with the Exodus. In many ways, Israel's story finds its center in God's act of deliverance in

The Story of Israel...

Notice how these recitals, typical of others found throughout the Old Testament, feature the story of the Exodus:

> When your children ask you in time to come, "What is the meaning of the decrees and the statutes and the ordinances that the LORD our God has commanded you?" then you shall say to your children, "We were Pharaoh's slaves in Egypt, but the LORD brought us out of Egypt with a mighty hand...."
>
> *Deuteronomy 6:20–24*

> And Joshua said to all the people, "...I sent Moses and Aaron, and I plagued Egypt with what I did in its midst; and afterwards I brought you out. When I brought your ancestors out of Egypt, you came to the sea; and the Egyptians pursued your ancestors with chariots and horsemen to the Red Sea. When they cried out to the LORD, he put darkness between you and the Egyptians, and made the sea come upon them and cover them; and your eyes saw what I did to Egypt.... I gave you a land on which you had not laboured, and towns that you had not built, and you live in them; you eat the fruit of vineyards and olive groves that you did not plant."
>
> *Joshua 24:2–13*

Other story recitals can be found in Deuteronomy 26:5–9; Nehemiah 9:6–37; Psalms 78, 105, 106, 135:8–12, 136; 1 Chronicles 16:8–36.

17

the Exodus. So in thinking about the story of the church, it's appropriate to begin where Israel often did when telling its story—at the dry banks on the freedom side of the Red Sea.

Moses and Miriam led the people in praise the day God drowned Pharaoh's army in the Red Sea. Those who passed through the waters were raised from a life of abject slavery to a new life of trusting freedom before the God who delivered them. What else could occur on the dry banks of freedom but liberated praise? God's mighty act of deliverance created a new community.

> Then Moses and the Israelites sang this song to the LORD:
> "I will sing to the LORD, for he has triumphed gloriously;
> horse and rider he has thrown into the sea.
> The LORD is my strength and my might,
> and he has become my salvation;
> this is my God, and I will praise him,
> my father's God, and I will exalt him."
>
> *Exodus 15:1–2*

The song of the redeemed breaks out in Exodus 15 because the Lord has heard the cries of the oppressed. The redeemed praise God because oppressors have been destroyed, "horse and rider thrown into the sea." The people who passed through the waters find themselves in a new place. Their praise punctuates the realization of a new world, a world not ordered by Pharaoh and his chaotic interests. The Exodus demonstrates that God can be moved to establish a new order in the view of all nations. The Lord is not the patron of the status quo working for the interests of those in power. This one who redeemed slaves will overcome chaos for the praise of his glory. In the Exodus, God delivers a people for the world-ordering work of praise.

It might seem odd to begin a book on the church in Exodus. Churches of Christ have been, after all, interested in the New Testament church. In fact, many of our traditional understandings of Scripture depict the Old Testament as the constitution for Israel and the New Testament as the constitution for the church. Such a conception, however, ignores the fact that the New Testament writers find their images of the church in the portraits of God's people found in the Old Testament. No portrait of God's people in the Old Testament is more prominent than the one that emerges in the Exodus story.

Crossing the sea on dry ground. Drinking water from a rock. Eating manna from heaven. The mighty acts God performs for his people form the backdrop for the dramatic words of covenant offered to Israel at the foot of Mt. Sinai (Exodus 19:1–9). In this dramatic moment, God claims a people. Here a people commit to the way of the God who has rescued them.

> **The New Testament Uses Old Testament Images…**
>
> Peter, an apostle of Jesus Christ, *To the exiles* of the Dispersion in Pontus, Galatia, Cappadocia, Asia, and Bithynia, who have been chosen and destined by God the Father and sanctified by the Spirit to be obedient to Jesus Christ and *to be sprinkled with his blood….*
>
> *1 Peter 1:1–2*
>
> May grace and peace be yours in abundance. Come to him, a living stone, rejected by mortals yet chosen and precious in God's sight, and like living stones, *let yourselves be built into a spiritual house, to be a holy priesthood,* to offer spiritual sacrifices acceptable to God through Jesus Christ.
>
> *1 Peter 2:4–5*

The words spoken by God set the framework for the relationship with his people that runs throughout Scripture. Covenant, holiness, worship, mercy, community, and service to the world all come into view in this momentous scene as God calls Israel to be a "holy nation" and a "priestly kingdom." Unpacking what this calling means reveals a lot about Israel's vocation in the world—and about God's purpose for calling his people to a new land.

Holy Nation

Israel is called to be holy *as God is holy*. That is, Israel's life reflects the character of God. And what does Israel know of God's character? They know Yahweh as the one who redeemed them from slavery. As such, they discover that Yahweh is holy. He is not like the gods of Egypt who sponsor the interests of the powerful. Nor is he like the god-pretender Pharaoh, who out of fear and the need to control

19

requires more bricks with less straw. Yahweh hears the cries of the slaves and works against the way things are to bring a new state of affairs for those oppressed. He is holy.

"Everything the Lord has spoken we will do" is Israel's stunning reply to God's offer of covenant at Sinai. Their response is stunning because they agree to obey the voice of God before they hear even a single command. All they know of Yahweh is his merciful act of deliverance. It is enough. They agree to obey his covenant because they want the story of the Exodus to continue. They become his partners in history because they want the world of the God who hears the oppressed to emerge and order their new lives. They want to be his community of salvation. Israel will be holy. Just as God is not like the other gods, so Israel will not be like the other nations.

Israel will live by a different script than the nations surrounding them. That script is formed by the words of God. We should not think of the law, therefore, as a set of lifeless ordinances. It is connected to the character and work of the deliverer God, and it represents his intentions to live in covenant relationship with a people committed to holiness. While some of the requirements of the law seem odd to us, their overall purpose is to bring God's deliverance experienced in the Exodus into every aspect of Israel's life. In everything from sexual purity to dietary stipulations, Israel's attention to the words of the law allows them to tie together God's deliverance and his holiness.

> **God's Just People...**
>
> For the Lord your God is God of gods and Lord of lords, the great God, mighty and awesome, who is not partial and takes no bribe, who executes justice for the orphan and the widow, and who loves the strangers, providing them with food and clothing. You shall also love the stranger, for you were strangers in the land of Egypt.
>
> *Deuteronomy 10:17–19*
>
> Religion that is pure and undefiled before God, the Father, is this; to care for orphans and widows in their distress, and to keep oneself unstained by the world.
>
> *James 1:27*

Notice how deliverance and law are held together in the giving of the ten commandments. "I am the Lord your God who brought you out of the land of Egypt, out of the house of slavery; you shall have no other gods before me..." (Exodus 20:1-3). The law is full of reminders of Israel's experience of Egypt. Take, for example, Exodus 23:9: "You shall not oppress a resident alien; you know the heart of an alien, for you were aliens in the land of Egypt." Unlike the experience of life under Pharaoh's rule, no one is to become marginalized among God's people. No one is to horde power or possessions. Israel will be different because they care for the widows, orphans, and the poor. As Israel obeys God's voice and keeps his covenant, they will continue to live out the story of the One who frees the oppressed. Israel will be holy as God is holy.

A Priestly Kingdom

I have treasured possessions. For example, I have a Julius Erving rookie basketball card. It is kept in a plastic sleeve to protect it—to keep it in mint condition, to preserve its value. No one is allowed to handle it. I keep it hidden away so that would-be burglars cannot plunder my treasure. But I have treasure of another kind. I have a Dick MacAulife autograph model, infielder's baseball glove. I've had it since Little League. It's beautiful. The weathered leather is creased into a perfect pocket, the product of oiling it, sleeping with it under my mattress (a ball tucked in the sweet spot), and hours of long toss and hot box. My Erving rookie card and MacAulife ball glove are both treasures, but there's a difference. The basketball card is something to admire. It is an end in itself. But, the glove is an instrument that allows me to participate in a larger world. It is my partner, an extension of my very self, allowing me to participate in the great game of baseball. It is treasure of a different sort.
—Mark 21

Admittedly, baseball gloves and Israel are not often equated. The simple point of comparison here is that God treasures Israel not as a trophy to be admired, but as a partner with whom he will work in the world. Israel's life is not an end in itself. Israel is God's chosen partner in caring for all of his creation: "If you obey my voice... you shall be my treasured possession out of all the peoples. The whole earth is mine, but you shall be for me a priestly kingdom..." (Exodus 19:5–6). Yahweh places Israel's priestly duty in the context of "the whole earth." The people of God are not delivered to rule the world or to ignore the world, but to share in God's concern for the world.

What does it mean to be a priestly nation? A priest stands between two parties. Israel's priests stood between God and the people, bringing the gifts of the people to God and pronouncing the blessings of God to the people. In the same way, Israel will be a priest to the nations. On behalf of all the peoples of the earth, Israel will offer praise to God. And by living God's way in the world, Israel will extend the blessings of God to all of creation. Consequently, worship is central to Israel's identity as a priestly nation. In worship, Israel both honors God and witnesses to the world. Through worship, Israel also offers on behalf of all nations the praise that is due God. It is little wonder that Israel's first great act this side of Egypt is praise. The people of God, his kingdom of priests, discover their vocation through worship.

Unfortunately, few churches today display this notion of priesthood in their worship. Specifically, there is little sense that worship is for the sake of the world. We tend to think of worship as existing for the sake of the individual. From this perspective, worship's purpose is primarily inspirational, enriching "my life" so that I can know the blessings of God more fully. Priestly worship, in contrast, has more than the individual in mind. Priestly worship is for the sake of the world. What a difference it would make to be reminded each week at the beginning of the service that we represent all of creation as we gather for worship. In the same way, it would make a great difference to be reminded at the end of each service that God's blessings do not exist for our sake alone, but for the sake of the world. So much of worship renewal seems to focus on our personal enjoyment in worship. Worship renewal might

22

look very different if we remembered that we worship on behalf of and for the sake of the world.

So that's what it means to be a *priestly* nation. But what does it mean to be a priestly *nation*? When we think of priests, we often think of individuals. Even when we read 1 Peter, "you are a royal priesthood," we interpret that to mean that each one of us individually is a priest. But the biblical notion is different: "you" is plural. All of Israel—woman, man and child—taken together constitute a priestly nation. Not the king alone. Not only the clergy. But all the people, living in covenant, represent God and become his blessing to the world by performing justice, loving mercy, and walking humbly before God (Micah 6:6).

Craig Van Gelder has written that Christians in North America have substituted worship for church. In other words, we tend to limit church to what we do together on Sunday morning and diminish the idea that church is primarily about living together in a distinct way in the world. Recovering our priestly vocation would require not only that we have the world in view when we gather on Sunday mornings but also that we view church as a community committed to an intentional way of life.

> The church is a people shaped by the redemptive reign of God. The church is not an end in itself. It has a distinct calling—to demonstrate the reality of God's redemptive power in the world. It has a unique nature—to live as a fellowship that demonstrates kingdom values and expresses kingdom power. It has a distinct purpose of carrying out a ministry of participating fully in the redemptive work of God in the world.
>
> *Craig van Gelder*
> The Essence of the Church: A Community Created by the Spirit, 2000

Exodus & Beyond

As strange as it may seem, God's formation of his people into a priestly nation takes place not in the comfort and safety of an established kingdom but while they are on the move. The offering of God's name, the extending of covenant, and the giving of the law all occur while Israel

23

is landless, living a nomadic existence. God's people are formed apart from what they have known—before they have found a lasting home. Granted, the land left behind at this point in the story is a land of bitter bondage and oppression. Still, in the precariousness of the wilderness, God's journeying people long for Egypt, for the security of fleshpots and portions of bread (Exodus 16:3). They long for the stability of a known world even though it's a world of slavery and oppression. Yet God's chosen people learn trust in him as they seek a lasting city (Hebrews 13:14).

Still, in spite of the centrality of the Exodus to Israel's identity, the story of God's creation of a holy people does not begin in Egypt or in the Exodus. Although it serves as a lens through which we can glimpse God's plan for all people, the Exodus is part of a story that is already well underway, a story that begins with creation itself.

From the Beginning

The picture of God's people from Exodus is no surprise if we know the stories in Genesis. The rich themes of the creation story reveal a God who brings life out of chaos. "Let us make humankind in our image," God says to those gathered around his throne. While the identity of the others in these important verses is open to debate, what is clear from the very beginning is that God creates *in* community *for* community. From Genesis 1 we learn that male and female together bear the image of God. From Genesis 2 we learn that a lone human falls short of God's desire for companionship. Both chapters reveal God's intense desire for relationships of mutuality and trust to be central to his created order. God intends humankind to be bound to him, to each other, and to all of creation.

Unfortunately, the sin of Adam and Eve disrupts all of these intended relationships and separates them from their divine tasks of procreation and cultivating the earth. The world no longer moves according to God's creative intent.

The stories of Genesis, however, reveal a God unwilling to abandon a world no longer moving to the rhythms

24

of trust and mutuality. Throughout the biblical story, God answers the fickleness of humankind with the constancy of his steadfast love. This redeeming love is on full display in God's election of Abraham. In response to the desire of Adam and Eve for autonomy from God, God invites Abraham into a relationship of binding promise and interdependence. In response to the desire of Adam and Eve to live life with primary concern for themselves, God invites Abraham into a life of blessing for the sake of others. God responds to a creation run amuck by calling into covenant an aging, barren couple to bless all nations.

> **Let Us Create...**
>
> Before the coming of Jesus, readers of this passage would have envisioned God as a king surrounded by his heavenly ruling council, a recurring picture of God in the Old Testament. Christians read this text and think of the Trinity and of Jesus' involvement in creation.
>
> For many, this picture from the first chapter of Genesis forms the basis for understanding the nature of the church, for as God exists in community, so we find our proper place in community. The church also understands its mission in relation to the Trinity: As the Father sends the Son and the Son sends the Spirit, so the church is sent into the world through the Spirit by the Son for the Father (John 14–17).

Notice the similarities between the concepts found in Exodus 19 and the promise God makes in Genesis 12:1–3 to the one he will later call Abraham.

> Now the Lord said to Abram, "Go from your country and your kindred and your father's house to the land I will show you. I will make you a great nation, and I will bless you, and make your name great, so that you will be a blessing. I will bless those who bless you, and the one who curses you I will curse; and in you all the families of the earth shall be blessed."

Like Israel, Abraham is an unlikely covenant partner. God promises Abraham numerous descendants, even though all the text tells us about Abraham at this point in the story is that his wife is barren and they are both old. The story depends on God's ability to create, not Abraham and Sarah's. Thus, the story of covenant is a story of grace.

25

Like Israel, Abraham is chosen not for his sake alone, but for the sake of all creation. Abraham is blessed so that he in turn will be a blessing. As amazing as this sounds, God's choosing of Abraham is for the sake of all the families of the earth.

Like Israel in the Exodus, Abraham formally covenants with God while on a journey—a journey where God demonstrates his faithfulness even in the face of Abraham's fickle trust. Abraham's covenant relationship with God begins with the call to leave the land that he knows and to seek another—"Go from your country and your kindred and your father's house to the land I will show you" (12:1).

The Genesis and Exodus stories establish a pattern of God's plan for redeeming his creation. God has always worked for salvation by calling a distinct community to live in covenant with him for the sake of all creation. Community is not secondary to God's strategy for salvation. Community is not merely a support group for those who honor God. On the contrary, God saves us by calling individuals out of self-centeredness into a community of people who live not for their own sake but for the sake of God and his creation.

While the stories of Abraham and the Exodus both develop notions of community in the context of a journey, both stories also anticipate a promised land: "Go ... to the land I will show you...," God says to Abraham. Through their wilderness wanderings, the rescued Israelites long for a land "flowing with milk and honey" (Exodus 3:8). The promised land carries the assurance of rest and belonging before God. However, security in the land also brings with it temptations that threaten Israel's mission to be a blessing to all nations.

God's People in the Land

In John Steinbeck's classic novel, *Of Mice and Men*, the main characters, George and Lennie, are transient ranch hands moving from job to job, from bunkhouse to bunkhouse. At various points throughout the story, Lennie, a large, powerful, mentally handicapped man, asks George to tell him about a future day when they will have a ranch of their own—a time when they will "live on the fatta the lan.'" George describes the ranch in great detail. "Well, it's ten acres," George dreams aloud. "Got a little win'mill. Got a little shack on it, an' a chicken run. Got a kitchen, orchard, cherries, apples, peaches, 'cots, nuts, got a few berries." Lennie knows the list as well as George. He turns the promise of land—a place to belong, a place to stop wandering—over and over again in his head. As George describes this promised land, Lennie always interjects, "An' rabbits, George." "Yes. Lennie. You will care for the rabbits."

Steinbeck's tale touches a place in all of us. Places that bring a sense of belonging, identity, and purpose are important to us all. And places that connect us to God fulfill an even greater longing.

> *I remember walking into the Duomo in Florence, Italy and immediately being captivated by the high arching vaults of stone and light, transfixed by the long aisle that led from darkness to light to the table where this cross-shaped cathedral found its gravitational center. This space spoke to me of the majesty and mystery of God. I have also known sacred space on a hiking trail above Latourell Falls in the Columbia River Gorge that divides Oregon and Washington. The sound of rushing water combined with the vision of shafts of light amid large green boughs from overhanging trees speaks to someplace deep in me. I go there as often as I can to be still before God.*
>
> *One last picture of sacred space: I have a black and white picture of my son emerging in my arms from a shallow Oregon creek. A baptismal picture. I can't tell you the name of the creek or even of the nearby campground where our congregation camped that weekend. But this picture denotes sacred space, not only because God met Josh there that day, but because the ring surrounding us in the picture is comprised of the faces of the people of God. Wherever I am with these people, I feel at home with God. All of us have a spiritual geography.*
> —*Mark*

27

Though called and formed in the wilderness, Israel's destination is the promised land. Canaan. A land flowing with milk and honey. A place to rest from traveling. Beginning with the promise made to Abraham, the biblical story moves toward land and all it represents. God will not leave Israel in the wilderness. There is a promised land that offers them a new kind of belonging and security.

The promised land, however, represents more. The land provides God's stage upon which Israel can model an alternative way of life. Imagine a nation where the poor are privileged, debts are routinely canceled, and land cannot be accumulated. Imagine a nation that does not trust in the stockpiling of military assets or the threat of a standing army. Imagine a nation that views the king as equally committed to read and obey the law of God. Such a nation would be holy as God is holy. This was God's purpose for Israel, and his law—the Torah—calls for just such a society. Not only does God want them to find rest in the promised land, but he intends for Israel to live as a priest among the nations.

Before we move with Israel to the promised land, however, it might be good for us to pause at the biblical boundary between Egypt and Canaan, between exodus and conquest, to listen again to what it will mean to be God's people in the promised land. In the book of Deuteronomy, Moses speaks to the people of God to remind them of what has gone before and what lies ahead—and how the two are connected. Before they "tread the verge of Jordan," God's people always do what they must when they live faithfully—they remember their story.

They pause at the boundary of the promised land because the land brings with it not only great promise, but also great risk. The risk is stated clearly in Deuteronomy 6:10–12:

> When the Lord your God has brought you into the land that he swore to your ancestors, to Abraham, to Isaac, and to Jacob, to give you—a land with fine, large cities that you did not build, houses filled with all sorts of goods that you did not hew, vineyards and olive groves that you did not plant—and when you have

> eaten your fill, take care that you do not forget the
> Lord who brought you out of the land of Egypt.

When you have eaten your fill. The threat of the land is bound up with its promise—satisfaction. It seems that satisfaction apart from memory dulls the senses toward God. The threat of land is that the security of cities and homes and vineyards will cause Israel to forget that their life and values were forged in their deliverance from slavery in Egypt and in the covenant and community formed in their journey—to put their trust in things rather than depending on God.

Temple & King: Blessings or Threats?

Two of the greatest symbols of security in the promised land also pose the greatest threat—temple and king. This might seem surprising. The idea of temple brings to mind the glory and splendor of the one Solomon builds and of that awesome scene in Isaiah 6:1–5 where God's robe fills the temple and the seraphs call to each other "Holy, holy, holy is the Lord of hosts." And when we think of king, we think of David, a man after God's own heart, with whom God made a covenant like no other: "Your house and your kingdom shall be made sure forever before me, your throne shall be established forever" (2 Samuel 7:16). If we had a slide show of great moments in the promised land, king and temple would appear often.

After all, few aspects of a community's life provide greater opportunity for God's glory than worship and leadership. Israel took the Exodus story as evidence of the nearness of God: "Who else has a God so near?" Still, experience of the presence of an invisible God requires concrete symbols and practices. We might say that Israel's religious life is the practice of the presence of God. When Israel worships in the temple, the presence of God becomes concrete and visible. The temple reminds Israel that God's presence is its most vital national resource. Worship in the temple often focuses Israel's faith on God's rule over all of creation. All kingdoms, including Israel's,

29

are reminded in worship that their rule is only legitimate in relation to God's.

Israel's king, therefore, possesses the opportunity to mirror God's ruling intentions among his people. Through the administration of justice, mercy, and steadfast love, Israel's king serves the rule and reign of the kingdom of God. Undoubtedly, no aspects of life in the land occupy Israel more than king and temple.

Still, king and temple pose great temptations for Israel—temptations noted by Yahweh himself. When David proposes to the prophet Nathan that he construct a dwelling for the Lord, it seems like a good idea. After all, David is living in a house of cedar while the ark of the covenant is housed in a tent. God's response to Nathan, however, is not warm to the idea of a permanent dwelling. "I have not lived in a house since the day I brought up the people of Israel out of Egypt.... [D]id I ever speak a word with any of the tribal leaders of Israel, whom I commanded to shepherd my people Israel, saying, 'Why have you not built me a house of cedar?'" (2 Samuel 7:6–8). A holy and free God has a natural resistance to houses made with human hands. He seems to prefer the precarious trust and the "journey" mentality that go along with a tent.

In the same way, God is not thrilled when Israel cries out for a king. He interprets their desire for a king as a rejection of his own rule of their life (1 Samuel 8:7). The prophet Samuel sees the coming of a monarchy as a return to the ways of Egypt—as moving backward in the story by forgetting Israel's exclusive covenant with God. According to Samuel, kings are kings whether in Egypt or in Jerusalem, and their uses of power run counter to the ideals of Israel, where no person is exempt from the demands of covenant. Samuel predicts that under a king, Israel will once again cry out as they did in Egypt. The subsequent stories of Israel's and Judah's kings prove Samuel's concerns justifiable.

30

King and temple both afford Israel opportunities for covenant faithfulness and provide reassuring symbols of Yahweh's favor and care. Like the imagined aspects of George and Lennie's ideal farm in *Of Mice and Men*, temple and king are important features of Israel's sense of place before God. Still, both provide occasions for stumbling. Without insistent reminders, God's people too easily settle into the security of the land and its blessings rather than trusting God to guide them on their journey.

The Rise of Prophets

It is no coincidence that the rise of the monarchy in Israel was accompanied by the rise of the prophets. Think of all the dramatic encounters between prophets and kings in Israel's story: Samuel and Saul, Nathan and David, Elijah and Ahab, Micaiah and Ahab, Isaiah and Hezekiah, Amos and Jereboam, Jeremiah and Jehoiakim. These stories reveal the tendency among kings to care more for self-preservation than for covenant fidelity with Yahweh. Power tends to dull a monarch's memory so that the foundational stories of the faith are forgotten, and old covenant standards of justice and mercy are overlooked. Prophets typically stand outside the circle of royal power and demand that the king have a memory. Remember Egypt! Remember the poor! Remember the law! Remember Yahweh is the source of your life!

The prophets understand that only a holy Israel can serve God's interests among the nations. To the extent that Israel acts like the nations around them, they lose their ability to function as a priestly nation that represents God to the world.

According to the prophets, this happens when the people of God:

+ place trust in other gods;
+ place trust in other nations and political alliances;
+ place trust in military might;
+ place trust in temple and worship rather than in justice and mercy;
+ place trust in status so that humble origins are forgotten;
+ place trust in "chosenness" so that covenant belonging creates a sense of privilege rather than responsibility.

31

Each of these is a temptation born of being too settled, of turning the focus inward on Israel's own needs and desires.

While many stories reflect the prophets' concerns, matters between prophet and king come to a head in the ministry of Jeremiah. God calls Jeremiah to ministry in Judah during a time of great political turmoil. Jeremiah preaches that the threat of Babylonian conquest is God's judgment against Jerusalem. The temple will be destroyed, and the king will be carried into captivity. The prophets and priests who serve the king denounce Jeremiah as a heretic, shouting down Jeremiah's prophecies of judgment with slogans of safety: "the temple of the Lord, the temple of the Lord, the temple of the Lord"

> The prophets frequently address those who place their trust in the temple and the trappings of religion rather than in God:
>
> Oh that one of you would shut the temple doors so that you would not light useless fires on my altar! I am not pleased with you, and I will accept no offering from your hands.
>
> *Malachi 1:10*
>
> Other examples can be found in Micah 2:6–11 and Amos 5:21–24.

(Jeremiah 7:14). They have committed the ultimate sin. They have used the things of God as a hedge against God himself, wrapping themselves in king and temple while refusing to live in the ways of God.

Ultimately, the prophets view Israel's life in the promised land as a failure. The experiment has gone awry. The temptations related to land, king, and temple have proved greater than Israel's willingness to keep covenant, and the shadow of Zion has eclipsed the memory of the Exodus. Satisfaction has trumped memory to the point that Israel no longer lives in a distinct way in the world. They are no longer holy and can therefore no longer serve as a kingdom of priests.

This failure is the reason prophets play such a vital role among the people of God. All human communities tend to gather power in ways that privilege some and abuse others. Too often, institutional aspects of a community's life become an end in themselves, overshadowing the community's mission in the world. Doctrines become self-serving, and worship becomes propaganda. The prophet stands in relation to the household of God as memory and conscience. The people of God cannot live faithfully within his promises without prophets.

The People of God in Exile & Beyond

In 587 BCE, God's people again take on a new form—one not of their own choosing. By God's choice, they become a people in exile, once again unsettled and uprooted as they had been in the Exodus. They will live away from the land, away from Zion, as the Babylonians' captives. What will it mean to be God's people in exile? What will it mean to honor Yahweh in a land where someone else's rule is recognized as ultimate? Will Israel remember its covenant with God and its purpose as a blessing to the world? And how will Israel practice the presence of God apart from land, temple, and king, unsure even of God's continuing presence in exile?

Jeremiah makes it clear that 587 is the end. Judah is beyond reformation or rehabilitation. There is no longer a repentance that will put the story back on the right track. "Your hurt is incurable / Your wound is grievous" is Jeremiah's diagnosis (Jeremiah 30:12). No hope for Judah, Jerusalem, or the temple remains. The poison of covenant infidelity has reached Judah's very heart. They are dead on arrival.

However, though Judah is dead, the story is not. Jeremiah's language is remarkable for both its lack of hope and its ultimate optimism. Jeremiah's confidence isn't in Israel's ability to keep covenant or to be better next time around but in the healing character of God, who can raise up a new, obedient Israel. So, in a single breath Jeremiah proclaims "Your wound is incurable" and "I will heal you" (Jeremiah 30:17).

Jeremiah's stunning message is that God's wounding of Judah is also the source of its healing. Because God is a God of everlasting love, not even death is final. Jeremiah's images of hope, rooted in the nature of God, are irrepressibly optimistic. Even the circumstances of exile can become the stage for God's covenant activity; even death

33

can result in life. In losing their land, Israel will rediscover something far more important.

Jeremiah 31 speaks boldly of a resurrected Israel. The people of God will be gathered again and a new covenant established:

> "The days are surely coming," says the Lord, "when I will make a new covenant with the house of Judah. It will not be like the covenant that I made with their ancestors when I took them by the hand to bring them out of the land of Egypt—a covenant that they broke though I was their husband," says the Lord. (31:31–32)

The new covenant will produce an obedient people because God will write his law directly on human hearts. God will guarantee relationship by dwelling within them: "I will be their God, and they shall be my people" (31:33).

God's resurrected people will transcend labels like "least" or "greatest." Instead of being divided into social categories, members of this community will find status in their mutual knowledge of the Lord. "No longer shall they teach one another, or say to each other, 'know the Lord,' for they shall all know me, from the least of them to the greatest, says the Lord" (31:34). And God's resurrected people will live in the full realization of the mercy of God. The new covenant promise of Yahweh

---

From the Least to the Greatest

Peter, standing with the eleven, raised his voice and addressed the crowd.... "This is what was spoken through the prophet Joel, 'In the last days it will be, God declares, that I will pour out my Spirit upon all flesh, and your sons and daughters shall prophecy, and your young men shall see visions, and your old men shall dream dreams. Even upon my slaves, both men and women, in those days I will pour out my Spirit....'"

Acts 2:17–18

Jesus called the twelve, and said to them, "Whoever wants to be first must be last of all and servant of all." Then he took a little child and put it among them; and taking it in his arms, he said to them, "Whoever welcomes one such child in my name welcomes me, and whoever welcomes me welcomes not me but the one who sent me."

Mark 9:35–37

34

is: "I will forgive their iniquity and remember their sin no more" (31:34).

Like Jeremiah, Ezekiel imagines a relationship between Israel and God beyond the death of exile. In the memorable vision of Ezekiel 37, Israel is depicted as a valley of dry bones—"and they were very dry" (verse 2). But in a remarkable scene of resurrection, the spirit of God brings life to a vast multitude, "the whole house of Israel." As with Jeremiah, this resurrected Israel will stand within a new covenant relationship with Yahweh: "I will put my spirit within you and you shall live" (37:7–14).

From Ezekiel's perspective, the failure of covenant lies at the feet of unfaithful shepherds who serve their own interests rather than those of the flock of God (34:1–31). In the day of new covenant, God will gather his flock and give them one shepherd, "my servant David" (34:23). Ezekiel emphasizes that the renewed people of God will be led by one who serves not himself but the interests of God and his people.

Death has come to Israel. However, hope in Yahweh extends beyond the grave. He will not forget his promises, nor will God give up on establishing a community for his purposes. This renewed community will possess the very spirit of God—a spirit manifest in a community of forgiveness led by a faithful shepherd—and it will remember its role as a blessing to the nations. Exile is not the final word.

Looking Forward

The vision of the prophets of exile is important. They no longer look back in history to find an ideal Israel to restore. Instead, they increasingly look to the future, to the Day of the Lord, when God himself will establish his reign. They envision a pure Israel in the fullness of time and live faithfully to that picture in the present. This does not mean that the prophets forget the past; the new work of God will be in keeping with his mighty acts in history. However, the people of God will pattern themselves not on a past vision of human achievement, but on one of God's future achievement. This future vision, by its very nature, will be a source of constant critique and renewal for the people of God. They will never be able to say, "we have arrived. We are now perfectly the people of God." Instead, they will always be pulled into the greater vision of God's resurrected community, seeking a city with true foundations.

Exile profoundly shaped Israel's faith. Not only did the people of Israel have to struggle with their notions of God and their own place within his covenant purposes, but they had to imagine ways of living faithfully apart from land, temple, and king. Many have suggested that in the exile Israel became a textual community. In other words, the enactment of God's presence no longer came through temple observance but through the reading and keeping of God's Word. Much of the Old Testament was either written or came to its final form during or after the exile. The synagogue came into being as the place where Israel read Scripture and worshipped. Through Scripture and prayer, Israel kept its covenant identity alive as aliens in a foreign land. Just as the habits of the wilderness prepared Israel for its life in the promised land, so ways of life learned in the exile were preparing God's people for their return to Jerusalem.

God's People After the Exile

"Comfort, O comfort my people" are the hopeful words given to the prophet in Isaiah 40:1. God is leading his people home. He has not forgotten Israel. The way home, however, might seem a little surprising. There is a new imperial power on the block. Cyrus, the Persian emperor, has overthrown the Babylonians and is opening the way for exiles to return home. From one perspective, Cyrus is God's chosen one. "The Lord ... says of Cyrus, 'He is my shepherd and he shall carry out my purpose'" (Isaiah 44:28; see also 45:1–13; 46:11). Cyrus, as God's anointed, will subdue nations, strip rulers of their robes, and rule the nations—all for the sake of Israel.

36

For some, this new turn of events is about restoring Israel's fortunes. A return to the land will be a return to a former way of life centered on king and temple.

Rebuild the temple. Find a descendant of David. Purify the bloodlines. Determine lineages. Restore the original land arrangements. Soon Israel will regain its former glory and will rule the nations.

But there is another vision of Israel's future in Isaiah. The common refrain of the prophet is "do not remember the former things" (43:18). God is doing something new, something different. Though the theme of the story remains the same, the plot has shifted. Israel must never again become an end in itself. God's people must never again equate chosenness with privilege or superiority; instead, God has determined that his new work will affirm Israel's role as a servant-priest to the nations. In fact, the surprising word of the prophet is that exile is more than just God's punishment. Exile is God's way of positioning Israel to join in his work for the sake of all nations.

Central to Isaiah's vision of the new work of God is the image of the servant. The servant is God's chosen instrument. "Here is my servant," Yahweh proclaims, "whom I uphold, my chosen, in whom my soul delights" (42:1). Four different passages, referred to as the "servant songs," describe the role of the servant in God's design (42:1–9; 49:1–6; 50:4–9; 52:13–53:12). While the exact identity of the servant is subject to great debate, at the very least Israel is to understand its role in direct relation to the servant's. God has greater plans for the servant

The Servant Songs

The "servant songs" consist of four passages in Isaiah that talk about the special role of the servant of the Lord in Israel's future. To whom do these songs refer? Sometimes the servant is clearly a personification of Israel, and sometimes he seems to be an individual. In some texts, the work of the servant seems to be in the present. In others, the servant's time of ministry is undetermined. New Testament writers clearly saw Jesus in texts like Isaiah 52–53.

Possibly all of these identifications of the servant are legitimate. Certainly, the image of the servant provided Israel with a new way to think of its life among the nations in light of the exile. While God clearly calls individuals to this ministry, he also calls his people as a whole to see its work in the world as the work of a suffering servant.

37

than merely restoring Israel to its glory: "It is too light a thing that you should be my servant to raise up the tribes of Jacob and to restore the survivors of Israel." God has bigger things in mind. "I will give you as a light to the nations, that my salvation may reach to the ends of the earth" (Isaiah 49:6).

As God writes the script of salvation, the starring role belongs to the servant, not to Cyrus. To all other observers, Cyrus seems to be the one who determines history. He rolls over nations like a rolling pin over soft dough, shaping them to his will. However, the real star, the servant, makes no such grand gestures; he "will not lift up his voice, or make it heard in the street." Instead, the servant cares for "bruised reeds" and "dimly burning wicks." While it might appear that Cyrus is the one who determines justice, the servant possesses the spirit of the Lord and "will bring forth justice to the nations" (42:1–4).

This marks a significant turn in Israel's understanding of themselves as the people of God. Just as Christ will later do fully, Israel is called to be God's partner in the world, the one who will help bring salvation to the nations. Returning once again from exile, Israel must continue to live a broken existence for the sake of others. The exile has turned proud, isolated Israel into missional Israel, forcing them to live among the nations and bear the judgment of God. Though often unaware of its missionary existence in exile, Israel was living out its missional purpose in ways it never could have done cloistered in the promised land. Israel is God's covenant with the nations—given up for the sake of all people.

Not surprisingly, the nations are slow to recognize the epic story God is telling through his people. The homeward procession of the exiles in Isaiah 52:7–53:12 is nothing less than a second Exodus, and the messenger of God stands on the ruined walls of Jerusalem and announces that the return of the exiles is the salvation of God, saying, "The Lord has bared his holy arm before the eyes of all the nations, and all the ends of the earth shall see the salvation of our God" (51:10). However, the returning band of dispirited exiles is hardly an impressive sight. No longer smug and privileged but lowly and humbled,

Israel has "no form or majesty that we should look at him, nothing in his appearance that we should desire him." The returning exiles, like the future Christ, look less like God's chosen one and more like God's rejected one, "a man of suffering and acquainted with infirmity; and as one from whom others hide their faces, he was despised and we held him of no account" (53:1–3).

Ultimately, though, recognizing the disfigured servant as God's chosen one will also cause the nations to see themselves in a new light. "He was wounded for our transgressions, crushed for our iniquities; upon him was the punishment that made us whole. All we like sheep have gone astray; we have all turned to our own way, and the Lord has laid upon him the iniquity of us all" (53:4–6). The striking number of references to the nations indicates that this new work of God recovers his concern for the whole earth.

Because God's plan to use a chosen people to save the world has not changed, the new work of God in the return from exile borrows heavily from the imagery of the Exodus. While this future vision makes only bare reference to the promise made to David, Exodus language abounds. For instance, God's power revealed in the Exodus is often referred to throughout the Old Testament as the revealing, or baring, of his arm. Also, the familiar image of God as shepherd is often tied to his wilderness provision for Israel. So, when the prophet proclaims in 40:10–11, "See, the Lord God comes with might, and his arm rules for him; .... He will feed his flock like a shepherd; he will gather the lambs in his arms, and carry them in his bosom," pictures of the Exodus come to mind.

> **God's Concern for the Whole Earth**
>
> Many times in Isaiah, God exhibits concern for the nations:
>
> Listen to me, my people, and give heed to me, my nation; for a teaching will go out from me, and my justice for a light to the peoples. I will bring near my deliverance swiftly, my salvation has gone out and my arms will rule the peoples; the coastlands wait for me.
>
> 51:4–5
>
> Other instances include 41:1; 42:9; 44:5; 45:22; 49:1–6, 14–22; 61:11; 66:22–23.

39

And what listener wouldn't think of the Exodus when the prophet announces, "When you pass through the waters, I will be with you" (43:2), or think of God's wilderness provision for Israel when they hear the words, "'The Lord has redeemed his servant Jacob.' They did not thirst when he led them through the deserts; he made water flow for them from a rock..." (48:20–21)? The Exodus is Israel's best memory and the one most trusted to create a faithful future.

The vision from Isaiah for God's people after exile raises questions of courage. Will God's people finally relinquish notions of being in control and claim their brokenness before the world? Will they embrace God's judgment on themselves and the world? Will the people of God bear more than they deserve for the sake of others? Will they give up protesting their loss of status and choose instead to live among the bruised reeds and dimly burning wicks? Will they live among the suffering even if this means that those in power will see them as weak and insignificant? Will God's people believe that the role of suffering servant is the lead role in the unfolding drama of salvation?

Conclusion

What can the church today gain from the perspective of the Old Testament? First, the people of God live out the story of the saving work God performed on their behalf. While many biblical stories speak of Israel's salvation, the story of the Exodus provides a faithful script from which not only Israel but the church can understand its identity and live in relation to God and to the nations. Like Israel, the church's life might best be summed up this way: as we were saved, so shall we live.

God's plan has always been for his chosen people to be holy. But what does this holiness entail? Unlike the rest of the world, God's people will honor him as the one true God. They will not trust in their own might but in God's daily provision. Refusing to allow power and possessions to be the property of only a few, the people of God will provide for the poor, the widow, the alien, and the sojourner. Like Israel, the church is called to live not for its own glory nor for its own sake, but for the glory of God and for the sake of all creation. In this way God's people will be holy, his prized possession.

The witness of the Old Testament for the church is clear in another way: the formation of a distinct community is central to God's saving work. Israel is not simply to revel in the blessings of God on its own behalf. Rather, it is to live as a blessing to the nations. The holiness to which God calls his people unites them not only with one another, but with those around them as they perform the priestly function of uniting God and humanity. For the people of God in Israel and in the church today, unity of purpose in serving others is the foundation of community.

In the Old Testament, the people of God take on many forms. The Israelites live with judges, under kings, and under foreign powers. They live in the wilderness, in the promised land, and in someone else's land. Still, wherever they live and in whatever specific form they take, they are to live as they did in the wilderness—a life of daily trusting in God's care and provision. Monarchy and temple, while great blessings, also made this difficult. For us as well, forms that institutionalize God's presence can become temptations to self-trust rather than trust in God. Some forms are more conducive than others to helping God's people maintain their reliance on him.

Finally, the Old Testament teaches us that God's people live for his future. They do not live in relation to some idealized past. Rather, in a state of exile and suffering, they live expectantly and humbly in anticipation of the great day of the Lord. From the perspective of that day, the role of the suffering servant is the starring role. The people of God lend themselves to his work of salvation by bearing the wounds of the world.

The prophetic images of exile in the Old Testament help us understand the next chapter in the story—the coming of Jesus—but they also provide helpful orientation for the circumstances that confront the church today. As we will argue in chapter seven, Christians increasingly find themselves in a kind of exile, living the faith in a culture that no longer values the Christian story. We live in a post-Christian North America and will need to learn again to view our lives in light of God's provision for a wandering people. Instead of lamenting the loss of the past, let us, like Isaiah before us, look forward to the discovery that God's chosen role for us as his people in the world is that of the servant.

The People of God & the End of the Age

And suddenly from heaven there came a sound like the rush of a mighty wind, and it filled the entire house where they were sitting. Divided tongues, as of fire, appeared among them, and a tongue rested on each one of them. And all of them were filled with the Holy Spirit and began to speak in other languages, as the Spirit gave them ability. Now there were devout Jews from every nation under heaven living in Jerusalem. And at this sound the crowd gathered and was bewildered, because each one heard them speaking in the native language of each.... But Peter, standing with the eleven, raised his voice and addressed them, "Men of Judea and all who live in Jerusalem, let this be known to you.... This is what was spoken of in the prophet Joel:

> In the last days it will be, God declares, that I will
>   pour out my Spirit on all flesh,
> And your sons and daughters shall prophesy
> And your young men shall see visions
> And your old men will dream dreams....
> Then everyone who calls on the name of the
>   Lord will be saved.

Acts 2:1–21

When my son was four years old we watched the movie Field of Dreams *one evening on television. The next day I came home from work to find Josh in his room, playing. He had conscripted every toy he owned into the service of replicating the set of* Field of Dreams. *Toy soldiers stood as cornrows just beyond the outfield. Lego®-constructed bleachers trimmed the first base line. Ninja Turtles® stood*

in for Shoeless Joe and the other ballplayers who emerged
from the toy soldier cornfield. "What are you playing?"
I asked him. "Field of Dreams," he replied proudly. But
then his face turned into a question mark and he asked,
"Daddy, what's this movie about, anyway?" It's possible, it
seems, to duplicate the playing field in exacting detail and
lose track of the meaning of the story.

—Mark

Imitating the New Testament church is less about reset-
ting the scene in exacting detail and more about living
out the meaning of God's story. Like those exiles who
returned to the land under Cyrus, the church cannot be
content simply to reproduce literally the specific characters, actions, locations, and practices of the past, nor
would it be possible to do so. Rather, the church lives the
often-improvisational art of extending the meaning and
action of the story in its own time and place. The church
is the community that continues to live the story even after
the final credits of Scripture roll across the screen. As we
have seen, that story began with a chosen people whom
God shaped through exodus and exile to be a priestly
nation, bringing his salvation to the world through those
he was teaching to be suffering servants. In the church, he
was calling for a new chapter to this story—one with new
scenes and characters.

Some might object that efforts to extend God's story
in new ways diminish the importance of biblical details
and make the witness of Scripture less important to the
task of being the church today. Just the opposite is true.
To continue living the story in faithful ways requires
deep and prolonged engagement with God's word. Like
those who watch a favorite movie over and over, noticing
with each viewing new details and how they intercon-
nect, our continuing engagement with Scripture reveals
God's narrative more richly. Like those movie viewers
who learn which details are vital and which are less significant, we learn more productively how to read God's
story and what our roles in it are. Those who give careful

44

attention to God's story learn to think not only about the characters, but to think with them, and that's closer to the business of the New Testament church than any wooden-soldier cornfield.

Jesus & the Nearness of the Reign of God

The story of God's people in the New Testament is best understood in light of the first Christians' belief that the coming of Jesus, and the subsequent coming of the Spirit, marked a decisive "turn of the ages." Jesus' announcement of the nearness of the kingdom signaled God's intent once again to gather a people to live under his reign for the sake of all creation. Now the nature and character of God's reign would be manifest most clearly in a new kind of king and a new kind of temple made possible by the death and resurrection of Jesus. To understand New Testament Christianity is to understand the church's conformity to this new chapter of God's story.

Initially many misunderstood the nature of this "new chapter." Jesus came proclaiming the reign of God. "The time is fulfilled," he preached. "The kingdom of God has come near. Repent, and believe the good news" (Mark 1:15). At the end of the previous chapter, we left Israel asking questions about God's presence in the wake of exile. For centuries, Israel had lived under someone else's reign. Imagine the dramatic impact of Jesus' announcement concerning God's approaching reign. For so long, Israel had prayed for God to visit his people in power once again. According to Jesus, the time had finally arrived when God would act in power on behalf of his people.

The description of the aged prophet, Simeon, captures well the longing of Israel's collective heart. Simeon, a man righteous and devout, was "looking for the consolation of Israel." When he held the Christ child in his arms, he echoed the hope of the prophets of the exile:

45

> Master, now you are dismissing your servant in peace,
>   according to your word;
>   for my eyes have seen your salvation,

> which you have prepared in the presence of all peoples,
> a light for revelation to the Gentiles
> and for glory to your people Israel. (Luke 2:25–32)

For Simeon, God's great work of salvation involved restoring Israel's glory in the presence of all peoples. Just as God had formed Israel before, so now in the "fullness of time" Israel was being restored to be a light of revelation to the Gentiles.

For those who shared the hope of the prophets of former days, the depth of their historical humiliation would be more than compensated for by the glorious outpouring of God's saving work in and through Israel. God's coming kingdom brought with it the dawn of a great day of salvation, one signaled by the gathering of scattered Israel, the exaltation of Jerusalem as the teaching center of the universe, the granting of forgiveness of sins, and the exaltation of the poor. For those keeping score, these signs would be evidence of a glorious day of salvation for Israel.

> **The Prophets Predict the Nearness of the Kingdom...**
>
> Thus says the Lord God: "Now I will restore the fortunes of Jacob, and have mercy on the whole house of Israel.... Then they shall know that I am the Lord their God because I sent them into exile among the nations, and then gathered them into their own land.... I will never again hide my face from them."
>
> *Ezekiel 39:25–29*
>
> Thus says the Lord: "In a time of favor I have answered you, on a day of salvation I have helped you...." Sing for joy, O heavens, and exult, O earth.... For the Lord has comforted his people and will have compassion on his suffering ones.
>
> *Isaiah 49:8, 13*

Jesus' ministry was in many ways in keeping with these expectations associated with the fullness of time and the "turn of the ages." For instance, he called twelve disciples, the same number as the tribes of Israel, an unmistakable sign that he intended to gather God's scattered people. He reinforced this sign by pronouncing forgiveness of sins, casting out demons, healing the sick, finding fellowship with the poor, and teaching the righteousness of God with authority. Jesus came not only preaching the reign of God but also demonstrating that reign by gathering a people to serve this emerging kingdom.

However, in other ways, Jesus' ministry ran counter to popular expectations. Though Jesus announced the coming nearness of God, the nature and shape of God's presence came as a surprise to many. For instance, those familiar with Israel's story expected the presence of God to be associated with the coming of a Davidic ruler and through renewed emphasis on the temple and observance of the law. After all, these had been elements of God's story with Israel, and the prophets had anticipated their renewal. Jesus' relationship to these elements was both personal and unconventional, though. For example, he saw himself fulfilling the law (Matthew 5:17) but was seen by many as a lawbreaker and pushed his own followers to pursue a righteousness beyond the letter of the law (for example Matthew 5:21–48; 12:1–8). He honored the temple as a place of prayer as he threw out the money-changers (Matthew 21:12ff), but saw himself as the very replacement of the temple (John 2:19–22). He was born son of David in the city of David—God's chosen ruler, the Messiah (Matthew 1)—yet he came not to be served, but to serve and give himself for others (Mark 10:45). His kingship, representing the rule of God, was not a rule from above, but from below. In other words, Jesus did not hold court with princes and nobles, but with tax collectors and sinners.

For those longing for God's consoling presence among his people, Jesus offered himself. "Something greater than the temple is here," he proclaimed (Matthew 12:6). The practice of the presence of God now would revolve not primarily around temple rituals or observance of the law, but rather around learning the way of Jesus, who is Emmanuel—"God with us" (Matthew 1:23). The ideal role that temple and king should have played in Israel's past now found fulfillment in Jesus as this new chapter in God's story emerged.

47

The Cross & The Nearness of God

Jesus' unconventional ministry is seen most clearly in his stated mission—to suffer and die for others. As the Gospel writers make abundantly clear, the way of Jesus always leads to the cross. Luke's report that Jesus "set his face to go to Jerusalem" (9:51) is one of many examples in the Gospels that shows the story of Jesus moving inexorably to the cross (see Matthew 16:21–28; Mark 8:31–38; John 3:14). New Testament writers, including those who penned the Gospels, were often occupied with the problem of a crucified messiah—"a stumbling block to Jews and foolishness to Gentiles" (1 Corinthians 1:23).

> How grievous a thing it is to be disgraced by a public court; how grievous to suffer banishment; and yet in the midst of any such disaster we retain some degree of liberty. Even if we are threatened with death, we may die free men. But the executioner, the veiling of the head and the very word "cross" should be far removed not only from the person of a Roman citizen but from his thoughts, his eyes, and his ears.
>
> *Cicero*
> Pro Rabirio, *63 BCE*

Even to Jesus' closest followers, the prospect of a crucified messiah was a scandal. Remember Peter's reaction to Jesus' announcement that the "Son of Man must undergo great suffering...and be killed" (Mark 8:31). "Peter took him aside and began to rebuke him." Peter's script for Israel's renewal didn't include a suffering messiah. But for Jesus, any view of God's rule—or his ruler—that didn't include radical self-giving was Satanic. "Get behind me, Satan!" Jesus responded. "For you are setting your mind not on divine things but on human things" (Mark 8:32–33). Though Peter properly identified Jesus as the chosen one of God, he badly misunderstood the job description. God had always intended his people to serve and save others, and here and throughout the Gospels, Jesus takes great pains to prevent the term "messiah" from being detached from the image of a suffering servant.

So in the ministry of Jesus, the nearness of God came in a surprising and significant form. Remember, while the law, temple, and king clearly conveyed God's presence to Israel, they also constituted Israel's greatest temptations—namely, to confuse the signs of God's presence for the actual presence of God and to allow the trappings of God's presence to give them a sense of privileged status in the world. Jesus took Israel's most prominent signs of chosenness and reinterpreted them in light of his own life—a life that forsook privilege for the sake of others. Any community, therefore, serving the interests of God's kingdom would by necessity be one to forego privilege for the sake of welcoming those without. Where the kingdom of God exists, led by a suffering messiah, the last are first and the first are last.

Those who answer the call to follow Jesus, an unconventional messiah, choose an unconventional life. Just as Israel was called to live a distinct life among the nations, so Jesus calls his followers to live together with unique values. The followers of Jesus turn the other cheek, give to everyone who begs from them, and practice unlimited forgiveness. The followers of Jesus are not content just to keep the letter of the law. They live a more demanding righteousness. So they keep commandments, not just by avoiding acts of murder or adultery, but by guarding their hearts from hatred and lust. The way of the kingdom always pulls the followers of Jesus deeper into the life of God and neighbor. Those who choose the reign of God for their way of life care for those who are vulnerable—the poor, the sick, children, and outsiders. In these ways and more, those who follow Jesus strive to "be perfect as [their] heavenly father is perfect" (Matthew 5–7).

Needless to say, living out the implications of the kingdom is hardest for those with the most to lose. Jesus' welcome of those on the outside—the poor, the sick, tax collectors and sinners—clearly challenged those with an investment in the status quo. Perhaps the greatest challenge for the first followers of Jesus involved his insistence that the reign of God encompassed the Gentiles. In Luke's Gospel, Jesus' first sermon announced the inauguration of the year of the Lord's favor (Luke 4:16–30). His audience would have interpreted that to mean two things: the restoration of Israel's glory and vengeance against their historic oppressors—Gentiles. Not only does Jesus avoid quoting in this sermon the part of Isaiah 61 promising vengeance, but he ends his sermon with examples from the Old Testa-

49

ment where God showed exclusive favor to Gentiles. Upon hearing this, his hearers sought to throw Jesus off of a cliff. While it is certainly true that Jesus' earthly ministry was primarily to the lost house of Israel, he did not intend to inaugurate a kingdom that "lorded over" others. Rather, he sought to restore Israel to its original purpose in God's plan. As the new king suffered and served, so must the chosen people who followed him and served his kingdom.

As we noted earlier in this chapter, the prophet Simeon saw in Jesus the coming of the salvation of God. He also saw that the coming of Jesus would mean "the falling and rising of many in Israel" (Luke 2:34). From Simeon's point of view, relationships are different in the kingdom of God. To follow Jesus and embrace his offer of salvation, those who are first must become last and the last must become first. At the turn of the ages, the coming of Jesus as the agent of God's salvation means the creation of a new kind of community.

Clearly, God's sending of Jesus marks a dramatic turn in the plot of the biblical story. His coming, however, is not the end of the story, but rather the exciting opening of a new set of chapters. God's sending of the Spirit comprises a crucial second act in the portrayal of the people of God at the turn of the ages. In the first act—the sending of Jesus—God gathers a renewed people to learn the distinctive way of Jesus, and in the second act—the sending of the Spirit—God sends out his renewed people to live as a blessing among the nations. As Jesus ascended into heaven, he told his followers, "You will receive power when the Holy Spirit has come upon you; and you will be my witnesses in Jerusalem, in all Judea and Samaria, and to the ends of the earth" (Acts 1:8). The promised coming of the Spirit would allow the story of Jesus to continue in powerful ways.

The Coming of the Spirit: Breaking Down Barriers

We know the scene well. During Pentecost, the mighty wind of the Spirit blows across the gathered crowd and reorders the world. Men and women from many nations witness tongues of fire from heaven rest on twelve common men from Galilee. Each one in the crowd—whether Mede, Parthian, or Elamite—hears the explanation of this event in his or her own language. This bestowal of tongues from heaven transcends all ethnic boundaries so that a new kind of community is created.

Peter says this much in his famous Acts 2 sermon. This new utterance is no human phenomenon. "These men are not drunk," he advises the crowd. Rather, a new day has dawned—a day no longer characterized by the distinctions of human communities. With the coming of the Spirit, the salvation of God has appeared, cutting across lines of Jew and Greek, male and female, young and old, slave and free. We know best the end of Peter's sermon and the offer of repentance and baptism found there, but the first part of his sermon is essential as well. A new community is now possible through the free movement of the Spirit of God. "God has poured out his Spirit on all flesh," Peter explains from the prophet Joel. "Your sons and daughters shall prophesy, and your young men shall see visions and your old men will dream dreams. Even upon my slaves, both men and women, in those days I will pour out my Spirit; and they shall prophesy" (Acts 2:14–18).

As we read further in Acts, the prophecy of Joel is worked out in a variety of ways, and the Holy Spirit leads the way. The Spirit constantly moves the church beyond geographic, ethnic, and other human boundaries. In fact, one might say that the church is always a few chapters behind the Spirit in Acts. A great case in point is the series of stories beginning with Cornelius' conversion and culminating with the deliberations of the Jerusalem council (Acts 10–15).

Through visions and dreams, the Spirit works to bring Cornelius, a Gentile, and Peter together. As Peter preaches, it becomes apparent to all present that the Spirit has come upon Cornelius and his household. The Jewish believers who accompanied Peter "were astounded that the gift of the Holy Spirit had been poured out even on the Gentiles." At once, Peter offers baptism to Cornelius and his entire household (Acts 10:44–45).

Yet not everyone was prepared for these new realities of the kingdom. When the report of Peter's activity reached the church in Jerusalem, the "circumcised believers" criticized Peter, not for preaching to or baptizing Gentiles, but for eating with them since they were people perceived as perpetually unclean. Preaching was one thing, but eating together showed a level of acceptance and an equality of status that threatened some people's understanding of God's story.

Meanwhile, as Peter was causing a stir with the church in Jerusalem, a young missionary named Paul was taking the gospel to places like Antioch and planting ethnically diverse churches (Acts 11). The movement of God's Spirit among the Gentiles brought the church to a point of crisis. How could the community of God live faithfully to both its past as recorded in Scripture (including Scripture's boundary markers like circumcision and diet) and be faithful to its missionary future among the Gentiles? This question occupied the Jerusalem council in Acts 15. In the end, the church decided what the Spirit had indicated to Peter five chapters earlier: "by giving them the Holy Spirit ... and in cleansing their hearts by faith [God] has made no distinctions between them and us" (Acts 15:9). The conclusion to those gathered that day,

> James replied, "My brothers, listen to me. Simeon has related how God first looked favorably on the Gentiles, to take from among them a people for his name. This agrees with the words of the prophets, as it is written,
> 'After this I will return,
> And I will rebuild the dwelling of David, which has fallen;
> From its ruins I will rebuild it, and I will set it up,
> So that all other peoples may seek the Lord—even all the Gentiles over whom my name has been called.
> Thus says the Lord, who has been making these things known from long ago.'
> Therefore, I have reached the decision that we should not trouble the Gentiles who are turning to God, but we should write to them to abstain only from things polluted by idols and from fornication and from whatever has been strangled and from blood."
>
> *Acts 15:13–20*

"It seemed good to the Holy Spirit and to us...," indicates their belief that they lived in a privileged age—an age in which the Spirit was reordering relationships and working for the salvation of all.

The Jerusalem council forced the early church to ask very important questions. Was the gospel strong enough to break down human boundaries? How could the church relax standards related to the long-established practice of the law and still uphold the promises of God made to Israel? What does it mean to follow the leading of the Spirit of the risen Jesus? From questions like these arose vital understandings of what it meant for the first Christians to be the people of God.

The coming of the Spirit at Pentecost launched a missionary church—a community crossing boundaries for the sake of gathering a people suited for the Kingdom of God. The New Testament records the efforts of the early church to negotiate the new social and cultural realities of God's reign. In particular, the story of the New Testament chronicles the challenges that emerged in taking the message of a Jewish Messiah to a Gentile world. The first Christians found themselves constantly in the creative opportunities afforded by both the continuity and discontinuity of God's past actions on Israel's behalf and the leading of the Spirit to the ends of the earth.

To God Be Glory in the Church: Paul & the Gentiles

Nowhere is the leading of the Spirit to transcend human boundaries more clear than in the imposing figure of Paul, the apostle to the Gentiles. Paul's letters clearly indicate that many of his views of salvation and the church arise from his conviction that God had called the Gentiles to be full partakers in the covenant promises of God. Paul saw the church as the people "on whom the end of the ages has come" (1 Corinthians 10:11). From this vantage point, the mystery of God's plan for the fullness of time comes into view: namely, that through Christ, God has created one new humanity in place of two. Paul sees himself as an agent of this new,

53

emerging reality. In particular, he has given up his privilege as a Jew to become a "prisoner of Christ for the sake of the Gentiles" (Ephesians 3:1–8). Entire writings, like Romans and Galatians, take great pains to explain how the gospel makes room for both Jew and Gentile in the offer of God's salvation at the end of the age. Many of our most striking pictures of the early church are painted against the backdrop of Paul's concern for the full inclusion of the Gentiles.

Take, for instance, the image of the church as the new temple of God. For Paul, the old structure signifying God's presence is abolished in the flesh of Christ (in this context, "the law with its commandments and ordinances"). In the place of this wall that divided people, a new dwelling place for God "is joined together and grows into a holy temple in the Lord; in whom you also are built together spiritually into a dwelling place for God" (Ephesians 2:14–21). According to Paul's vision, when the church overcomes the barrier of Jew and Gentile, the wisdom of the mystery of God is put on display before the entire universe. The rich variety of the church becomes evidence even to the rulers and authorities in the heavenly places of God's ability to "gather all things up in (Christ), things in heaven and things on earth" (Ephesians 1:10; 3:8–10). No wonder Paul's beautiful prayer in Ephesians 3:14–21 ends with the exclamation, "to [God] be glory in the church and in Christ Jesus to all generations, forever and ever. Amen."

Paul marvels over the church in a similar way in Romans: "O the depths of the riches and wisdom and knowledge of God! .... For from him and through him and to him are all things. To him be the glory forever. Amen" (11:33–36). What sends Paul into this flight of fancy? In Romans, Jesus is a second Adam, the progenitor of a new race. By the Spirit of Jesus, God is creating a new humanity—one no longer subject to the power of sin and death, but a humanity under the dominion of grace for the sake of righteousness (5:12–21). While the way of the first Adam led to alienation between Jew and Gentile (1:18–3:21), the new way of faith in Jesus brings Jew and Gentile to a place where "together you may with one voice glorify the God and Father of our Lord Jesus Christ. Welcome one another, therefore, just as Christ has welcomed you, for the glory of God" (15:6). At the end of chapter eleven, Paul marvels at the wisdom of God who through Christ has brought Jew and Gentile to a place of mutual dependence.

The Spirit's work goes beyond overcoming barriers between Jew and Gentile. It also applies to old and young, male and female, slave and free. The Spirit is always leading the church deeper into the peace of God revealed in Christ Jesus. While the predominant challenge for the first century revolved around Jew and Gentile, other social relationships are transformed within the church as well. In our recent past, the Spirit's reconciling work led the church to move beyond the distinctions of slave and free. While these movements are sometimes slow and painful, the church is the place where God pours his Spirit out on all flesh, both sons and daughters, young and old, and upon both men and women slaves (Acts 2:16–21). Paul states things this way: "As many of you as were baptized into Christ have clothed yourselves with Christ. There is no longer Jew or Greek, there is no longer slave or free, there is no longer male or female; for all of you are one in Christ Jesus" (Galatians 3:27–28).

Is the church only about overcoming human barriers? After all, some bowling leagues and motorcycle clubs cross human boundaries as well. Clearly, the church is committed to a particular way of life—a life in Christ—that makes it different from other communities. This distinct way of life will be the focus of the rest of the chapter. Still, it is important to recognize the pervasive belief of the earliest Christians that the coming of Jesus and the subsequent coming of the Spirit created a new social reality reflecting God's purposes for the end of time.

The Baptized Life: Living the Story of Jesus   55

In the previous chapter I wrote briefly about the baptism of my son, Josh. There are many images I will carry with me from that day. Nancy, my wife, and I stood with Josh

*ankle deep in a cool stream. Our hearts were full with
joy. Josh had chosen the way of the cross as his way of life.
As we stood there, surrounded by our church community,
we spoke to him of the way of life he was entering. And we
gave him gifts to remind him of the kind of story he was
joining. Nancy gave Josh a ring composed of intertwined,
never- ending strands. He was never to think of himself
as an isolated individual. He had joined a story of intertwined lives stretching into eternity. I gave Josh a wooden
cross on a leather strap that I had worn around my neck
for years. It was made from wood native to the country
of Belize, a place where I had done mission work. As a
baptized person, Josh was choosing to take up his cross
and follow Jesus, no matter where that might lead him.*

*After Josh's baptism, members of our congregation
spoke blessings to him and gave him glimpses of both the
promise and peril of the way he had chosen. And they
promised to be with him. These were baptized people
as well. They too had joined the story of Jesus and were
committed to living the way of the cross in the world. On
that great day, God washed Josh's sins away. But more
happened that day. Josh pledged his allegiance to living
the way of Jesus in the power of the Spirit within a community committed to the same story.*

—Mark

With the coming of Jesus and the subsequent coming of the
Spirit, a new and decisive chapter in the story of God came
into view. This new chapter signaled nothing less than a
decisive turn of the ages, bringing with it the offer of God's
salvation. Participation in a new story—a story marked not
by human failure but by the righteousness of God—was
now possible. One could now be a part of a community of
salvation that lived in keeping with the final purposes of
God for all of creation. But how do humans become actors
in the drama of salvation or characters in the unfolding
of God's story of salvation? How do they show that they
belong to the end of the ages? Baptism is the casting call for
those who want to be actors in the Christian story.

John the Baptist prepared people for the coming reign of
God by offering baptism for repentance and the forgiveness

of sins (Matthew 3:6). Baptism properly belongs to the end of the ages. As John's baptism indicates, the new age of the kingdom requires new lives—lives that are both forgiven and committed to new ways of living. But John's baptism anticipates a greater one—the baptism available in Jesus. Like John's, this baptism also prepares people for the kingdom of God by offering forgiveness and calling for a new way of life, but it is more than a change of spiritual status from lost to saved. The baptism of Jesus also brings the power of the Holy Spirit. A new age, requiring new lives, also requires a new source of power—the Spirit of God. Through baptism, God welcomes people into the story of Jesus and that of the Spirit.

When Paul describes baptism in Romans 6:1–11, he portrays it as a death to an old life and a resurrection to walk in "newness of life" (6:4). This new life, however, does not leave the cross of Jesus behind. Rather, it takes the cross as the road map by which Christians find themselves traveling in the story of God. In baptism, Christians proclaim that the way of life that led Jesus to the cross is their way of life as well, and this means taking up one's cross by sharing Jesus' suffering concern for God's creation and his self-abandonment for the sake of others. The baptized life shares Jesus' complete trust in God by dying to all forms of self-trust, so that we say, like Paul, "I am crucified with Christ, and it is no longer I who live but Christ who lives in me" (Galatians 2:19–20). Paul lives as a baptized person by living the way of the cross.

> We are…always carrying in the body the death of Jesus, so that the life of Jesus may be made visible in our bodies. For while we live, we are always being given up to death for Jesus' sake, so that the life of Jesus may be made visible in our mortal flesh.
>
> *2 Corinthians 4:8–11*
>
> I want to know Christ and the power of his resurrection and the sharing of his sufferings by becoming like him in his death.
>
> *Philippians 3:10*

The way of the cross is a radical way of life in our self-absorbed world. A set of luxury condominiums near a busy interstate in Dallas woos possible owners with a large banner

57

that reads "Live to Be Served By Others." This is not the baptized life! Those who live the way of the cross live not for themselves, but for others. By having the same mind as Christ, the baptized learn to do "nothing from selfish ambition or conceit, but in humility to regard others as better than [them]selves." Paul urges them, "Look not to your own interests, but to the interests of others" (Philippians 2:3–4). In another place, Paul appeals to Christians to consider themselves "living sacrifices," people who do not think "more highly of themselves than they ought to think" (Romans 12:3). Living sacrifices love genuinely with mutual affection, outdoing one another in showing honor. They bless those who curse them. They rejoice with those who rejoice and weep with those who weep. Refusing haughtiness, they associate with the lowly. They show hospitality to strangers and share their possessions with others in need (Romans 12:1–21). This kind of service to others indicates more than church membership; it illustrates lives completely transformed by the story of Jesus.

As these passages point out, the baptized life cannot be lived in isolation from others. In an environment where Christians live according to their baptisms, a rich community emerges full of faith, hope, and love. Though poured out and spent for one another as suffering servants, these living sacrifices find that their lives do not evaporate or become dry husks. Though Christians live all day long as lambs being led to the slaughter, they learn that they are more than conquerors (Romans 8:36–37). Through living submissive lives, they find themselves amazingly alive. This is so because the God who raised Jesus from the dead is present to all those who "lose their life for [Jesus'] sake and the sake of the gospel" (Mark 8:35). The power that raised Jesus from the dead is put to work in the church, bringing God's life to those who willingly lay down theirs for the sake of others (Romans 5:1–11; 2 Corinthians 5:14; Ephesians 1:20–23).

However, the disciples of Jesus do not live the way of the cross only toward each other. As Israel was meant to bless all nations, the life that disciples learn in the community of faith is meant to be lived toward all of God's creation. The baptized person follows Jesus into the world as a suffering servant. The crucified one does not avoid places of shame or suffering. Rather, in keeping with the portrayal of the Servant of God in Isaiah, he bears the suffering of others for their healing (Isaiah 53:4–6). The church's task is not to live a privileged life in a gated community above the sin and strife of the world. God's desire for his chosen ones is not that they somehow step around the trouble of the world. Rather, they are to follow Jesus into the world to bear its suffering with the enduring love of God. As the writer of Hebrews urges, Christians are to leave the city—a place of honor and security—and go to Jesus outside the camp—a place of rejection and shame—and bear the abuse he endured for the sake of the world (Hebrews 13:14).

So, the baptized know that the church's life is not an end in itself. The church does not exist to make all the rules, to be in charge of others, nor to glorify itself. It does not seek its own privilege or comfort or preach only about the good life, nor is it simply a support group for those who have already been saved. Rather, the church forms the very stage upon which God's salvation is enacted and embraced. The church, like its Lord, is sent into the world, not to be served, but to serve and give itself up for others. The baptized are those who willingly enter the suffering of all creation with the redemptive love of God.

> ### Discipleship
>
> [Discipleship in Hebrews] means living like the heroes of the faith who lived as strangers and aliens on the earth, seeking God's city.... It means following in the path of the suffering Jesus, and being transformed through God's power, as he was, into genuine children of God through the obedience of faith.... It means enduring for the sake of an education (12:7). It means "going forth to him outside the camp and bearing the abuse he endured" (13:13).
>
> *Luke Timothy Johnson in Fleer & Bland's* Preaching Hebrews, 2003

The Baptized Life: A Spirit-Empowered Story

In baptism, the same power that raised Jesus from the dead fills the life of the believer. The baptized not only experience a death in baptism. They are also raised to a new way of life—life in the Spirit. In fact, a life conformed to the death of Jesus is sustainable only through the power of the Holy Spirit. The baptized share in the great blessing of God's indwelling Spirit: "If the Spirit of him who raised Jesus from the dead dwells in you, he who raised Christ from the dead will give life to your mortal bodies through his Spirit that dwells in you" (Romans 8:11).

However, the Spirit not only fills individuals but also dwells within the community of faith as a whole. For instance, when Paul reminds his readers that they are the temple of the Holy Spirit in 1 Corinthians 3:16–17, he is referring to the church as a whole. In another of his most memorable images, Paul refers to the church as the "body of Christ" (1 Corinthians 12–14). What is striking about this image is that the body of Christ comes into view by the ministry of the Spirit. The body is composed of many parts, but unified by one Spirit. It is the Spirit that provides the gifts for the functioning of the body. Apostles, prophets, teachers, miracle workers, healers, helpers, leaders, and gifted speakers all receive their ministry through the provision of the Spirit.

To the extent that the Spirit works among the members of the church, the body of Christ can be seen and Christ's ministry furthered. Still, the presence of spiritual gifts is no guarantee that the church will function as the body of Christ. Without the community and sacrifice essential to the family of God, spiritual gifts become to the church what king and temple were to Israel: signs of God's presence which have replaced the presence of God himself. Jesus warned that "On that day many will say to me, 'Lord, Lord, did we not prophesy in your name, and do many deeds of power in your name?' Then I will declare to them, 'I never knew you; go away from me, you evildoers'" (Matthew 7:22–23). The presence of impressive gifts is no guarantee that their use is being inspired by the same Spirit who granted them. Such gifts are not given for the glory of the individual, after all, but rather for the good of the community. Paul reminds the Corinthians that "each is given a

60

manifestation of the Spirit for the common good" (1 Corinthians 12:7). God is not as interested in Spirit-inspired individuals as he is in a Spirit-inspired community.

So the Spirit-inspired community lives not only by gifts, but also by Spirit-inspired virtues. In fact, without these virtues, the Spirit's gifts are little more than "noisy gongs and clanging symbols." The church emerges as a sign of the age that will not pass away when it lives in faith, hope, and love (1 Corinthians 13:1–13). The church shows itself to be a community of God's own possession when it bears the fruit of the Spirit: love, joy, peace, patience, kindness, generosity, faithfulness, gentleness, and self-control (Galatians 5:22–23). The presence of the fruit of the Spirit allows the cruciform life, or a life conformed to the way of the cross, to emerge in community. For instance, surely patience, kindness, and generosity are necessary to considering "others better than yourselves" or doing "nothing from selfish ambition or conceit" (Philippians 2:3–4). And surely gentleness and self-control are necessary for repaying abuse with blessing. Without the virtues given by the Spirit, holiness would be impossible. As the Spirit's virtues are employed, a community of the cross emerges in which God is pleased to dwell.

As a community serving the resurrection, the church learns that the way of the Spirit is the way of life—the way of healing, peace, and acceptance. When the Spirit leads the church, therefore, its members learn to look at life differently. For instance, as the church lives in the fruit of the Spirit, the real meaning of power becomes apparent. The self-emptying way of love provides the freedom necessary for transformed lives. Generosity extends goodness to others. Gentleness creates welcoming, hospitable space for a community of peace to emerge. Living in the Spirit, the church learns that humility is not the precondition for experiencing the power of God; humility is the power of God. In the same way, patience isn't merely a preparation for acting in power; patience is a powerful action.

Because the world tends to define power in different ways—ways that lead to control, fragmentation, violence, and death—those who live by the Spirit's power will always see themselves as exiles in this world. As the Israelites followed God through the wilderness in search of a new land, so resurrection people—those who have abandoned modes of power set on self-preservation for modes of power related to self-sacrifice—seek a different city, the one that is to come.

The Baptized Life: A Family Around the Table

Baptism is not the only practice that defines what it means to be a people of God at the end of the ages. When Jesus shared the Passover meal with his disciples before his death, he looked forward to the day when they would "eat and drink at my table in the kingdom" (Luke 22:14–30). Those who meet around the Lord's table eat in anticipation of the great feast to be fulfilled in the kingdom of God. It is around the Lord's table that God's people learn what it means to be a people of the last days.

As with any family, the family of God is bound both by birth and by practice of family life. And nothing is more central to family life than mealtime. In the New Testament, the people on whom the end of the ages has fallen gather for worship not around an altar, but a table. In worship, Christians reenact God's merciful hospitality around a table that knows no distinctions. Notice that when Jesus observes how his contemporaries throw banquets, jockeying for seats of honor and inviting only those who can in turn enhance their community standing, he offers the vision of a new banquet befitting the kingdom of God where invitation is extended only to those who can offer nothing in return. Those who eat at the Lord's table do so in anticipation of that great day when "the poor, the crippled, the lame, and the blind" will eat bread in the kingdom of heaven (Luke 14:13).

The view of Jesus around the table in Luke's Gospel is mirrored by the table practices of the church in Acts. Luke is fond of showing his readers that the movement of the Spirit in conversion is followed by the movement of people to eat around a common table—an intimate act that shows true acceptance and community. Notice that the Christians who experienced the outpouring of the Spirit at Pentecost devoted themselves to "the breaking of bread" and found themselves "day by day" breaking bread together (Acts 2:42–47). One of the tests of the gospel in Acts seems to be whether allegiance to the story of Jesus is powerful enough to bring people around a common table to share a common life. Remember, Peter's preaching to Cornelius was followed by table fellowship (Acts 11:3). In the same way, notice Lydia's challenge to Paul after her conversion in Acts 16: "If you have judged me to be faithful to the Lord, come and stay at my home" (16:15). Or notice just a few verses later that the Philippian jailer, upon his conversion, "brought them up into his house and set food before them; and he and his entire household rejoiced that he had become a believer in God" (16:34). In Acts, the story of Jesus became visible in gatherings around table.

For Paul, gathering around a table without distinctions stands as a proclamation of the death of Jesus until he returns (1 Corinthians 11:26). Because the death of Jesus is for all, everything that would divide people must be put to death. When Paul realizes that the Corinthians' practice of the Lord's Supper divides the rich from the poor, he concludes, "When you come together, it is not really to eat the Lord's Supper" (1 Corinthians 11:20). Table etiquette at the Lord's Supper demands that the rich wait for the poor so that all may share a common meal. It is around such a table that Christians learn what it means to be a people of God's possession.

New Testament authors liberally use the language of family to describe the people of God at the end of the age. For Paul, Jesus is more than a Moses figure, bringing reformation through teaching or instruction. He is the firstborn of a new family. In Paul's letters, he writes to brothers and sisters and his children in the faith. These kinships are not defined by blood but by the waters of baptism, which, for Paul, are thicker than blood. Those who share in the family inheritance of Abraham are defined by the righteousness

63

that comes through the faith of Jesus Christ. God has called a new chosen people, a new family. The creation of this new family occupies Paul's prayers offered to "the Father, from whom every family in heaven and earth takes its name" (Ephesians 3:14).

Jesus also used the language of family to describe his followers. Who are Jesus' mothers, brothers, and sisters? Not those who share blood ties. Rather, Jesus proclaims, "Whoever does the will of my Father in heaven is my brother and sister and mother" (Matthew 12:50). Significantly, the designation "father" is missing from Jesus' description of the new family. This is due in part to Jesus' teaching that only God merits the title "Father" (Matthew 23:9). But the absence of this term also indicates that the new family invites those without power or privilege to be fully included among God's new people. In an ancient world that favored fathers and husbands, Jesus imagines a family of mothers, brothers, and sisters. His ministry is remarkable for attracting those who lived without social standing or privilege. Women, children, the poor, the sick, and Gentiles all prominently follow Jesus and constitute a family for the last days. Community through the bond of the Spirit is both the end and the means by which God is telling his story.

> **Community**
>
> The Christian community is described in many ways. James calls Christians "friends of God." In the ancient world, the notion of friendship went well beyond affection or positive regard for others. "The word 'friend' was regarded as a particularly intense and inclusive kind of intimacy." For writers of James' day, friendship meant to be of "one soul" with another, which meant a sharing of values, attitudes, and perspectives.
>
> *Luke Timothy Johnson*
> Brother of Jesus, Friend of God: Studies in the Letter of James, *2004*

What Does This All Mean for Us?

So the final credits of the New Testament story have scrolled across the screen. What would it mean for today's church to continue in the story? How does the church today live in light of the coming of Jesus and the sending of the Spirit? What does it mean to live as the people on whom the end of the ages has fallen in today's world? How can we live to extend not just the forms of the story, but its meaning? These questions will be addressed more fully in Chapters 7–9. Still, it is important here to notice some of the initial implications.

First, the church of the Spirit is an evangelistic community. In the time of the early church, the movement of the Spirit always created opportunities for the church to witness to what the risen Lord was doing in the world, and the same is true now. Too often, modern Christians think of evangelism as a human endeavor, one person teaching another. The view from Acts would confirm John Wesley's conviction that God is the great evangelist in the world. We are merely witnesses to the movement of Jesus through the working of the Spirit. The followers of Jesus will find as they go into the world that the presence of the Spirit goes ahead of them, convicting the world of sin and creating opportunity for the proclamation of the gospel (John 16:1–11).

The first Christians recognized God's movement in the world because the Holy Spirit is the continuing presence of the risen Jesus. Though free of the control of the church, the Spirit is not a free agent but serves to extend the ministry of Jesus. We, too, need to be open to the leading of the Spirit, trusting him to open doors for teaching and witnessing. Missions programs and other evangelistic efforts fall flat when we don't rely on the Spirit to prepare the way.

Of course, to be open to the Spirit's leading demands that we live spirit-filled lives. Christians are not merely the recipients of the salvation of God, but the sign or demonstration of that salvation. In classic studies on the church, one might find an entire chapter devoted to the "mission" of the church. Studies that divide the church into categories tend to separate mission from issues like worship or church governance. Mission becomes an activity of the church, set apart from other activities of the church. In fact, many would suggest that mission is what happens outside the walls of the church, distinguished from the church's "inward" life, which is something other than mission. The church's mission in the world is to live in the salvation made manifest in the coming kingdom of God. Therefore, "mission" is not a program of the church. Mission is who the church is. Talk of the church's mission too often focuses on how the church will enhance its own survival. In contrast, the mission of God calls participants, even the church, to give up their very lives for the sake of his reign. The mission of the church involves living the way of the kingdom before the world.

To the extent that the people of God live within the way of the kingdom, the salvation of God becomes visible to others. As sins are forgiven, sick and broken lives are healed, the poor are honored, and children are welcomed, the salvation of God is realized in a merciful community. As God's people turn the other cheek, love their enemies, and refuse to lord power and privilege over others, God's salvation becomes visible in a peaceful community. As praise of God replaces boasting about ethnicity, the salvation of God becomes visible in a new family of rich diversity. On the other hand, when God's people live by the standards of an age that is passing away, the opportunity to experience the salvation offered by God is diminished, both for the church and for others. So, for instance, when leaders seek to dominate others, or preference is given to those with an abundance of possessions, or children are marginalized, then a community merely participates in the world already made available by the principalities and powers of this age. Such a community misses the opportunity to live in the salvation extended in the ministry of Jesus.

Second, the church must eat together as a family. Unfortunately, our experience of the Lord's Supper often falls short of the significant role it played in defining the people of God in the New Testament. Our practice of the Lord's Supper typically features silent meditation, a time of self-introspection or meditation on the death of Jesus "for me." We have little sense that Jesus has welcomed all of us around the table to become a Spirit-empowered community. As a result, our churches tend to display little diversity among members. The power of the table to bring together all kinds of people is curtailed, and as a result, our congregations tend to drift towards social, cultural, and ethnic uniformity. Turned silently inward, we fail to share the intimate community that early Christians expressed around the table. What would happen if the table became less a time of individual meditation and more a time of recognizing community? What if it became the occasion when the church prayed for the sick, confessed sins, extended blessings, or shared its possessions? These practices might help the church recover the first Christians' sense that by the power of the Spirit, God was breaking down human barriers around a table set by Jesus.

Third, in order to be true to God's call, we must not only practice baptism, but we must view it in the way God intended. Churches of Christ have certainly been interested in the baptismal practices of the first Christians. However, we still have some work to do in understanding how baptism formed the first Christian communities. In our traditional baptismal practices, forgiveness of sins is always mentioned. The authors seldom witness a baptism where this sign of the new age is not offered. However, less frequent is the mention of the presence of the Holy Spirit, the powerful partner who allows us to participate in the new age being revealed. Furthermore, almost always missing in our baptismal practice is language about repentance—that participation in a new age requires a new way of life, namely the way of the cross. Too often, our baptisms reveal little interest in anything other than changing our "eternal status." Certainly, baptism marks a movement from death to life, but for the first Christians, it was primarily a call to live a distinct life in keeping with the emerging reign of God. For the early church, baptism was more than a ticket to heaven; it was the door to a new way of life.

Fourth, the church needs to act as a servant, not existing for its own comfort, but taking the message of God to the dark, unpleasant places where hurting people live. If the purpose of the church is to be big, then the suburbs

67

are the place to be. However, if its purpose is to live in the story of one who was born in a cattle stall, then the church might find itself choosing lowlier accommodations. Of course, nothing is wrong with having churches in the suburbs. However, in a day and age when churches frequently sell their buildings to relocate to more plush surroundings, it is essential that we not abandon neighborhoods where life is a bit grittier. As followers of Christ, we have a servant's duty to plant and maintain churches in the lowliest of circumstances. They may be smaller or larger, but they will always be closer to the natural habitat of God's coming into the world.

Fifth, the church must live as a family in community, excluding no one. Michael Emerson, in his provocative book *Divided By Faith*, notes that no hour in American life is more segregated than the Sunday morning worship hour. Emerson writes particularly of the racial segregation that is maintained in our congregations. However, this segregation moves in other directions as well. Sunday worship is the occasion when the poor meet with the poor, the rich meet with the rich, the young meet with the young, and the old meet with the old. Church growth theory even encourages this demographic division, noting that churches grow fastest in homogenous groupings. Moreover, as Emerson notes, individualistic understandings of salvation tend to undermine visions of the church that cross ethnic, racial, and other social boundaries. When "personal salvation" dominates our understandings of the salvation of God, Christians are prone to think, "As long as I'm saved and you're saved, there's really no need for us to worship together." Emerson demonstrates how far the contemporary church is from Paul's vision of a church that intentionally overcomes the boundaries presented by Jew and Greek, slave and free, and male and female.

Conclusion

In the New Testament, we encounter the church as the people on whom the end of the ages has come. With the sending of Jesus and the subsequent sending of the Spirit, God has acted decisively for the salvation of all. As Jesus was sent to be God's suffering presence in the world, so God sends the church. As a cross-bearing people, the church lives deeply engaged with a hurting world. However, because the way of the cross stands opposed to worldly definitions of power and success, those who live this way in the world will never be "of the world." 1 Peter describes the church's existence aptly as resident aliens (1 Peter 2:11). Resident aliens live in the world but have citizenship in another—a world emerging at the turn of the ages. By imitating the story of Jesus, particularly his death and resurrection, and by living in the power of the Spirit, the church becomes both a sign and foretaste of the salvation of God. In the fullness of time, God is gathering nothing less than a new humanity to live under his reign so that his nearness might be experienced among all nations.

Still, while the church experiences the salvation of God in the here and now, it must never confuse its own life with God's salvation. Jesus' preaching is clear: the kingdom of God is both present and coming. It is present in the ministry of Jesus, as he indicates when he tells his opponents, "If it is by the Spirit of God that I cast out demons, then the kingdom of God has come to you" (Matthew 12:28). On another occasion, Jesus answers the query of the Pharisees concerning signs of the coming of the kingdom by announcing that the "kingdom is among you" (Luke 17:21). Still, while Jesus indicates that the kingdom is present in his ministry, it is also still a future reality. Jesus teaches his followers to pray for the coming of God's kingdom (Matthew 6:10), a reality that will not be completely revealed until "the Son of Man comes in a cloud with power and glory" (Luke 21:27–33). Because the kingdom is both present and coming, the church serves the reign of God by constantly practicing repentance, knowing that it will never fully experience the salvation of God until Jesus returns. Consequently, the church must see its own life in temporary terms. As the writer of Hebrews puts it, "Here we have no lasting city, but we are looking for the city that is to come" (Hebrews 13:13). The church cannot seek its own power and privilege, nor can it become too comfortable here in the present age. It is a community on the move, a priestly nation that has left behind comfort and security to follow the leading of God's Spirit into the world.

4 Keeping the Story Straight

My first car was a '68 Mustang. What a great first car! There's just something cool about a Mustang. Mustangs were cool when they first rolled off the assembly line in 1965, and they are still cool today. I recently had the opportunity to rent an '04 Mustang convertible for a weekend. The convertible is a very different car than my old '68. In many ways they are not the same car. The new Mustang has a much more powerful engine than the engine my car packed under the hood. When I lifted the hood to inspect the 200 cubic inch engine in my '68, I could see the ground below. When you lift the hood on a new model, you have to search and search just to find the dipstick. My little Mustang didn't have an FM radio, much less a 5-CD stereo system. Unlike the new models, it didn't have cruise control, or a five-speed transmission, or air bags. In some ways they are very different cars.

Still, there is something about both cars that undeniably says "Mustang." A Mustang is not a pick-up truck. Nor is it a station wagon, or minivan, or family sedan. You would never mistake a Mustang for a Cadillac Seville, not then and not now. And a Mustang is even different from other sports cars. You'll never confuse a Mustang for a Trans-am or Corvette. A Mustang is a Mustang, whether it's a '68 or an '04. Though the models have changed from year to year, the image of the car is the same. Sports coupe. Sunglasses. Rock and roll. Cool.

—Mark

71

In a way, the church is like the Mustang. As with all metaphors, this one has its limits. I am not speaking of the church as a sports car as opposed to a luxury sedan or family car, and I'm not saying that the "later models" of church are more or less advanced than earlier editions. Instead, I mean to suggest that, like the Mustang, the church exhibits both consistency and variety from "model" to "model." Not all churches are exactly the same. Not even in the New Testament. Churches can be strikingly different from context to context. Yet, despite these differences, churches can still be unmistakably faithful to what it means to be a church. Like the Mustang, the church will always bear certain features that set it apart from all other communities, even while there are significant differences from church to church. In this chapter, we want to look at the New Testament church and notice how its features display both variety and consistency.

Faithful Practices

In chapter three, we suggested that the church is the community living in the story of Jesus at the turn of the ages. In other words, the church expresses its life as the continuation of the ministry of Jesus through the guidance of the Holy Spirit. Indeed, this book is committed to the notion that the church is a story-formed, story-living community. The question we want to consider in this chapter is: "can a narrative approach to understanding the church adequately account for the rich set of practices we find in earliest Christianity?" We believe that asking questions about practices in relation to the Christian story holds some promising advantages over other approaches.

Other approaches to understanding the church tend to define it by categories, such as the worship of the church, the polity or structure of the church, the mission of the church, and so on. Defining the church in relation to categories presents two problems. First, categories value organization, and organization values similarity. Too often, sorting the church into categories sifts out diversity, viewing variety only as aberration. On the other hand, because a story includes both continuity and discontinuity, narrative approaches can more easily account for diversity as something other than an aberration. Second, categories tend to take on a life of their own. For instance, worship can be treated in isolation from ethics and the connections between the two overlooked. This lack of integration can also lead to a lack of shape or proportion, with all categories seeming equally important. In contrast, by giving attention to plot, narratives clarify relationships and try to take into account which aspects of a story are most vital to the plot at any given time. Some aspects of the story might move to the foreground while others recede into the background. For these reasons, a narrative approach holds great promise in helping us understand the practices of the church.

Many of the habits and practices we find in the New Testament are designed to help the church keep the story straight as it struggles to be true to the past and follow the Spirit's leading for the future. If the church's task is to live faithfully to the story, then keeping the story straight is an indispensable aspect of the church's life, both for the early Christians and for us today. The practices of the earliest Christians did not serve only as guardians marking the boundaries of the faith. They served as invaluable guides, carrying the story in important ways.

By accounting for practices of the first Christians according to their connection to the story of Jesus, we avoid two extremes. The first extreme flies under the banner "we've never done it that way before." From this viewpoint, the practices of the church are seen as fixed and set in stone. In turn, the work of the church becomes preoccupied with defining and defending "the way we do things." Faithfulness consists of doing things the way they've always been done.

A second extreme runs in the opposite direction, and its slogan might be "out with the old, in with the new." Here, practices are mere forms that can be changed like one changes clothing. Or the faith is like an ear of corn, with a disposable husk of practices formed around the essential kernels of belief. In either case, faithfulness

73

here is defined as jettisoning old practices to make way for the new.

Both of these extremes separate church practices from the story and thereby lose the ability to manage faithfully issues of continuity and change. The "we've never done it that way before" extreme says "yes" to continuity and "no" to change. The "out with the old, in with the new" extreme says "yes" to change and "no" to continuity. However, by understanding the relationship between practices and the story, the church lives in the tension of both continuity and change, of both consistency and variety—a tension we see at work in the first Christians.

The first Christians trusted a fairly predictable set of practices to help them keep the story straight. Yet these practices were not carried out in rigid uniformity from church to church. On the contrary, the New Testament witness exhibits impressive diversity. For example, all churches trusted worship to keep the story straight, but not all churches worshipped in exactly the same way. As we will see, what was true for worship was also true for other aspects of church life from congregation to congregation.

Keeping the Story Straight

The earliest Christians clearly trusted worship to help them keep the story straight. Through praise, confession, and ritual, New Testament communities rehearsed the Christian story when they assembled for worship. But they trusted more than worship. They trusted Scripture as well—the Old Testament—to help them understand what it means to be God's people. The church also trusted faithful leaders: men and women whose lives flowed from the story of God because they lived out the Christian story in their daily lives and so could be trusted to keep the story straight.

74

We are accustomed to thinking of worship, Scripture, and leadership as essential aspects of church life, just as the first Christians did; but they also emphasized other elements that Churches of Christ have tended to downplay, such as the role of ethics—or holy living—and the work of the Holy Spirit. The early Christians were aware that they lived differently from those around them because they believed a different story; and the belief that Jesus continued to live with his people through the presence of the Holy Spirit gave the church confidence that they would remain faithful to the story.

Worship, leadership, Scripture, ethics, and the Spirit form a multi-strand rope that kept the early church tethered to the story of God. While this list might be described differently by others, and while, given further reflection, we might add more items ourselves, the point worth considering is that the earliest Christians looked to several intertwined aspects of their life to keep the story straight. These aspects are like inseparably intertwined strands in a good rope. For instance, Scripture alone is not enough to safeguard the story. The church's reading of Scripture is aided by obedient lives, trustworthy teachers, and the illumination of the Spirit. Without these other aspects, Christians can come to view Scripture as little more than a rule book. Neither is the direction of the Spirit alone sufficient in keeping the story straight. Because the leading of the Spirit is sometimes difficult to distinguish from our own wishes and desires, discerning the spirits is necessary and cannot be done apart from worship, Scripture, and an obedient way of life. Ethics without life in the Spirit too easily becomes legalism; worship apart from ethics devolves into formalism and even blatant hypocrisy, while Scripture apart from the living witness of the Spirit becomes biblicism. The point is, these elements are interrelated and together keep the church living faithfully within the story.

Formalism and Biblicism

"Formalism" defines things according to their formal, or external characteristics, and overlooks or downplays other definitions. For instance, Paul accuses his opponents of "holding to the outward form of godliness, but denying its power" (2 Timothy 3:5).

"Biblicism" limits the revelation of God to the pages of Scripture. Jesus accuses some who follow him of biblicism when he says, "You search the Scriptures because you think that in them you have eternal life; and it is they that testify on my behalf. Yet you refuse to come to me to have life" (John 5:39–40).

75

The idea that worship, leadership, Scripture, ethics, and life in the Spirit were vital elements of the early church's life is not a new one. However, what is often not noticed is the way that each of these elements helps the church live within the story of Jesus. What is the connection of each of these aspects of the church's life to the story of Jesus? That is the essential question that occupies this chapter.

Trusting Worship

Through praise, prayer, confession, recital, and ritual enactment, Christians remember the story that called them into existence. By "remember," we mean more than calling events to mind or jogging the brain's stores of information. For Christians, remembering means to relive or to participate anew in the act being remembered. Take, for instance, the Lord's Supper. When Christians "do this in memory of [Christ]," they do not simply recall the Last Supper or the death of Jesus mentally. Rather, through meaningful ritual they participate again in the story. What is true of the Lord's Supper is true of baptism and other aspects of worship as well. Worship exists to help us reenact the Christian story. Though not all songs or prayers or readings make direct reference to a particular story or set of stories, all of worship functions to maintain a view of the world in which God has acted to redeem his creation. We might say that worship is where the first Christians learned their lines to become characters in God's continuing story.

While we have very little description of the earliest Christians' actual worship assemblies, the New Testament is liberally sprinkled with language used in early Christian worship. We find in various places hymns, blessings, baptismal language, and confessions. These confessions served week-in and week-out to provide the grammar by which worshippers interpreted their lives in light of the Christian story. Notice, for instance, how the great confession in Philippians 2 traces the story of Jesus:

76

> Let the same mind be in you that was in Christ Jesus, who, though he was in the form of God, did not regard equality with God as something to be exploited, but

emptied himself, taking the form of a slave, being born in human likeness. And being found in human form became obedient to death—even death on a cross. Therefore, God has highly exalted him and gave him the name that is above every name, so that at the name of Jesus every knee should bend, in heaven and on earth and under the earth, and every tongue should confess that Jesus Christ is Lord, to the glory of God the Father." (Philippians 2:5–11)

Here and in other places (for example, Colossians 1:15–20; 1 Timothy 2:5, 3:16), New Testament writers demonstrated the early church's concern to find words to guide the church into the future.

Such a concern for future faithfulness is explicitly tied to a series of confessions in the pastoral epistles (1 and 2 Timothy, Titus). "The saying is sure" is Paul's preface to each of these confessions (1 Timothy 1:15, 3:1, 4:9; 2 Timothy 2:11–13; Titus 3:4–8). These faithful sayings stand in contrast to the false teachers' empty words that "eat away like gangrene." Instead, Timothy is to give the church "healthy words" (translated in some versions as "sound doctrine") that will help them keep the story straight. All but one of these trustworthy sayings feature language about the work of Jesus that stands at the heart of the Gospel. Take for instance 2 Timothy 2:11–13: "If we have died with him, we will also live with him; if we endure, we will also reign with him; if we deny him he will deny us; if we are faithless, he remains faithful—for he cannot deny himself." Where does the church learn and rehearse these trustworthy sayings (especially in an oral culture)? In worship.

Each Lord's day, Christians gather to remember the story by which they live their lives. Too often, we worship without an awareness of the story-sustaining role of our Sunday assemblies. Worship can be thought of as the performance of certain acts that keep us in good standing with God. This view of worship can result in a lack of appreciation for the role worship plays in allowing Christians to participate in the life-giving story of God. The first Christians worshiped not to satisfy a list of requirements but to participate in the story of the faith.

Trusting Leaders

Evidence of the importance of authoritative teachers appears frequently in the New Testament. For instance, the church as described in Acts places a high premium on the teaching and authority of the apostles—those who participated most directly in the earthly ministry of Jesus. Though not one of the Twelve, Paul also makes appeal to apostolic authority due to his experience with the risen Lord as he brings the gospel to the Gentiles. To the extent that Paul's authority was recognized among the churches, his delegates—Timothy, Barnabas, Silas, Tychicus, Epaphroditus, and Phoebe—were welcomed by the church as authoritative figures.

> Paul, an apostle—sent neither by human commission nor from human authorities, but through Jesus Christ and God the Father who raised him from the dead....
>
> *Galatians 1:1*
>
> Still, I think it is necessary to send you Epaphroditus, my brother, co-worker and fellow soldier....
>
> *Philippians 2:25*

The teaching authority of Paul and his delegates was essential for infant churches, primarily Gentile in composition, to make progress in the faith. That's why it's not surprising to see in one of Paul's lists of gifts for the building up of the church a heavy emphasis on the word of God: "The gifts that he gave were that some would be apostles, some prophets, some evangelists, some pastors and teachers, to equip the saints for the work of ministry..." (Ephesians 4:11–12).

Paul's churches, however, were not the only ones to emphasize the importance of trustworthy teachers. Matthew's Gospel reorients Christians experiencing transition as they move away from the patterns and teachings of the synagogue. Apart from the authoritative teaching of "those who sit on Moses' seat" (the scribes and Pharisees, Matthew 23:2), how will the church know it is living faithfully to the story of God? Jesus' teachings and deeds are offered in Matthew's Gospel to help his disciples recognize scribes trained for the kingdom of heaven. These teachers bring from their storehouse treasures both old and new (Matthew 13:51–52). Matthew's Gospel portrays Jesus as very concerned with finding leaders

78

who will teach disci-
ples "everything that I
have commanded you"
(Matthew 28:20).

From these brief
examples from Paul's
letters and Matthew's
Gospel, it is clear that
the first Christians
relied on trustworthy
leaders to help them
keep the story straight.
This is true in part
because teaching is so
important to the main-
tenance of any tradition.
However, Christian
leadership does not
keep the story straight

The Gospels and the Churches

What is true of the epistles in the New
Testament is also true of the Gospels. Matthew, Mark, Luke, and John were written
not just to set the record straight, but to set
churches straight. Part of what accounts for
the variety we find among the Gospels is
the fact that they were written with different contexts in mind. Although discussing
a Gospel's intended audience can be hard,
the power of the Gospels lies in their ability to allow Jesus to speak again to the new
and varying circumstances encountered
by his followers in subsequent generations
and locations. Because they shed light on
early Christian communities, the Gospels
should be considered when accounting for
the faith and practice of churches.

only through teaching. Christian leaders also display the
story in their leadership style. Notice that after Jesus predicts
his death and resurrection, he teaches his disciples that those
who are great in the kingdom of God are those who serve.
Christian leaders do not "lord it over" others as the Gentiles
do. Instead, those who follow the crucified one seek not to
be served, but to serve, to be the least among the people of
God (Mark 10:42–45). Peter echoes the words of Jesus when
reminding elders of their duties with respect to God's people:

> Now as an elder myself and a witness of the sufferings
> of Christ, as well as one who shares in the glory to be
> revealed, I exhort the elders among you to tend the flock
> of God that is in your charge, exercising the oversight,
> not under compulsion but willingly, as God would have
> you do it—not for sordid gain but eagerly. Do not lord it
> over those in your charge, but be examples to the flock.
> And when the chief shepherd appears, you will win the
> crown of glory that never fades away. (1 Peter 5:1–4)

79

These elders are to view their leadership as an extension of the
chief shepherd's. They are to view their work in light of the

sufferings of Christ and his glory to be revealed (death and resurrection). Their leadership style, therefore, is an enactment of the story of Jesus. As those who follow the crucified one, they do not lord it over those in their charge but willingly serve as humble examples of selfless service to the flock of God.

What we find in the Gospels and in 1 Peter are manifest other places as well. Paul's letters express his own understandings of leadership in relation to the death and resurrection of Jesus. When Paul claims to know nothing among the Corinthians except Christ and him crucified, he is speaking of more than just his message (1 Corinthians 2:1–5). He is also speaking specifically of his ministry style. In contrast to others who would display the message of Christ with brilliant rhetorical flourish, Paul is willing for his weakness to be the proper vehicle to carry the gospel of a crucified Savior. Consistently challenged to defend the authenticity of his ministry, Paul never appeals to any standard other than his conformity to the death of Jesus. His leadership style carries the story of the gospel and, therefore, helps the church keep the story straight.

> Paul's opponents say, "His letters are weighty and strong, but his physical presence is weak..." (2 Corinthians 10:10).
>
> Paul counters, "...but [God] said to me 'my grace is sufficient for you, for power is made perfect in weakness.' So, I will boast all the more gladly of my weaknesses, so that the power of Christ may dwell in me...for whenever I am weak, then I am strong" (2 Corinthians 12:9–10).

Certainly through their teaching, early leaders helped the first Christians continue in the story. Beyond their teaching, however, these leaders displayed their confidence in the death and resurrection of Jesus in their leadership style. Through submitted love and selfless care for others, early Christian leaders lived out the story of the crucified one before the people of God.

Trusting Scripture

As with all New Testament writers, Paul believed that the story of Jesus was in keeping with the story of Scripture. Jesus lived, died, and was raised "in accordance with the scriptures" (1 Corinthians 15:3–4). While not every detail in the Old Testament points directly to Jesus, New Testament writers saw in Jesus nothing less than the culmination of the story of the Old Testament. For Matthew, Jesus came not as the end of the law, but as its fulfillment (5:21). Paul's extended argument in Romans makes virtually the same claim (Romans 2–5) and demonstrates specifically how Jesus' story is the fulfillment of the promise made to Abraham. Early Christians found great comfort in knowing that both the story of Jesus and the story of the church were anticipated by the Old Testament. By knowing the story of Scripture deeply, the church found its own place in the story of God in new circumstances.

Committed to the belief that the story of Jesus was best understood in light of the story of Israel, Gospel writers took great pains to tell their story in ways that highlighted echoes from stories in the Old Testament. For instance, one cannot read the story of the angel's announcement to Mary without hearing several other birth announcements in the Old Testament, particularly that of the birth of Samuel to his mother Hannah. In the same way, one cannot hear Jesus' infancy story in Matthew without thinking of the birth of Moses. Both stories involve Egypt, a despotic ruler, and the killing of first-born males. Examples like these are multiplied time and again throughout the New Testament. New Testament documents constantly bring to readers' minds the stories of Abraham or David or Isaiah or even Melchizedek. The first believers, after all, were Old Testament Christians. Knowing Jesus helped them understand Scripture better, and knowing Scripture gave them better insight into the life and significance of Jesus.

Because of their emphasis on Scripture, very early on Christians began to collect stories and sayings from the life of Jesus (first oral, then written), as well as Paul's letters and other significant writings. While the formation of the New Testament as we know it was still generations away, the earliest Christians were a textual community, trusting the writings of the Old Testament and their own emerging written witness to the work of God to help them keep the story straight.

81

The earliest reference to the New Testament in the form we now have it comes from an Easter Letter by the early theologian Athanasius in 367 CE. Athanasius' list was formally accepted by a Roman council in 393. However, the debate over which writings should be considered Scripture lasted long beyond this council's decision. The Eastern church did not adopt the same list until the agreement of a council in Constantinople in 692 CE.

Churches of Christ have traditionally been known as a "people of the Book," deeply committed to the Scripture. However, in order to be like the earliest Christians, we must maintain and strengthen this focus. Too few of our worship assemblies today feature the reading of Scripture, and Sunday school classes too often seem more interested in topics other than the study of God's word. Regrettably, study of the Old Testament—the Bible of the first Christians—frequently gets downplayed or completely ignored. We hope that churches will again heed the admonition of 1 Timothy 4:13 to "Give attention to the public reading of Scripture, to exhorting, to teaching."

Trusting a Distinct Life

Often biblical writers orient their readers to the Christian story by comparing their attitudes and behaviors as Christians to those they had before. Notice, for instance, Paul's appeal in Colossians "to put to death whatever in you is earthly.... These are the ways you once followed when you were living that life. But now you must get rid of such things" (3:5–8). The stark contrast between their old and new patterns of life provided evidence that they were living a different story and belonged to a different age.

The first Christians were aware that their behavior made them different. 1 Peter's language is striking in this regard: "I urge you as aliens and exiles to abstain from the desires of the flesh that wage war against the soul. Conduct yourselves honorably among the Gentiles, so that, though they malign you as evildoers, they may see your honorable deeds and glorify God when he comes to judge" (1 Peter 2:11–12). As aliens and exiles, Christians find themselves living squarely in the story of God's redeeming work begun in Israel. Like Israel, the church's distinctive life marks them as a "chosen race, a royal priesthood, a holy nation, God's own people" (2:9).

Simply living differently, however, is no guarantee that one's life is helping to keep the story straight. By tying ethics directly to the story of the death and resurrection of Jesus, early Christians gained confidence that they were living faithfully. For instance, New Testament writers placed a great deal of emphasis on the practice of loving enemies. For Paul, love of enemies was directly tied to the cross of Jesus. He makes this connection explicit in Romans: "For while we were still weak, at the right time Christ died for the ungodly ... God proves his love for us that while we were sinners Christ died for us.... For if while we were enemies, we were reconciled to God through the death of his Son, much more surely, having been reconciled, will we be saved by his life" (Romans 5:6-10). When Paul urges his readers to "bless those who persecute you; bless and do not curse them," he is recalling the story of God's love expressed in the cross (Romans 12:14). In a similar way, 1 Peter calls Christians "not [to] repay evil for evil or abuse for abuse; but, on the contrary, repay with a blessing" (3:9). Why? "For Christ also suffered for sins once for all, the righteous for the unrighteous, in order to bring you to God" (3:18). Again, Christian behavior is tied directly to the death of Jesus.

Jesus' own teaching on loving enemies anticipates his death—a death for sinners. As Christians act kindly toward those who hate them, bless those who curse them, and pray for those who abuse them, they know they are following the one who died for God's enemies. When they turn the other cheek and offer their shirt to those who demand their cloak, they know they are entrusting themselves to the one who raised Jesus from the dead. As Christians love their

> The term "ethics" is used here to denote the values and behaviors that define Christianity as a way of life.

83

enemies, expecting nothing in return, they keep the story straight (Luke 6:27–36).

Sometimes New Testament authors use ethical commitments, like loving enemies, to show how distinct Christians were from those around them. At other times, ethical commitments are expressed in customary forms to draw connections between Christian behavior and the larger culture. For instance, when discussing domestic relationships, early Christian writers often imitated a typical form of advice literature known as "household codes." Just as Greek or Roman moralists would address husbands and wives,

"Household codes" similar to those in the New Testament can be found in ancient writings like Aristotle's *Politics*, Xenophon's *Oeconomicus*, and Hierocles' *Oikonomikos* (all from the 4th century BCE), and Seneca's *Epistle* 94 (from the 1st century CE). For more information, see David Balch and Carolyn Osiek's *The Early Christian Family* (2003).

masters and slaves, and fathers and children, so New Testament writers offer admonitions for living within the household of the first century world (see Ephesians 5:21–6:9; Colossians 3:18–4:1; 1 Peter 2:11–3:7).

However, while the form of household codes might be familiar within that culture, in the epistles the traditional relationships are reinterpreted in light of the death and resurrection. Notice how Paul uses the Christian story to define the relationship of husband and wife in Ephesians 5. "Submit to one another," he begins, "out of reverence for Christ." This call to submission would be a common feature of advice to wives in traditional household codes of the time; however, here it is placed in the context of discipleship to Jesus. While in traditional portrayals, husbands would not have been expected to submit to their wives in return, Paul applies the submission of Christ to both husband and wife: "Wives, be subject to your husbands *as you are to the Lord*. . . . Husbands, love your wives, *just as Christ loved the church and gave himself up for her*" (Ephesians 5:21–33). The italicized portions demonstrate how both wife and husband are given instruction in the context of the Christian story. Seen from this perspective,

84

marriage now becomes a primary place where Christians live out the script of the death and resurrection. Husbands and wives, living distinctively in a mutually submitted relationship, help the church keep the story straight.

Other examples could be offered of early Christian ethical commitments that flow directly from understandings of the death and resurrection of Jesus. For instance, the first Christians understood hospitality as an extension of the welcome they received from God through Christ Jesus (Romans 12:1; 13; 15:7). The extravagant New Testament teachings on forgiveness found their source in the extravagant forgiveness offered to Christians in the death of Jesus (Colossians 3:13). Embedded in practices like hospitality, forgiveness, marriage, and loving enemies, the Christian story was preserved through a distinctive life.

Trusting the Risen Lord

The belief that Jesus continues to live in his church through the Holy Spirit gave the first Christians confidence to take the gospel faithfully into uncharted territories that presented new challenges. As we noted in the previous chapter, the book of Acts chronicles for Theophilus "all that Jesus began to do and to teach." The church's awareness of and reliance upon the Holy Spirit guaranteed that the story begun in Jesus would continue along the same lines. At several points, Luke's narrative makes it clear that the direct influence of the risen Lord guides the church and keeps it living faithfully.

For Paul, the presence of the Spirit in the community of faith gave evidence that the gospel had found its mark. In Thessalonians, for example, he reminds the church: "For we know,

> **The Spirit in Acts**
>
> While Peter was still thinking about the vision, the Spirit said to him, "…Now get up, go down to them and go with them without hesitation" (Acts 10:19–20).
>
> "They…were prevented by the Holy Spirit from speaking the message in the province of Asia" (Acts 16:6).
>
> For other descriptions of the Spirit's work, see Acts 8:39; 10:4, 13; 11:12; 13:2; 20:22.

85

brothers and sisters beloved by God, that he has chosen you, because our message of the gospel came to you not in word only, but also in power and in the Holy Spirit and with full conviction" (1 Thessalonians 1:3–5; see also Galatians 3:1–5). Paul urges his converts to pursue a Spirit-cultivated life, praying "in the Spirit at all times in every prayer and supplication" (Ephesians 6:18). Paul is confident that the Spirit is present with Christians in both worship and evangelism, giving them speech, discernment, and confidence that Jesus is in their midst (see Ephesians 6:17–20; 1 Corinthians 2:14; 12–14). For Paul, there is no community of the last age apart from the intimate guidance of the Spirit of the risen Lord.

Communities influenced by the Gospel of John also looked to the spirit for guidance, taking seriously Jesus' words, "But the Advocate, the Holy Spirit, whom the Father will send in my name, will teach you everything, and remind you of all that I have said to you" (John 15:26). 1 John reinforced this message. Remarkable declarations like "You have no need for anyone to teach you" inspired Christians to proceed confidently in the Christian life because of the anointing that was within them (1 John 2:18–27). Since the Holy Spirit played such a key role for these early Christians, they recognized the importance of testing "the spirits to see if they are from God" (1 John 4:1). They knew that the Spirit of God would continue to lead them in very direct ways while keeping them in tune with their role as God's chosen people.

It might be tempting for us to say that the Spirit works in the church simply through worship, ethics, leadership, and Scripture, but not through direct intercession. It is certainly true that God's Spirit is at work in these areas. However, throughout Scripture God refuses to be limited to the trappings of religion. Churches of Christ have traditionally viewed with distrust claims about interaction with the Holy Spirit's present-day workings, largely as a reaction against abuses and extremes. While we must certainly avoid abuses and be careful to discern the Spirit's will from our own, it is equally important to realize that we can err in the opposite direction and attempt to put

God in a box. The Spirit of God is not limited to the pages of Scripture, appointed places and times of worship, or the religious practices of the church. In John 3, Jesus tells Nicodemus that the Spirit is like the wind, which "blows where it chooses, and you hear the sound of it, but you do not know where it comes from or where it goes" (John 3:8). The Spirit's presence is in many ways a mystery. Still, the first Christians trusted that Jesus would live among them through his Spirit, helping them keep the story straight.

A Witness to Diversity

To a greater or lesser degree, every New Testament community trusted worship, leadership, Scripture, distinctive ethics, and the leading of the Spirit to help them remain true to their calling and purpose, and these elements provided a kind of broad consistency from congregation to congregation. Still, as we suggested before, this does not mean that all churches were organized alike or worshipped alike. The first converts in Acts were Jews. Their acceptance of Jesus as Messiah most likely did not initially alter significant aspects of their worship practices. For example, in the early chapters of Acts, the church was clearly continuing to live within the structures of the temple (3:1; 6:1–7). What we know of worship in those contexts is very different than the worship service described in 1 Corinthians 14:26–39. The highly structured liturgies of temple and synagogue are a far cry from a service where "each one has a hymn, a revelation, a tongue, or an interpretation" (1 Corinthians 14:26). Although very few detailed descriptions of early Christian worship exist, it is unlikely that either the example of the Jerusalem or Corinthian church served as a model for all churches in the New Testament period.

What was true for worship was also true for leadership structures. The seven men appointed to care for widows in Acts 6 do not represent an innovation in organizational structure and should not be thought of as the first "deacons"—a designation common to special servants among Paul's churches. As "almoners" appointed to care for the

Hellenist widows present in Jerusalem due to the events of Pentecost, these men fulfilled leadership roles already established in traditional Jewish temple life. The point is the church in Jerusalem continued to participate in the traditional patterns of Jewish life.

In contrast, churches begun by Paul existed largely in urban, Greco-Roman centers where the *ecclesia* (the Greek word for gathering, and the word we translate "church") formed the heart of civic life. These churches trusted a combination of local leaders (elders) and itinerant representatives of Paul's mission—people like Timothy, Silas, Tychicus, Epaphras, and Phoebe—to exercise the authority of the gospel. Given their Greco-Roman, urban context, it is not surprising that these churches appear less "Jewish" than their counterparts in and around Jerusalem.

Because we often tend to read all New Testament documents according to the patterns we find in Paul's letters, we may skim over other examples of structural diversity within the New Testament. Take for example what we read concerning leadership and congregational structure in Matthew and 1 Peter. Matthew's Gospel has much to say about leadership, offering insight about how that leadership might function in an actual community. In contrast to the "scribes and Pharisees" who "sit on Moses' seat," Jesus hopes to produce scribes "trained for the kingdom of Heaven" (Matthew 23:2; 13:52), who do not tie on heavy burdens, do their deeds of piety to be seen by others, or take on honorary titles like rabbi, father, or instructor (23:4–10). In contrast, these emerging churches trust a community made up of "brothers" to exercise the authority of the risen Jesus in ways that honor mercy over sacrifice (Matthew 9:13; 11:7; 18:15–20; 28:18–20). While Matthew defines leadership in contrast to the Jewish structures from which these churches are emerging, the language used to describe emerging patterns of life is still decidedly Jewish. It is difficult to imagine that two churches—one taking Matthew as its guide and another taking 1 Timothy—would end up with similar leadership structures.

This kind of diversity continues throughout all the churches of the New Testament. When we cross the moun-

88

tains away from the urban centers of Paul's mission areas and examine churches in the more remote areas of "Pontus, Galatia, Cappadocia, Asia, and Bythinia" (1 Peter 1:1), we find yet another kind of vocabulary at work in describing the people of God. Missing in 1 Peter is the language of the *ecclesia*, an organizational structure more prominent in Romanized urban areas. Instead, these Christian "exiles" are described in the traditional language of the household. Together, they form the *oikos*, or household of God. Like all ancient households, they look to elders for direction (1 Peter 5:1–5) and call each member to serve as *oikonimoi* (household servants, or stewards; 1 Peter 4:10). Although the epistles of the New Testament were not intended to reveal all aspects of congregational leadership and structure, it is at the very least striking that the language used to describe churches varies significantly from context to context and likely represents an impressive variety of practice among the first Christians. Their leadership and worship practices tend to reflect not only the Christian story but also the social and cultural contexts in which they lived.

> The population of Asia Minor was and remained a predominantly rural population.... This is indicated by the use of agrarian, herding, and domestic metaphors ... and the striking absence of *polis*-related terminology for the Christian community such as Paul's preferred term *ekklesia*....
>
> *John Elliott*
> A Home For the Homeless, *1990*

A Variety of Recipes

While the details of congregational life found in the New Testament certainly varied from church to church, variety among early Christians ran even deeper. Though the first Christian communities all trusted, to one degree or another, worship, Scripture, leadership, ethics, and life in the Spirit to help them keep the story straight, the emphasis given to each varied from congregation to congregation.

In other words, some communities trusted formal leadership more than others, while some gave more weight to the direct influence of the Holy Spirit. Some communities emphasized their alien status in the larger culture, while still others focused more on their purpose, in Paul's words, to "be all things to all people" in order to save the most. While the basic ingredients were the same from church to church, the specific recipes were different.

Let's take 1 John and 1 & 2 Timothy as an example of this variety in church recipes. In one aspect, these letters address a similar circumstance: church practice beyond the life of founding apostles. How will the church keep the story straight once their founding leader is no longer around? These letters address this problem differently. In preparing Timothy for this eventuality, Paul reveals three striking emphases: find trustworthy words; find trustworthy leaders; live a distinctive life. The first two of these most clearly highlight the differences between 1 & 2 Timothy and 1 John.

The pastoral epistles are liberally sprinkled with trustworthy sayings. Paul seems to be drawing upon and expanding a confessional heritage that will serve the church well beyond his ministry. This emphasis on keeping trustworthy sayings before the community is coupled with an emphasis on finding trustworthy teachers. Paul's instructions to Timothy are clear: "What you have heard from me through many witnesses entrust to faithful people who will be able to teach others as well" (2 Timothy 2:2). Those who prove to be "apt teachers" or who "hold fast to the mystery of the faith with a clear conscience" are to be recognized in an official way as elders and deacons. Through the exercise of their recognized ministries, these leaders will safeguard the teaching of the church. What will allow the community of faith to survive the absence of a founding apostle? In the pastoral epistles, the emphasis is on recognizing and empowering leaders who will pass down authoritative teachings.

90   1 John reveals a very different focus, though. In this letter, Christians are encouraged to discern the spirits to determine if they are from God. They are to trust the "anointing [they] have received from him who abides in [them]" which allows them "to know all things" (1 John 2:20–27). Like the pastorals, 1 John

is concerned that these believers hold on to certain teachings they have known from the earliest days. Indeed, the anointing they receive from the Spirit allows them to abide in the teachings they have heard from the beginning. Unlike the pastorals, however, there is no interest in identifying office holders to maintain the traditions handed down from previous witnesses. To the contrary, the beloved elder in 1 John reminds these Spirit-directed Christians that they have no need for anyone to be their teacher (1 John 2:27). How will the church in 1 John keep the story straight? By finding and ordaining leaders? Not primarily. Rather, this church will survive the loss of their founding leader chiefly by trusting the anointing they have received and by testing the spirits to see if they are from God.

These different emphases in 1 & 2 Timothy and 1 John also occur in other communities described in the New

Toleration of Diversity

As a collection, the New Testament writings themselves witness to the significantly different visions of life that were forged out in this period...diverse beliefs, practices, rituals, community structures, ethical guidelines, and ethnic identities.... The later Christians who decided which writings to include in the Christian canon were well aware of the differences among the books they selected. Instead of choosing only those books that agreed with one theology and church structure, they chose those books closest to Jesus in time and influence, and they allowed the pluralism to stand.

David Rhoads
The Challenge of Diversity, 2003

There was no evidence in [the New Testament writings] that a consistent or uniform ecclesiology had emerged. Rather, writings addressed to different New Testament communities had quite diverse emphases.

Raymon Brown
The Churches the Apostles Left Behind, 1985

Our study has also forced us to recognize a marked degree of diversity within first-century Christianity. We can no longer doubt that there were many different expressions of Christianity within the New Testament...the same faith in Jesus man and exalted one had to come to expression in worlds in a variety of different individuals and circumstances.

James D. G. Dunn
Unity and Diversity in the New Testament, 1990

91

Testament. For instance, language about the leading of the Spirit is largely missing in Matthew's Gospel (in contrast, for example, to Luke's Gospel). In this sense, it resembles the pastorals more than it does 1 John. However, unlike the pastorals, Matthew is very suspicious of officially recognized leaders. "Call no one on earth rabbi... father... or instructor" is Jesus' counsel to the church emerging from the influence of the synagogue. Rather, the church is a collection of "brothers and sisters" who together share the responsibility of binding and loosing in the name of Jesus (Matthew 23:8–12).

This diversity, not only in practice, but also in emphasis, reveals a vibrant picture of New Testament churches. No single community in the New Testament fully embodies everything it means to be a congregation of God's people. The unity of the church in the New Testament did not involve uniformity of practice. Instead, these local communities tailored their practices according to their understandings of the death and resurrection of Jesus and the challenges presented by their specific cultural contexts. The strength of the New Testament church lay not in the "sameness" of congregations from place to place, but precisely in the freedom of the first Christians to live out the story of Jesus in diverse ways appropriate to their varying contexts.

While the practices of the church are necessary for the people of God to keep the story straight, they are never to be thought of as ends in themselves. When the practices of the church become greater than the story they serve, the church loses its way. Moreover, when one practice becomes the exclusive way the church seeks to keep the story straight, the church can also lose its way. Finally, when one "recipe" of the church is seen as the "complete" or final expression of what it means to live as the people of God, the church loses its way.

92   New Testament Christians

Such diversity in the New Testament church may come as a surprise to many of us who have learned to speak of it as a monolithic entity with all churches organizing, worshipping, and behaving alike. Since we strive to imitate the earliest followers of Christ, what does the diversity found in the New Testament teach us about what it means to be the church? How are we to account for this diversity in the quest to resemble the first Christians?

Both in the first and the 21st centuries, the church exists to find its place in the story of God at the turn of the ages by conforming its life to the story of Jesus. This understanding of the church helps explain its necessary diversity in two ways. First, the very story that Christians live, the story of the death and resurrection of Jesus, calls the church not to see its own life as an end in itself. Like Jesus, the church is sent into the world to empty itself of all privilege so that it might serve others (Philippians 2:5–11). Its posture, therefore, is not only a speaking posture, but also a listening one. In every culture, the church is willing to give its life away to see what the gospel might look like raised to life in each new setting. As the early church spread from Jerusalem to Ephesus to Rome, it learned to ask the question, "What does it mean to live the story of the death and resurrection in this particular context?"

This sensitivity to culture does not mean that the church is merely faddish, though, changing its appearance, practices, and values to make itself more fashionable or palatable to the dominant culture. The church's question in each context is not "what will make us popular?" but "what would a servant-church look like here?" Therefore, the church learns to ask, "Where are the servants' quarters in this context? Where are the places of brokenness in this setting? What patterns of trust in God would stand against this culture's insistence on self-preservation and autonomy?" Since sacrifice and servanthood lie at the core of the gospel, churches give up their rights for the sake of others, including the right to form a congregation for the primary purpose of meeting members' own needs for comfort. Early Christian churches looked different from context to context because they understood that the church exists not for itself but for the neighbor for whom Christ died. As a result, they allowed the gospel to find an expression appropriate for their time and place.

93

Second, the first Christians defined their lives in relation to the present and coming kingdom of God. Seeing themselves drawn into the future of God, they realized that no single expression of the church fully accounts for God's future reign, which will come only with the return of Jesus. Therefore, as the first fruit of a new creation, the church is a seeking community, yearning for the fullness of God's kingdom when all of creation will be revealed in glory. With the cry of *Maranatha* (Lord, come quickly), the church shares the apocalyptic faith of many of the prophets, urging the people of God to live toward a perfect future—a lasting city—rather than an idealized past. As a result, the earliest church possessed a nimble faith that was open to God's future. If we want to be like the early Christians, we must also be a forward-looking church focused on allowing and even expecting variety and change as God pulls his people further into his reign—and by extension, a forward-looking church is less likely to view a previous expression of the church as the complete pattern for all subsequent churches. The end of the church is not to serve itself, but to serve God who calls the church into existence.

Conclusion: Looking Back, Looking Forward

Mere discussion of the ideas laid out in this chapter gains nothing unless we can find successful ways to implement them. Although the response of today's church will be discussed more fully in the last chapters of this book, we can draw some general observations about what it means to be God's people based on the parts of the story we have explored so far.

First, as we've seen, God's people find their place in the world by constantly reenacting the story of their deliverance. This is true whether the story of deliverance is the Exodus or the death and resurrection of Jesus. The people of God live distinctive lives because they live according to a distinctive script—the story of God's saving work on behalf of all creation.

Second, community is clearly essential to God's redeeming work in creation, and his saving work always involves

94

calling a distinct community to live for the sake of the world. The church, therefore, is more than just a collection of people who are saved; it is the community in which people discover what it means to be saved.

Third, God's people are typically at their best when they live daily trusting in the mercies of God. These conditions occur most often when God's people are on the move, leaving what is familiar for the adventure of serving God in the world. Settled people tend to be satisfied people with reduced capacity to trust. Seeking people tend to be trusting people, and in turn are more open to God's mission in the world.

Fourth, when the church's life, or any aspect of the church's life, becomes an end in itself, God's people have wandered into idolatry. Just as Israel put its trust in temple and king rather than in God, the church's practices—such as baptism, communion, musical styles, and so on—can become detached from the story that authorizes them. As vital as those practices are, if we rely on them for understanding our identity, God's people are susceptible to confusing the things of God with God himself.

Fifth, the community of faith best fulfills the mission of God in the world when its eyes are fixed on God's in-breaking future. When the church sees itself serving the final purposes of God for all creation, its vision is clear. While the stories of early Christians are certainly authoritative guides for all subsequent generations, the church today, like those first believers, is always being pulled into God's future. Christians seeking to imitate New Testament Christianity are a future-oriented people, guided by but not bound to the past.

Sixth, while the church always lives the same story, it does so in varying times and places, adapting and responding to each new cultural context it encounters in its effort to bring the blessing of God to all people. Comprised of a people of the kingdom, the church is always living in both continuity and discontinuity, in the already but not yet. As such, it displays remarkable variety as God's missionary people in the world. 95

The story of the chosen people of God began with Israel, and later with the early church, but it doesn't end there. For the 20 centuries that followed, the church lived in the story of Jesus, sometimes effectively and sometimes not. Unfortunately, teaching and studying church history and practice after the close of the New Testament have not generally been high priorities in Churches of Christ. We need to change that. A church that sees itself in perspective—as a small chapter in a much greater, on-going story—is less likely to succumb to provincialism or to view itself as the only acceptable form of Christianity, an attitude that clearly conflicts with the spirit of God in the early churches.

5 The Story Continues

These things happened to them to serve as an example, and they were written down to instruct us, on whom the ends of the ages have come. So if you think you are standing, watch out that you do not fall.

1 Corinthians 10:11–12

It is my purpose to write an account of the successions of the holy apostles, as well as of the times which have elapsed from the days of our Savior to our own; and to relate the many important events which are said to have occurred in the history of the Church; .... From afar they raise their voices like torches, and they cry out, as from some lofty and conspicuous watch-tower, admonishing us where to walk and how to direct the course of our work steadily and safely.

Eusebius of Caesarea, Church History, *4th century CE*

When I received word from the registrar's office that I would be required to take a year of remedial church history classes to get into a graduate theology program, I was not happy. My impression of history from high school and college classes was that it was boring and irrelevant. To force me to pay for two semesters of church history was nothing short of an injustice. But, I did as I was told and began the class.

Within weeks my attitude about the course and about church history had begun to change rather dramatically. In every set of readings and every class meeting there was at least one "ah-ha!" moment. "So that's how the doctrine of the Trinity developed; so that's why we say what we *do in the Lord's Supper; so that's the reason John Calvin developed his teaching on predestination; so that's where conflicts over baptism came from." I began to see amazing connections—stories that told how each generation of Christians had struggled to be faithful to Christ from the days of the Apostles until now.*

I'm not sure when it actually dawned on me that the body of Christians to which I belonged also had a history—that Churches of Christ were part of a long heritage that has shaped us too in profound ways. But when that realization hit me, it was an awakening. To discover how we were formed, to have a sense of the connections we have to those who came before us, was liberating and encouraging! It showed me as never before the truth of Christ's promise that nothing would ever destroy his church.

This experience made me realize how important it is for Christians to develop what might be called a "spiritual historical consciousness," to use their God-given ability to know and understand something about the people to whom they owe so much. The next two chapters provide glimpses into the church's journey through the last two thousand years that can help instruct, admonish, and direct us as we seek that lasting city.

—Doug

Ignorance is Not Bliss

We are a "people of the Book," but the story of the church continues to unfold long after the close of Scripture. The story of God's people has continued through the centuries—not so much because those who professed Christ were always faithful, but because God is faithful. Just as Jesus' work in the New Testament grew out of God's work in the Old, the formation of the church in the New Testament was the springboard for its continuing journey through the history that followed.

Every aspect of the Church's pilgrimage is part of who we are today. All those who have gone before us—all of the saints and the sinners—have shaped the church in real and significant ways. Acknowledging this doesn't mean we must whitewash the past or pretend that everything said and done in the name of Christ was good or right. Human pride and lust for power have always had the potential to cut off the fruit of the Spirit and produce the works of the flesh instead. True, the gates of hell have never prevailed against Christ's church, but sometimes people claiming to follow Christ have perverted the story and distracted the church from its journey. Yet in the midst of this always imperfect, often failing church, God has always worked to cleanse and shape into the likeness of Christ those who together, in the words of 1 John, are "walking in the light." Walking—that means that the people of God are travelers.

It's nothing new to claim that we've been shaped by our past. No one denies being profoundly formed by genetics and by the habits, advice, and instruction of parents, teachers, and friends. The people who had a hand in shaping us, in turn, were themselves formed in their thinking and habits by others, and so on back to the beginning. God designed us this way, and it is a blessing from him to recognize these connections with our past.

However, admitting that we have been shaped by our past doesn't mean we are trapped by it—in fact, the opposite is true. Knowing our story releases us from thinking we have reached perfection. Knowing our story liberates us from the assumption that our ways of acting and thinking are above critique. Through the centuries, Christians who remained ignorant of their past have been imprisoned by it, assuming that their ways were necessarily God's ways. Scripture always condemns that mentality; if a church thinks it is "standing," it is in grave danger of a fall (1 Corinthians 10:12).

Knowing how and why the church of the past made specific choices provides crucial insight for discerning when the church has kept the story straight—when it has continued to seek that lasting city—and when it has failed to do so. Such knowledge is essential for Christian leaders when faced with critical decisions today. When has this matter come up in the history of the church, and why? How has the church in the past dealt with this issue when it arose? Asking questions like these helps present-day

99

leaders tap into the experiences and wisdom of centuries of Christians who have walked before us and on whose shoulders we stand.

We do need to be clear, however, that past events and current situations are not identical. Studying history is not so the church can simply duplicate today what others did in another time and place. Rather, it helps Christians discern both similarities with the past and unique aspects of the present—a crucial awareness for helping the church today act in ways appropriate for its own times.

The danger is that pride will sneak in, enticing us to believe that we know better than those poor ignorant folks who came before us, and that we are finally going to get everything right. Every generation is charged with being faithful to the story in its own circumstances. Although Christians can't condone anything in the church's history that was unfaithful to the Christian story, it is not our business to demean those who have struggled to be faithful in their own situations. Again and again, church history reveals what we also see in Scripture—communities of faith struggling to live faithfully to the Christian story in their own circumstances. We face the same task today.

In the church's journey toward the lasting city, it has often encountered challenges in keeping the story of Christ straight. In the last two chapters, we've seen how the first Christian communities reflected wide diversity as the story encountered new cultures. While this diversity was necessary for the church to be faithful, it also posed the danger

> Like it or not, we are heirs of [a] host of diverse and even contradictory witnesses. Some of their actions we may find revolting, and others inspiring. But all of them form part of our history. All of them, those whom we admire as well as those whom we despise, brought us to where we are now. Without understanding that past, we are unable to understand ourselves, for in a sense that past still lives in us and influences who we are and how we understand the Christian message. Every renewal of the church, every great age in its history, has been grounded on a renewed reading of history.
>
> *Justo Gonzalez*
> The Story of Christianity, *1999*

of mixing the story of Christ with ideas that would destroy the gospel's distinctiveness. The church of the New Testament relied on Scripture, worship, faithful leaders, life in the Spirit, a focus on the risen Lord, and other elements to maintain its faithfulness. It contin-

Syncretism:

The merging of different and often opposing belief systems to form another that has elements of all. Syncretism was an important characteristic of Greek and pagan religion, and it was natural for early Christians from those backgrounds to tend to combine Christian and pagan ideas.

ued to look to those elements for keeping the story straight in the following centuries as well.

At first the church wrestled mostly with how to understand the story of Jesus in light of Judaism and the Hebrew scriptures. But as time passed and the church moved deeper into a Greek-thinking, Roman-administered world, it faced new challenges to its understanding of both its identity and Christ's identity. Much of what happened to the church on this part of its journey resulted from its interaction with this complex world.

Keeping the Story Straight—Heresies & Boundaries

Paul explained the heart of the Christian story in 1 Corinthians 15:3–4: "For I handed on to you as of first importance what I in turn had received: that Christ died for our sins in accordance with the scriptures, and that he was buried, and that he was raised on the third day in accordance with the scriptures." "The story" is the story of Christ. If anything has to be kept straight, it's who Christ is and, therefore, who and what his church is. Christ's identity and nature define his church as the redeemed people who, like Christ, give themselves for others. The doctrines about Christ are essential not simply because they are factually correct but because they make a difference in the way the church thinks and acts—in the very understanding of itself.

For example, in Roman society it was common for unwanted children, particularly girls, to be abandoned

101

to die after birth. Babies were not considered part of the family until formally accepted by the father in a special religious ceremony. So if there were too many mouths to feed, or the father didn't want to have to pay a dowry to marry off a daughter, the baby was "exposed"—placed out in the elements to die. Sometimes wicked people would take these children and sell them into slavery or prostitution. Not only did Christians reject the practice of exposing babies, many actively sought out these infants, took them in, and raised them as their own. They did this because they believed that God had come in the form of a defenseless human baby and believed that, to be Christ's church, they had to reflect his sacrifice for the helpless in their own lives.

Christ's identity influenced Christians' behavior in other ways as well. In the ancient world people were deeply concerned about getting a proper burial. It ensured rest for the departed soul and preservation of the person's memory. The rich had no problem with that, and even people of modest means often formed "burial clubs" as insurance; but many poor simply had no way to provide this service for themselves. Many Christians loved and cared for the poor in this way. According to Aristides (a Christian writer living in Athens in the 2nd century), whenever one of their poor died, Christians ungrudgingly contributed according to each one's ability and buried him or her. For Christians, the motivation to do this was not simply insurance for their own burial. They did this because of what they believed about Christ—that he had come in the flesh, that he had died and been buried in a borrowed tomb, and that they like Christ were willing to give themselves for the care of the poor and helpless.

Christians became known as those who cared for the sick. The early church historian Eusebius of Caesarea (275–339 CE) tells how Christians in Alexandria, Egypt cared for those dying of a plague, even willing to sacrifice their own lives. "They held fast to each other and visited the sick fearlessly, and ministered to them continually, serving them in Christ. And they died with them most joyfully, taking the affliction of others." The pagans, on the other hand, "deserted those who began to be sick, and fled

102

from their dearest friends. And they cast them out into the streets when they were half dead, and left the dead like refuse, unburied." In the mid-300s, the Emperor Julian (known as "the Apostate") tried to revive pagan religion in the empire and suppress Christianity. The problem was, he said, that the church had "been specially advanced through the loving service rendered to strangers and through their care of the burial of the dead." He called it a scandal that the Christians cared not only for their own poor but for pagans too, while "those who belong to us look in vain for the help we should render them." What could motivate people to act contrary to every human impulse for self-preservation? It was the conviction that Christ had had a fully human life and that he was willing to give it up for others. It was the conviction that the lasting city that gives true security is not in this world.

The church in every age, whenever it is seeking the lasting city, whenever it has kept the story straight, has been Christ to the helpless, providing care for the sick, food for the needy, and protection for the abandoned. This is not simply because of human kindness—it is because of who they believe Christ is. The right belief made all the difference, not simply because it was factually correct, but because it transformed them into people willing to give themselves totally for others (2 Corinthians 3:18).

Not surprisingly, then, the first major challenges to the story centered on this issue of the nature of Christ and therefore of his church.

Gnosticism

One of the earliest tests the church faced came from people we know as Gnostics. Gnosticism's origins remain obscure, but its ideas fit well with those of the Greeks, who made a sharp distinction between the physical and spiritual worlds. To the Greeks the physical was bad while the spiritual was good. The Gnostics taught that matter had been created by a low-level god (some said it was the god of the Old Testament) who was powerful enough to create but stupid enough not to know he shouldn't. From this

103

perspective, our physical bodies are evil, prisons of our real spiritual nature, and the object of life becomes getting out of the body and back to the spiritual realm. The Gnostics preached that Jesus, a divine being from the spiritual realm, came to reveal the secret of how to navigate that dangerous journey—but only to a select group of people able to receive it.

One reason Gnosticism was so dangerous was that it seemed in many ways to fit with the gospel story. The Bible itself says that the world is a place of toil and sorrow, subject to principalities, powers, and the "Prince of this World." At the very heart of the gospel is the belief that one from heaven came down with news that would release us from that bondage.

However, despite its façade of biblical accuracy, Gnostic teaching held devastating implications for the story of Christ. If, as the Gnostics said, matter and spirit are opposites and cannot mix, then the divine Jesus could not have had a physical body, which means he couldn't have gotten tired and hungry, suffered pain and death, or risen from the dead. And most devastatingly, Jesus couldn't really have given his life for the world at all—it was just an illusion.

Among early Christian Gnostics were the 2nd century Egyptian teachers Basilides and Valentinus. The church father Irenaeus attacked their teachings such as the claim that Jesus did not have a physical body but had switched places with Simon of Cyrene, tricking the crowd into crucifying Simon instead of Jesus. A library of Gnostic writings was discovered near the town of Nag Hammadi in Upper Egypt in 1945. These materials included texts thought to have been lost or destroyed, including the "Gospel of Thomas" and "Gospel of Philip."

Furthermore, Gnostics taught that Jesus came to reveal his secrets just to certain "spiritual" people who in turn would pass them on to others who "measured up." Many found this aspect of Gnosticism especially alluring, because receiving the secret knowledge put you into an "inner circle" that was above other "lesser" Christians. Pride, that most insidious of evils, created an attitude of elitism that divided the church, diverted it from its journey, and perverted

104

the story. What's more, the idea that the physical universe (including the human body) was evil led some to believe that true spirituality called for extreme neglect and abuse of their bodies. Still others believed that since their body was not really who they were, they could do anything "in the flesh" and it didn't matter.

Does this sound familiar? Gnosticism is relevant to us today because the attitude that fueled it still flourishes among us. Pride and elitism remain major temptations for Christians—and such attitudes are not confined to any one group. Popular notions of religion and worship tend to focus on the individual's private experience and preferences, largely disregarding and weakening the church. Christians who feel they've had a special revelation from God, or even those who are more educated, may see themselves as superior to "ordinary" Christians because of their experiences and knowledge. Also, some Christians and Christian groups completely disregard the care of the physical universe—a very Gnostic idea. Gnosticism perverted the story of Christ—not simply because it got the facts wrong but because it corrupted the heart and actions of Christians, making them arrogant and self-centered instead of self-sacrificing and Christ-like. Gnosticism undermined the church and diverted it from its journey. The attitudes of Gnosticism still do the same today.

Marcionism

Another early threat to the story was Marcionism. Marcion was a 2nd-century Roman Christian whose ideas sounded a lot like those of Gnosticism. For one, he made the same distinction between matter and spirit that the Gnostics did. Jesus

Marcion, a wealthy ship owner from Sinope on the Black Sea and son of a bishop, became a bishop himself in the early 2nd century. He moved to Rome around 135 CE and contributed large sums of money to the churches there. In 144 he was excommunicated for his teachings. No copies of his book *Antitheses* exists, but we know his teachings from quotes made in the five volumes *Against Marcion* written by the church father Tertullian in the early 3rd century.

did not have a human body—he only appeared to be born, grow up, die, and rise from the dead. Marcion despised anything Jewish, including the Old Testament and its God. He taught that any deity who would make bears kill the children who teased Elisha or establish a principle like "an eye for an eye" could not be the same God who said "let the children come to me" and "turn the other cheek."

Marcion compiled the first list of Christian scriptures for a "New Testament," perhaps his most significant contribution to Christian history. Reflecting his hatred for the Hebrew scriptures, Judaism, and the Law, he included the one Gospel written by a Gentile—Luke— (minus the parts about Jesus' birth and resurrection), and ten of Paul's books (minus the parts that referred to Abraham and other Old Testament characters). He wanted to distance Christianity from any connection with the Jewish faith.

As spiritual descendents of the early Christians who grappled with these issues, we have inherited Marcion's struggle with the relationship between the Old and New Testaments as well as his often selective view of how God can and ought to act. The hatred of the Jews reflected in Marcion's work and even among many "orthodox" Christians continued to have an impact not only on Christianity but on world history, and anti-semitism still exists among some Christian communities today. Also, like both the Gnostics and Marcion, many Christians characterize the troubles of the physical world—poverty, abuse, slavery, hunger, pollution—as "non-spiritual" and therefore not something Christians should be concerned about. Marcionism denied God's mighty works through time—his creation, his making a people for himself in Israel, his leading them out of bondage in the Exodus. This struck at the very nature of God and the heart of the story. Whether we realize it or not, when we dismiss the Old Testament as irrelevant for our own lives, discriminate against others, or ignore social justice, we follow Marcion, not Jesus.

106

Montanism

Still another threat to Christianity appeared in a movement begun by Montanus, a man who may have been a pagan priest for the Roman goddess Cybele before becoming a Christian. He began preaching around the year 172 CE, along with two women named Prisca and Maximilla. They claimed to be the mouthpiece for the Holy Spirit and for Christ, demanding unconditional obedience from their followers and rejecting any accountability to the larger church. Montanus required strict discipline, including extreme fasting, rejection of marriage, and seeking of martyrdom. He took advantage of a sense among many Christians of the day that the faith wasn't what it used to be. Some believed that the Spirit was being quenched as the church moved toward more formal structure, leadership,

Montanus and his companions operated from the village of Pepuza in Phrygia, today part of Central Turkey. Though little is known of the fate of Montanus and his companions, they gained one prominent follower from the main church—Tertullian. Increasingly disturbed by what he thought was a laxness in discipline creeping into the church, Tertullian embraced the extreme self-discipline of the Montanists.

and an authoritative collection of scriptures. Montanus and his followers, like many in the early church, preached that Christ's second coming was imminent, so the church did not need such "worldly" things.

While these ideas may sound far-fetched and unlikely as pitfalls for today's churches, the threat of Montanism still exists in the danger of over-reaction to structure. As we observed in the last chapter, God can and does work through formal structure and order, which played a vital role in keeping early churches faithful to the story of Christ. Without structure, the excesses of spontaneous, charismatic actions such as those of Montanus and his followers can quickly get out of control and lead to elitist attitudes, lack of accountability, unfaithfulness to the story, and diversion from the church's journey. Churches of Christ have traditionally placed a strong emphasis on proper structure in the church. Today, however, as many

107

long to breathe fresh life into our church practices, we must be aware of the danger that in our haste to change we may fail to conduct ourselves "decently and in order."

Jewish Christian Sects

Certain groups of Jewish Christians also held ideas destructive to the story. The New Testament clearly indicates that the first Christians were Jews, and the first churches met in synagogues. Naturally, Jewish believers brought into Christianity their own understandings about the Messiah and the kingdom of God. As the church struggled to understand who Jesus was, some Jewish Christians could not move beyond their earlier beliefs and practices. Judaizing teachers insisted that Christians observe the Jewish ceremonial laws, including circumcision. They held that Jesus was the messiah and therefore the savior sent by God, but he was not God.

These Jewish sects were identified by early Christian writers like Irenaeus and Eusebius as "Ebionites," though some seemed to be named "Nazarenes." They evidently had one written Gospel that was a version of the Gospel of Matthew minus the birth and infancy stories and which depicted Jesus as a vegetarian. Only a few fragments of this Gospel exist, quoted in the work of a late 4th-century writer named Epiphanius.

Like Gnosticism and Marcionism, such ideas cut at the very heart of Christianity—the identity of Jesus. The Christ of these sects became primarily a human teacher who came to minister to Jews, and so they struggled with arrogance and exclusivism that would not allow them to accept Gentiles or any Gentile practices that were different from their own. They perverted the story by refusing to allow faithful diversity. While most Christians today don't insist on maintaining Jewish practices, we have frequently committed the same error these Jewish-Christian sects did by insisting that our traditional ways of doing things embody the "true" requirements of God. In discerning matters of salvation from matters of preference, we must avoid the temptation to use ourselves as a yardstick by which we measure all followers of Christ.

108

The Church's Response

The church had to expose the unfaithfulness of these movements, each of which claimed to be true Christianity. Again, it was crucial for the church to eliminate these teachings not simply because they were factually wrong—intellectually off base—but because they distorted the church's understanding of Christ and therefore of itself and its mission, drawing it away from its journey toward the lasting city.

In the face of all these competing beliefs, how would the church keep the story straight and discern truth from error? The previous chapter explored five elements the New Testament church relied on for guidance, and subsequent generations of Christians would turn to the same ones. In different circumstances through the centuries, though, churches have looked more to some elements than to others. In the years immediately following the end of the New Testament era, the church met threats to the story in three principal ways—through its worship, through Scripture, and through faithful leaders.

In its worship, the church stayed on track by proclaiming Christ to be both divine and human, creator and redeemer, often by reciting trustworthy sayings handed down by previous Christians. One of the earliest statements of belief used in baptisms and Christian worship is known as the "Apostles' Creed." This statement of belief deliberately refuted what the Gnostics, Marcionites, and other groups were teaching about Christ and the physical creation, along with their exclusivism

The Apostles' Creed

I believe in God, the Father almighty, creator of heaven and earth.

I believe in Jesus Christ, his only Son, our Lord. He was conceived by the power of the Holy Spirit and born of the Virgin Mary. He suffered under Pontius Pilate, was crucified, died, and was buried. He descended to the dead. On the third day he rose again. He ascended into heaven, and is seated at the right hand of the Father. He will come again to judge the living and the dead.

I believe in the Holy Spirit, the holy catholic Church, the communion of saints, the forgiveness of sins, the resurrection of the body, and the life everlasting.

109

and arrogance. Reciting the Creed in worship constantly reminded Christians of these essential parts of the story—beliefs that defined and shaped the church.

Scripture also played a key role in helping the church avoid wrong teachings. As the church recognized the new Christian texts as authoritative, it embraced rather than rejected Christianity's Jewish heritage. As the essential first part of the story, the Old Testament revealed a God who loved and pursued those he had created, even when they rebelled against him. As the church came to appreciate the Hebrew scriptures in this new light, Christians saw at least two common themes in both "testaments" that contradicted the teachings of Marcion and others then threatening the story: the nature of creation, and the person and work of Christ. Christians understood from Scripture that the world, though fallen and in bondage to decay, was not meant to be that way (Romans 8:18–21; Colossians 1:20). The one, absolutely powerful, infinitely good God fashioned the physical universe, including the human body, declaring it and the entire creation "very good" (Hebrews 11:3; Genesis 1:1–31). From scriptures such as these, they held to the essential truth that Christ, the fully divine "Son of God," took on a body of flesh and became fully human, and that anyone who denies it perverts the story and is outside the bounds of the church (Colossians 1:15–19; 2 John 7). Christ truly died and was raised from the dead—if not, all is lost (1 Corinthians 15). Also, by understanding that Christ gave himself for all, Christians rejected the idea that the gospel story is just for an elite group of "spirituals" who get insider knowledge about how to get to heaven (Romans 5:18–19; 2 Peter 3:9).

In addition to worship and Scripture, the church turned to the preaching and writing of faithful leaders in their struggle to avoid error. Irenaeus of Lyons in particular wrote to refute the notion that Christ's message was a secret intended only for a "special few." Surely, he said, Jesus must have told the full story to the Apostles—his closest associates on earth and the ultimate "special few." After all, he had promised them that his Spirit would guide them into

110

all truth and charged them with taking the story to the whole world. He had even given them power to loose and bind on earth and in heaven. In turn, they passed on this "deposit of faith" to faithful leaders who would teach others. Irenaeus' reasoning was simple: go to a church established by an Apostle, he said. See what they teach. If what you are hearing from the Gnostics or anyone else is not in line with Apostolic teaching, you must reject it. The Apostles' ministry and teaching provided the standard for faithfulness—recorded in Scripture and reflected in the worship and practice of the church.

Irenaeus of Lyons (c. 135–200 CE) became bishop of a relatively new church in Gaul (today France) after the previous bishop was killed in a persecution in 177. Irenaeus was one of the most active church leaders in opposing Gnostic and other destructive teachings, especially in his five-volume work *Against Heresies*.

Yet once again, Irenaeus was not interested in mere intellectual precision; apostolic teaching was not simply correct facts. Right doctrine made a person like God. In book three of his writing *Against Heresies* he asked "how could we be joined to incorruptibility and immortality, unless, first, incorruptibility and immortality had become that which we also are, so that the corruptible might be swallowed up by incorruptibility, and the mortal by immor-

...we are in a position to reckon those who were by the apostles instituted bishops in the Churches, and [to demonstrate] the succession of these men to our own times; those who neither taught nor knew of anything like what these [heretics] rave about. For if the apostles had known hidden mysteries, which they were in the habit of imparting to "the perfect" apart and privately from the rest, they would have delivered them especially to those to whom they were also committing the Churches themselves.

Irenaeus
Against Heresies, *Book III, 1st century CE*

tality, that we might receive the adoption of children?" Christ became human so that humans could be transformed into the image of Christ (2 Corinthians 3:18).

Another Kind of Threat: The "Ultra-Faithful"

These early challenges to the story were in many ways direct assaults on the gospel and the church. They changed crucial parts of the story, and their acceptance led to actions and attitudes that were unfaithful to it. Yet another less expected kind of threat arose that led the church once again to draw boundaries to keep the story straight. This time, the danger came from people who were inside the boundaries the church had already drawn.

Ironically, sometimes Christians responded to threats by over-compensating for them, neglecting some truths of the gospel in order to emphasize the one they felt was threatened. As a result, the truth they tried to protect often became detached from the whole story, endangering the very story they sought to keep straight. The church labeled this "out-of-balance" approach heresy. Originally the word simply meant a "choice," but it soon came to mean a choice that put the story in jeopardy. Threats like Gnosticism and Marcionism were heresies too, but these new threats came at the church from an unexpected angle.

For example, we've seen repeatedly that the New Testament teaches Jesus' humanity in the Gospels, showing that he got tired and hungry, was crucified and died. 2 John 7 explicitly warns that anyone who denies that Christ came in the flesh is antichrist. In keeping with these teachings, the church rightfully condemned those who, like the Gnostics, rejected Christ's humanity. Accepting Jesus' humanity is not optional for Christians because it makes a tremendous difference in how we understand what Christ did for us and how we act as his followers. But if Christians were to detach this one aspect of the truth by emphasizing Jesus' humanity to the neglect of other important truths, the story would be perverted.

That is exactly what happened. In the struggle to fight the teachings of the Gnostics and others by preserving the notion of Christ's humanity, some groups of Christians taught that Jesus was born simply as a human and did not become divine until his baptism, when the Spirit of God came on him in the form of a dove. Jesus had not existed before his birth, they said, and his divinity came from

God's Spirit living in him. This explanation emphasized Jesus' humanity, from his birth to his death. Yet "adoptionism," as it came to be called (Jesus was "adopted" by God at his baptism), ended up making Jesus merely a special human being—a very special one, certainly, even unique, but not divine in any full sense. The adoptionists wanted to preserve Christ's humanity—a scriptural must. But ironically, in the process of focusing so intently on that truth, they perverted the full story and became heretics.

In the 4th century, Christians wrestled with and hotly discussed the question: how could the church worship Christ and the Father and still believe in only one God? Arius (250–336 CE), a popular preacher in Alexandria, Egypt, came up with what he thought was the solution— one that preserved both Christ's divinity and the Christian belief in one God. He reasoned that Christ was the first-born of all creation—the first thing God created. God then elevated Christ to his right hand, and Christ created everything else that exists. This theory emphasized two essential pieces of the story—that there is only one God, and that Christ is worthy of worship—but it twisted the story as a whole because it made Christ a created being who was obviously lower than the Father.

As with the earlier heresies, Arius' teachings posed more than simply an intellectual problem. They had implications for how Christians worshipped, prayed, understood salvation, and even saw their own human nature and abilities. Once again, the attempt to be faithful to an important truth led to unfaithfulness.

How can awareness of these ancient heresies help us today? First, such an awareness helps Christians understand that the church has always struggled to keep the story straight, and realizing this, we should be grateful for the gift of the written word that directs and strengthens us. Second, it ought to humble Christians with the realization that, even in the effort to be faithful, we may stray into unfaithfulness. And third, an understanding of these heresies reaffirms God's wisdom in creating communities of faith that make this journey together; it helps us appreciate his gift of wise,

113

loving, and godly leaders who know the living Word, are steeped in the written word, and are shaped by the Spirit. Far from being dry relics of history, the stories of these early heresies serve as danger signs, marking false paths along the road to the lasting home we seek.

Yet Another Kind of Threat: Becoming Accepted

The church, however, had yet another challenge besides Hebrew and Greek ideas that perverted the story and "ultra-faithful" Christians who detached and focused on one truth to the detriment of others. For three centuries, the early church had flourished as an underground movement, understanding itself as a pilgrim people—counter-cultural and persecuted exiles searching for a permanent city. But in the 4th century, something happened that completely changed that self-perception—Christianity became legal.

Its amazing move from persecuted minority to established majority composes one of the most significant events in the history of the church. In 313 CE the Emperor Constantine legalized Christianity and by his actions made it the favored religion, a shift that had major consequences for the church. Instead of the object of ridicule and persecution, the church became the place to be to get ahead in the world. The story of the crucified Christ—formerly a stark reminder of the gulf between the kingdoms of this world and the kingdom of God—now became acceptable with the church's "triumph" under Constantine.

> Constantine's "Edict of Toleration," also called the "Edict of Milan," declared religious freedom for the Empire. The early church historian Eusebius relates that Constantine had seen a vision of the cross with the words in Latin "By this sign you will conquer" before a crucial battle for control of the western Empire. After he won the battle, he issued the Edict of Milan that nullified all previous edicts against Christians and instructed Roman officials to restore all property previously confiscated from Christians to its rightful owners without delay.

114

The church experienced an identity shift—from an exiled people sent into the world to a settled and gathered people at home in the world. Before long, the church derived its identity primarily from the monarchy, and church offices often became seats of power rather than places of service. Images of triumph and monarchy are biblical. After all, Jesus is called the "Prince of Peace" and the "heir to David's throne." But when the church comes to understand those images in the way the world understands them, or when images like kingship become so dominant that others, like servanthood, are neglected or forgotten, the story suffers distortion. The Israelites made the mistake of replacing God with the institutions of temple and king, and with the legalization of Christianity, the church faced the same temptation. Whenever the church stops its journey, believing it has already reached its permanent city, its focus becomes itself rather than its savior, its mission, and its destination.

The Emperor Theodosius completed the "Constantinian shift" in 380 CE by making Christianity the official religion of the Roman Empire. Empires, whether religious or political, value order and conformity, tending to eliminate diversity. Control increases, and the concerns of the state become the concerns of the church. The church councils that took place in the next centuries were convened by emperors, not just to eliminate heresy, but to keep the *pax romana*, the peace of the Empire. The church's mission became less about bringing the story of God to people in new cultural settings and more about transplanting a Roman way of life. Not surprisingly, the structure of the church increasingly mimicked that of the Empire.

> It is our desire that all the various nations ... should continue in the profession of that religion which was delivered to the Romans by the divine Apostle Peter.... We authorize the followers of this law to assume the title Catholic Christians; but as for the others ... we decree that they shall be branded with the ignominious name of heretics.... They will suffer ... divine condemnation, and ... the punishment which our authority, in accordance with the will of heaven, shall decide to inflict.
>
> Code of Theodosius XVI, *438 CE*

In trying to remain faithful, the church now faced two conflicting developments: the need to impose order and

The *pax romana*, "Roman peace," was a period of about 200 years (27 BCE–180 CE—from Emperor Octavian to Marcus Aurelius) during which the Roman Empire controlled all the lands around the Mediterranean Sea and most of Northwest Europe. Relative stability existed throughout the Empire during this period, Roman culture and language spread, travel was relatively safe, and Christianity began and expanded throughout the Empire and beyond.

boundaries to defend the faith from intruding ideas and heresies that perverted the story, and the need to resist the heavy-handed order being imposed on the church by the Roman Empire—an order that often squelched the diversity important to be faithful to the story. Both of these needs tended to push the church toward relying on its leaders—on seeing "office" as most important for keeping the story straight. Certainly, reliance on faithful leaders has been one of the ways the church has maintained its faithfulness on its journey, and emphasizing one or more aspect (such as leadership) is often helpful and appropriate. But when other key elements, like Scripture, the Holy Spirit, worship, and holiness, get pushed to one side, Christians easily lose their way. As we've seen before, when one element of the church or of Christianity becomes detached and takes a life of its own, the whole story is often eclipsed.

Institutional Church—Institutional Leaders

Both the New Testament and other early Christian writings describe a church with elders (or bishops), deacons, and evangelists, with some congregations in the 2nd century designating widows and young men for specific duties, as well (see 1 Timothy 5). But as early as the end of

There were many writings by early Christians that were never accepted as Scripture, yet were cherished by the church. These were in the form of devotional guides, advice from wise leaders, sermons, descriptions of worship, teaching against heresies, and a host of other useful materials. Those interested in reading some of these early Christian writings can consult web sites such as "The Early Church Fathers" at <www.ccel.org/fathers2/>.

116

the first century, some churches began to identify a single leader (the bishop) above the other "offices." At first, these bishops were usually leaders of congregations in larger cities who also had charge over other congregations in the area.

This move from a shepherding leadership structure to a more hierarchical one occurred for many reasons, but one significant theological pressure in this direction was the need many Christians felt for a spokesperson who could defend the faith against heretics and represent the church to the world. The bishop even became, in the minds of some Christians, the mystical link to Christ himself, and without his authorization, no service was valid.

This concentration of the bishop's power over a region of churches led to a different kind of leadership. Undeniably, multitudes of Christians and leaders continued living faithfully to the story. Yet, whenever the office of bishop became a position of power for one man rather than a place of service for godly leaders, the church's journey was sidetracked. Even at the beginning of this shift in church leadership, many were coming to see the church as a settled institution that dispensed grace through its priests—a far cry from the vision of a pilgrim people seeking a city not of this world. Human weakness tempted Christians to pervert the story, even as they strove to strengthen the church by relying on faithful leaders.

During and after the time of Constantine, the church became, in the minds of most people, an institution ruled by bishops. The great Christian thinker Augustine (354–430 CE) strengthened the idea by insisting that the role of defining sin and the requirements for forgiveness belongs to the church. Salvation comes through the church, he said, and so being right with God involves

> Augustine of Hippo (354–430 CE) was one of the most influential leaders and writers of the early church. His conversion from an intellectual bent on satisfying his own desires to a church leader of immense power is told in his book *Confessions*. His *City of God* refuted the accusation that the fall of the Roman Empire was due to neglect of the ancient gods and made a sharp distinction between the kingdoms of the earth and the kingdom of God.

117

doing what the church (through the bishops and other officers) tells the individual Christian to do. Augustine sought
to defend the church of his day against groups like the Donatists and Pelagians, who insisted that they were the only true Christians. He did not intend to minimize holy living, Scripture, or worship. Yet others would use his writings to support the idea that obedience to the bishops took precedence over all other aspects of Christianity. The
church became the ultimate source of authority in religion, and
as a result, instead of viewing itself as the pilgrim community
saved by Christ and ministering to the world, the institutional
church became itself the central agent of salvation.

Donatists

A divisive North African movement that taught that their leaders and churches were the only true and pure ones and refused to recognize the baptism of other churches.

Pelagians

Followers of a British monk named Pelagius, they were accused of teaching that Jesus' life was simply to set a good example for humans, who have the ability to live a sinless life.

From our perspective, it's easy to identify mistakes many
Christians made during this part of the story. However, we
must remember that they strengthened the leadership offices
of the church in an attempt to keep the story straight under
the pressures of heresy and culture. Instead, over time the role of leadership easily became unbalanced and took control. Of course, even in the worst of times, diversity and faithfulness prevailed in many places. Although this book has focused only on the church in the West, the Eastern church had its own strengths and weaknesses, emphasiz-

The Eastern "Orthodox" Church and the western Roman "Catholic" Church moved apart relatively early. For one thing, the East and West had significant differences of culture and language that necessarily resulted in different ways of doing worship and understanding what was most important. In 1054 Pope Leo IX excommunicated the Eastern churches for heresy, and the Patriarch of Constantinople promptly returned the favor by excommunicating the western churches in league with Rome. Part of the tension surrounded the refusal of the Eastern churches to accept the universal authority of the Pope.

118

ing different elements to keep the story straight. Moreover, many Western Christians in this era saw the dangers in the institutional church, rejecting its favored status to live lives of self-denial, selling their possessions for the sake of the poor and choosing deliberately to live as humble ascetics. Yet by the Middle Ages, the church—by now termed Catholic—was largely defined by its offices of institutional bishops and clergy—not by its status as the pilgrim people of God.

In light of the considerable trust the Catholic Church placed in its powerful institutional leaders, it's not surprising that many Christians developed strong reactions to the resulting abuses. In the 15th and 16th centuries, the leaders of the Protestant Reformation strove to reorient the way people understood Christ, salvation, and the church. They insisted repeatedly on the principle of *sola scriptura*—that the scriptures alone, not the decrees of councils, bishops, or Popes, are the authoritative word of God. These reformers also proclaimed *sola fide*—that salvation comes not through obedience to the church's doctrines, but through faith in Jesus Christ and his saving work. In the eyes of leaders like Martin Luther and John Calvin, the New Testament taught "the priesthood of all believers," which they believed challenged the idea that only the institutional priests and bishops could approach God and dispense forgiveness.

The term "catholic" is from the Latin that simply means "universal." The early church, in writing to refute heresy, referred to the mainstream church as the catholic or universal church. Over time the term came to be associated with the western church that was associated with Rome, and in the division between East and West, catholic became "Roman Catholic" as opposed to "Eastern Orthodox."

As we have seen already, each of these "corrections" had the potential to become detached from the larger story and result in distortions to the story in different but equally destructive ways. If emphasized to the neglect of faithful leadership and a strong sense of the community, for example, the emphases on *sola scriptura* and the "priesthood of all believers" often resulted in every individual becoming his or her own authority. Fragmentation replaced faithful diversity as Christians over-compensated for abuses of

119

leadership by rejecting even healthy spiritual guidance. In the same way, if disconnected from an emphasis on holy living and obedience to Scripture, *sola fide* (faith alone) could become a license for selfishness and disregard for God's will.

Martin Luther, John Calvin, and other reformers wrestled with the distortions to the story they saw in the church of their day and gave their lives to reforming it. Yet they still perceived the church largely as an institution, a place where the gospel is preached and the sacraments rightly administered. They viewed it as a place to gather for worship, not as an exiled community living in distinct ways in the world. Both Catholics and Protestants continued (and often still continue) to see the church as it was seen in the "Constantinian" era—as a permanent city at home in this world.

Not all Christians held this view of the church, though. One movement in the Reformation radically reoriented its members' view of the church—the Anabaptists. While some violent extremist groups were originally included under this label, the Anabaptists that survived the era embraced pacifism as part of their understanding of the church as God's holy people. They rejected the Constantinian union of church and state and the infant baptism it required, instead viewing the church as a body of believers who had consciously accepted Christ and committed to live a simple and godly life. To the Anabaptists, holy living, not submission to church dogma, provided the chief evidence of one's Christianity.

Not surprisingly, the Anabaptists were hated by Catholic and Protestant alike, partly because they rejected the legitimacy of everyone else's Christianity,

> We have been united concerning the separation that shall take place from the evil and the wickedness which the devil has planted in the world, simply in this; that we have no fellowship with them, and do not run with them in the confusion of their abominations. So it is; since all who have not entered into the obedience of faith and have not united themselves with God so that they will to do His will, are a great abomination before God....
>
> *from the* Schleitheim Confession, *an early Anabaptist statement of belief, 1527.*

but also because they embodied the frightening vision of the church as a pilgrim people with nowhere to lay its head. However, in their attempts to correct the mistakes of others, the Anabaptists' heavy reliance on living a separate and holy life, although an essential part of keeping the story straight, sometimes became detached from the other elements of a healthy church. When this happened, their desire for holiness became itself a source of distortion, leading in some cases to a radical separation from the world rather than a mission to serve it.

Conclusion

In light of what we've just examined, how can anyone claim to be living the story faithfully? It seems that every attempt to eliminate distortions in the story has only resulted in more. In one sense, that's true. Humans are not perfect—the gospel story makes that clear. Sin is still sin—and admitting imperfection does not condone it. On the contrary, to be saved we must admit that we are sinful and can be redeemed only through the blood of Christ.

On the other hand, admitting humans are imperfect does not let us off the hook. It does not excuse Christians from continuing the journey toward the lasting city or striving with all our being to keep the story straight. God expects us to be traveling, not sedentary, always journeying and never permitting ourselves the smug sense that we have found our place in the world.

Simply put, continuing the journey toward the lasting city isn't easy. As we've seen, New Testament Christians relied on elements like Scripture, worship, leadership, holy living, and the Holy Spirit, all working in combination to ensure their faithfulness to God's purpose for his church. Emphasized in different combinations from congregation to congregation, these elements provided healthy diversity, as well as continuity, for the growing church. Churches must allow themselves the freedom in Christ to combine these elements in ways that make the most sense for their time, place, and circumstance. Such congregations aren't denying the authority of the first-century church to serve as our model; on the contrary, their approach aligns perfectly with the principles (if not the specific practices) that governed the early church. This kind of diversity ought to provide the opportunity for Christians to experience the richness and legitimacy of diversity in the church, grasping parts of the story we might otherwise ignore.

As we've discovered, though, with the freedom of diversity inevitably comes the threat of heresy. Even the most well-meaning attempts to avoid and correct dangers facing the church can result in an unhealthy imbalance that may derail us in our journey toward a lasting city. Both heresies and our over-corrections to them still threaten the church today, leading to attitudes and behavior that manifest the works of the flesh rather than the fruit of the Spirit. Studying the problems of the past makes us sensitive to those and similar problems when they reappear in new disguises. In response, we should fall before God in humility every day asking for wisdom and discernment, and praying that the fruit of his Spirit be seen increasingly in our lives.

Finally, in our efforts to be like Christ, we need to be wary of passing judgment on earlier Christians for their errors. While it's easy to see the speck in their eye, our business is to learn from their successes and failures so we can remove the log from our own. The Roman, Medieval, and Reformation-era churches made grave errors, certainly, but the story of our own Restoration Movement is full of both triumphs and mistakes, as well. Understanding our place in the vast, sweeping history of the church gives us the humility, experience, and perspective we need to examine ourselves—an essential part of remaining faithful to the story of Jesus and to our journey toward the lasting city.

6

Churches of Christ:
Being Faithful to the Story

We know that all things work together for good for those
who love God, who are called according to his purpose.

Romans 8:28

Tired of new creeds and new parties in religion, and
of the numerous abortive efforts to reform the reformation; convinced from the Holy Scriptures, from
observation and experience, that the union of the disciples of Christ is essential to the conversion of the
world, and that the correction and improvement of
no creed, or partisan establishment in Christendom,
could ever become the basis of such a union, ... a few
individuals, about the commencement of the present
century, began to reflect upon the ways and means to
restore primitive Christianity.

This cause, like every other, was first plead [sic] by
the tongue, afterwards by the pen and the press. The
history of its progress corresponds with the history of
every other religious revolution in this respect—that
different points, at different times, almost exclusively
engrossed the attention of its pleaders.

Alexander Campbell, Preface to The Christian System, *1835*

In my growing-up years, two local congregations pub-
lished papers titled the Gospel Defender *and the* Gospel
Contender *on opposite weeks from each other. The*
paper that was published one week got its content from
the previous issue of the other. Every copy was filled

123

with attacks and counterattacks on matters ranging from kitchens in the church building to congregational support of orphanages. I liked reading them; they were filled with clever insults and stirring denunciations that I thought might come in handy in future battles I would have to wage. And, frankly, it was exciting and entertaining to watch these verbal gladiatorial matches.

The two papers followed me to college, but as I continued to read them I became increasingly aware that something wasn't quite right. The writers modeled a spirit that appealed to something other than my higher nature. Instead of making me want to love others more and to treat people with kindness, reading those papers made me want to cut people down, to criticize them and focus on things I thought they needed to correct. These papers didn't make me want to take the gospel to others, nor did they bring about an increase in the fruit of the Spirit in my life. In fact, they made me want to be quarrelsome, factious, and divisive—characteristics specifically labeled works of the flesh.

It is certainly not bad to contend for the faith or to defend it—that is exactly what this book urges all Christians to do. But believing that it's advancing the faith to denounce one another over matters such as those highlighted in the Contender and the Defender (or hundreds of others like them) betrays a fundamental misunderstanding of Christ's church. Such an understanding assumes that "my side" has arrived; the task now is to defend the walls of our fortified city. Gone is the sense of mission and the continuing quest for the lasting city.

I stopped my subscriptions to the papers sometime during my college years—or maybe they just played themselves out and stopped publication; I don't remember. There were plenty of other papers that performed the same function. But the years of controversy and animosity represented by those publications was a reminder to me of how easy it is to think I am defending the gospel and the church while missing the very point of the story and the very mission of the church. God help us to have eyes to see and ears to hear.

—Doug

124

The Mind of Churches of Christ—Nineteenth-Century Formation

The early leaders of Churches of Christ wanted more than anything to keep the story straight. Believing that the Christianity of their day had abandoned or distorted some key elements of the story, they made a prophetic call for the church to return to God's mission, to seek again the lasting city. Like Christians through the centuries, these believers relied on Scripture, faithful leaders, authentic worship, an ethical lifestyle, and the spirit of Christ to keep the story straight, and their story deserves examination.

By 1831, Barton W. Stone and Alexander Campbell had known about each other's religious reforms for several years. The American-born Stone and the Irish-born Campbell first met in 1824 near Stone's home in Georgetown, Kentucky and developed a healthy respect for each other. Both shared the vision of a united church free from organizational structures that divided Christians, and both urged Christians to turn to the Bible alone for their beliefs and practices, rejecting sectarian creeds that forced believers into opposing camps.

Stone's "Christians" and Campbell's "disciples" (as the two groups were called) shared so many similarities, in fact, that many people began asking why they had not united with each other. Especially in Kentucky, where congregations of both movements often existed in the same town, calls for a formal union between the two movements increased in the 1830s. Stone broached the subject first in

Stone and the Campbells

Barton W. Stone (1772–1844) was born in Port Tobacco, Maryland and was baptized as an infant in the Anglican Church. While studying at a school operated by Presbyterian minister David Caldwell, Stone was converted and gave his life to the Presbyterian ministry. While serving two small churches in Kentucky, Stone and four others broke with the Calvinist Presbyterians and formed the Springfield Presbytery in 1803. But the following year they dissolved that body to be simply Christian Churches.

Thomas Campbell (1763–1854) and his son Alexander (1788–1866) were also Presbyterians, but from Ireland. In America they settled in western Virginia and soon separated from their Presbyterian body to promote unity among all believers.

125

the August 1831 issue of his paper, the *Christian Messenger*. The two groups were already united in spirit, Stone wrote; and he declared that the churches of his movement were ready to be united formally with Campbell's at any time.

He went on to claim, however, that a union had not occurred because the "disciples" objected to some opinions held by Stone's movement. The "Christians" taught and practiced immersion for the remission of sins like the disciples did, Stone asserted, but the disciples objected to having fellowship with unimmersed persons, while the "Christians" did not. Also, he pointed out that the "disciples" did not want to be confused with the various groups who called themselves Christian. In other words, Stone said, the two groups had not formally united because the disciples didn't want to. Stone closed his article on "Union" with these words:

> I have long thought, and seriously thought, whether a formal union on the Bible, without possessing the spirit of that book, would be a blessing or a curse to society—whether it would be better than faith without works, or than a body without the spirit—whether it would not rather be a stumbling block, a delusive snare to the world. O, my brethren: let us repent and do our first works—let us seek for more holiness, rather than trouble ourselves and others with schemes and plans for union. The love of God shed abroad in our hearts by the Holy Ghost given unto us, will more effectually unite than all the wisdom of the world combined.

Campbell quickly replied. In the September 1831 issue of his paper the *Millennial Harbinger*, he reprinted Stone's article and responded at length. In no uncertain terms, he denied that his reform movement was essentially like Stone's. Stone had claimed that Campbell's followers had "received the doctrine taught by us many years ago." Not so, exclaimed Campbell. Many groups in Europe and America had denounced sects, creeds, and human dogmas over the last two hundred years, but those movements had nothing to do with the movement he was leading. Other reformers had done "only the work of a pioneer ... clearing the forests, girdling the trees, and burning the brush."

Campbell insisted that he and his followers were about much more than rejecting creeds, councils, and sects. They wanted to discover the system he called "the ancient gospel and ancient order of things." In a letter to a critic published the month before, Campbell had declared "we contend that God has given us a Divine System, perfect as the system of the universe, and that both Testaments compose that system." This system of teaching and practice (the ancient gospel and order) easily distinguished his work, he insisted, "from every other cause pled on this continent or in Europe since the great apostasy."

This exchange between Stone and Campbell, occurring on the very eve of the union of their two movements, power-fully illustrates two different views in understanding Christianity and the church—views that have been part of Churches of Christ from our beginning. One saw the church primarily as holy community; the other empha-sized the church as biblical system. One emphasized a transformed and holy life as key to being faithful to the story; the other looked especially to order as key to keeping the story straight. While different, the two under-standings have been in many ways complementary—or at least they've had that potential. Without Stone's vision of holiness, the emphasis on order can obscure the sense of pilgrimage that is central to the church's identity. Without Campbell's search for order, there is danger of a lack of stable leadership, a neglect of serious study and of devel-opment of strong convictions. In studying the history of how Churches of Christ have struggled to deal with and integrate these two visions of the church in the last two centuries, we gain valuable insight into our own ways of thinking and acting in the present.

The Great Apostasy

"The Great Apostasy" was the term that had been used by Protestants since the Reformation to refer to the corruption and falling away they saw embodied in the Roman Catholic Church. This understand-ing reflected a specific historic interpreta-tion of New Testament scriptures such as 2 Timothy 3 and 2 Peter 3 that warned of a falling away.

127

Keeping the Story Straight Through the Church's Unity

American religion in the early 1800s might be described as chaotic. The young nation's ideals of independence and democracy, when applied to Christianity, produced a religious culture in which individuals had the right and ability to determine biblical truth for themselves. Naturally, this resulted in a bewildering increase in church divisions and a rise in the number of new churches and movements, each claiming to have the "truth."

The religious conflict of their day led Thomas and Alexander Campbell, Barton W. Stone, and a host of others to the conviction that being faithful to Christ demanded recognizing the unity of Christ's church and making that unity visible. They believed that in America, free from the corrupt state churches of the Old World, this Christian unity could become a reality. A deep desire to end sectarian divisions motivated both "founding documents" of the Movement, the "Last Will and Testament of the Springfield Presbytery" (1804) and the "Declaration and Address of the Christian Association" (1809). These writings attest to the deep desire of these people to fight against the selfish individualism and division that dominated American religion.

> We will that this body die, be dissolved, and sink into union with the body of Christ at large; for there is but one Body, and one Spirit, even as we are called in one hope of our calling.
>
> *"Last Will and Testament of the Springfield Presbytery," 1804*

> The Church of Christ upon earth is essentially, intentionally, and constitutionally one; consisting of all those in every place that profess their faith in Christ and obedience to him in all things according to the Scriptures, and that manifest the same by their tempers and conduct, and of none else; as none else can be truly and properly called Christians.
>
> *Thomas Campbell*
> Declaration and Address, *1809*

So the early leaders of Churches of Christ responded to division in faithful and biblical ways. The church cannot be divided and fighting against itself—it is one, they insisted. God has given it direction concerning how to live, worship, and structure itself. They emphasized careful study of Scripture to discern those truths, and they urged followers of Christ to love one another and to come together in every locality to work and worship in unity. As always happens, the elements of Christianity that engrossed their attention were those especially needed to be faithful to the story in their particular circumstances.

The early emphasis on unity led to the Movement's strong stand on two other issues: denominational systems, and creeds and confessions. The people of the Stone-Campbell Movement fought against denominational organizations and creeds because they believed that these separated Christians. Denominations tended to make people loyal to a church name rather than simply to Christ and led to structures and practices that separated them from other followers of Jesus. In addition, creeds and confessions of faith spelled out the doctrines and practices unique to each denomination, making the divisions even stronger. Such divisions are anti-natural, Thomas Campbell exclaimed in the *Declaration and Address*, exciting "Christians to condemn, to hate, and oppose one another, who are bound by the highest and most endearing obligations to love each other as brethren, even as Christ loved them."

The early leaders of the Movement insisted that believers must abandon human creeds and confessions as terms of fellowship, forcing the denominational structures to topple under their own useless mass; they encouraged all believers to go back to the Bible alone as the ultimate source for all we say and do. As Alexander Campbell said in the preface to his *Christian System*, no creed or any revision of one could bring about unity. To be faithful to the truth of the oneness of Christ's church meant trusting Scripture alone.

Keeping the Story Straight Through Faithfulness to Scripture

Rejecting human creeds and confessions and restoring the clear teachings of Scripture alone as the basis for visible Christian unity became the watchword for the churches of the Stone-Campbell Movement. Yet Barton W. Stone and Alexander Campbell took significantly different approaches to this goal.

129

Campbell focused on the recovery of correct doctrines and practices. He viewed the Bible as "a book of facts," by which he meant that Scripture, unlike human creeds and confessions, was not mere opinion or speculation. What Campbell meant by "facts" involved more than simple data, yet he clearly took a primarily intellectual approach to Scripture. If the Bible is essentially a book of facts, every Christian's primary duty is to use his or her reason and get those facts straight.

Campbell assumed, as did most Americans of his day, that every individual shared in the "common sense." When used properly, that ability would lead people to discover the facts in every area of life, including religion. Since the facts of religion were in the Bible, each person had the ability and the responsibility to study the Bible to discover and understand its facts. Campbell thought that, if they reasoned properly, everyone would arrive at the same truths about the church's beliefs and practices. On those truths alone, not on any human creed or confession, could the visible unity of the church be restored.

Stone, on the other hand, believed the church's restoration depended on lives transformed by God's Spirit. Only lives showing the fruit of the Spirit (love, joy, and peace) and rejecting the works of the flesh (quarrels, dissensions, and divisions) could bring unity. He understood the Bible to be much more than a book of facts; it was the living, active word of God, the sword of the Spirit, which takes hold of our hearts and minds and shapes us into the likeness of Christ. For Stone, "having all the facts straight" and stating doctrinal propositions correctly were not the primary marks of a true church; a true church, because of what it believes, lives a life turned toward God, exhibiting unselfish love and service toward others. A church like this would be united with all others that manifested that same Spirit of God.

130 Stone's vision of the church did not exclude concern for the "facts." He held the authority of Scripture as absolute and advocated serious study and thought. But he insisted that Scripture does not simply supply information—it transforms. Correct doctrines and practices involved more than "getting

it right" intellectually. To be right ultimately, doctrines must shape us into the likeness of Christ as our lives reflect the increasing harvest of the fruit of the Spirit. For Stone, this understanding of the church meant that differences on specific doctrines and practices would not be a reason for separation or division among those who manifest the spirit of Christ. In fact, such differences would be cause to stay together to learn from and strengthen one another.

Confronted with the stark reality of division among Christians, early leaders in Churches of Christ focused on the biblical call for unity of Christ's church. They believed that recognizing Scripture as their ultimate authority and rejecting divisive denominational structures and creeds would make the unity they sought visible. Yet from the beginning, two views of how Scripture guided the church existed together in the Movement—two views of the church and its unity. Both had as their object faithfulness to the story.

> The scriptures will never keep together in union and fellowship members not in the spirit of the scriptures, which spirit is love, peace, unity, forbearance and cheerful obedience. I blush for my fellows who hold up the Bible as the bond of union yet make their opinions of it tests of fellowship; who plead for union of all Christians; yet refuse fellowship from such as dissent from their notions.... Such anti-sectarian sectarians are doing more mischief to the cause and advancement of truth, the unity of Christians, and the salvation of the world, than all the skeptics in the world. In fact, they create skeptics.
>
> *Barton W. Stone*
> Christian Messenger, *1835*

Keeping the Story Straight Through Faithful Worship

The church through the centuries has looked to worship to help it keep the story straight, and the same was true of the early leaders of the Stone-Campbell Movement. They saw how competing worship practices among the churches served to separate and alienate Christians. Furthermore, they believed that the church had neglected certain worship practices vital for the church to remain faithful.

131

Barton Stone saw the worship of God primarily as the place where we humble ourselves completely before our Lord. In an 1841 article, he compared worship to the relationship between a dog and its master. While worship involves submission when we receive rebuke and correction, it is also a place of great joy as we come into the presence of our Master. In other writings, Stone argued that prayer was inherently an act of submission and humility—one that recognized our dependence on God and allowed us to show our gratitude for blessings received. As another key element of worship, preaching should not center on controversy, Stone believed, and singing should reflect a loving and giving God, not the angry, vengeful deity described in the hymnals of his day. Though in the earliest days of Stone's movement his churches had not observed the Lord's Supper every Sunday, by 1841 Stone argued for weekly observance using a single unleavened loaf, which symbolically represented the oneness of Christ's body.

Since he primarily viewed the church as holy community, Stone spent little time discussing the specifics of the worship service, but focused on the nature of worship as a place of humility and joy. Although they agreed on the importance of scriptural worship, Stone and Campbell differed in the way they spoke of it. Alexander Campbell's focus on the church as system led to a much more detailed focus on the acts of worship.

Between 1824 and 1830, in his journal the *Christian Baptist*, Alexander Campbell published a series of articles on restoring the practices of the ancient church. In the fifth article, he argued for a divinely authorized order of worship that is uniformly the same in every worship assembly. In the June 1838 *Millennial Harbinger*, Campbell gave a "general outline of worship in public assemblies, as is now generally practiced." The items he included were singing, reading, thanksgiving, teaching, exhorting, praying, blessing, breaking the loaf, contributing to the Lord's treasury, and preaching the word; but he added there might be other elements "as the occasion may require."

132

While he identified certain ingredients in the "ancient order" of worship, he did not formulate a rigid list of acts of worship as others later would.

To Campbell, the two parts of worship most in need of reform were the Lord's Supper and singing. He amassed convincing arguments for taking the Lord's Supper weekly, a practice that would become characteristic of all the churches of the Stone-Campbell Movement. However, Campbell differed from Stone regarding the nature of the Lord's Supper. In his book *The Christian System*, Campbell explained that the Lord's Supper's primary purpose is to "furnish arguments" that help us to live for God and resist sin. By "argument," he meant more than simply intellectual reasons, but also "example" or "model." Yet for Campbell, communion involved no mystical element, no special presence of Christ, no supernatural strengthening. Its importance in worship lay in its ability to remind us of Christ's sacrifice, providing arguments for why we should be his followers.

Campbell's view became the predominant understanding of the Lord's Supper in most churches of the Movement. The insistence on its weekly observance has been a great strength of Churches of Christ and is a faithful response to the story. Yet even in Campbell's own day, some acknowledged a deeper significance for communion than he admitted. People like Robert Richardson, for example, saw that the weekly Lord's Supper was central to the story—a virtual reenactment of the gospel. This was no mere ritual but an act that transformed the church into the likeness of Christ as they "remembered" God's ultimate sacrifice. Communion played an essential role in bringing the church to reflect Christ's attitude of self-sacrifice in its own life.

Concerning congregational singing, Campbell spent much time arguing against the use of hymns with unscriptural teachings. "Our hymn book is as good an index to the brains and to the hearts of a people as the creed book," he declared in 1827. He, like Stone, gave examples of hymn words that reflected Calvinist doctrine and so could not be accepted by the churches if they wished to be faithful to Scripture. While correct doctrine in song

133

lyrics continued to be important to Campbell and those who have come after him, the practice of unaccompanied congregational singing would become one of the most characteristic markers of Churches of Christ. Believing that the service should be fully participatory and accessible to every member, Campbell opposed choirs and other special music as well as formal ritual or liturgy that involved prescribed scripture readings, sermon texts, and written prayers. Campbell and other leaders insisted that rote repetition of formal services worked against active engagement of the minds and hearts of every member.

Campbell saw himself as steering a course that would avoid both the emotional extremes of the revivals and the cold, formal, and spiritless worship he observed in some of the establishment churches. Yet clearly Campbell favored rational and solemn services. Since he saw the church as a system, he believed worship should be, as he explained in 1835, "a display of the most rational and religious arrangement—a model, indeed, of the utility and beauty of perfect order."

Stone's focus on the church as holy community and Campbell's view of it as a biblical system deeply influenced their efforts to reform the church's worship. Both emphasized practices and understandings they believed had been lost or corrupted, threatening faithfulness to the story, and their ideas were not inherently antagonistic to each other. Yet holding the two visions together would prove to be a difficult task as the Stone-Campbell Movement continued to grow and develop.

Keeping the Story Straight Through Faithful Leaders—Elders

Like Christians before them, Stone and Campbell also looked to faithful leadership to help them restore the unity of the church. In previous centuries, leadership positions had often became places of power rather than of service, and the leaders of the Stone-Campbell Movement saw similar problems that threatened the church's journey in their own day. The Presbyterian heritage shared by all the founding leaders emphasized the importance of elders in every congregation. However, Presbyterian elders often had authority beyond their local congregation through the presbyteries, synods, and General Assembly of the Presbyterian Church. Stone and the Campbells had experienced the coercive power of these Presbyterian bodies—Stone in his fight with the Synod of Kentucky and Thomas Campbell in his expulsion from the Associate Synod in Pennsylvania. They were convinced that such organizations, as well as leadership bodies like the Methodist General Conference and the Episcopal General Convention, were contrary to Scripture and a hindrance to the church's journey.

Stone continued to

> The Presbyterian system has two kinds of elders and several "levels." Ministers are "teaching elders," while those not formally ordained to the ministry are "ruling elders." The elders in a local congregation are known as the "session." Elders from congregations in certain geographical regions are chosen to serve at the "presbytery" and "Synod" levels ("synod" is from a Greek word meaning "meeting"). In a full-blown Presbyterian system, the body known as the General Assembly brings elders together usually every year for a national gathering. These levels function as church courts to make decisions, guide the churches, and to license and ordain ministers. Stone got into trouble with the Synod of Kentucky when he and his companions held a revival meeting that included non-Presbyterians and seemed to contradict Calvinist doctrine. Thomas Campbell was censured and dismissed from his Synod when he insisted that the Bible rather than the Presbyterian creed—The Westminster Confession—was the only reliable source for teaching and for the unity of the church.

view the role of elders very highly, though. In the "Witnesses Address" of the "Last Will and Testament of the Springfield Presbytery," he and the other signers stated that they would continue to exercise their functions as ministers of the gospel (that is, as ordained elders), including ordaining pastors and other elders. In an 1827 article in the *Christian Messenger*, Stone insisted that only elders could ordain ministers, and that if a minister were accused of teaching false doctrine, he was to be judged by "the conference of bishops and elders" rather than simply by

135

the local congregation. In 1832 in Lexington, Kentucky, only a few weeks after the famous New Year's service when the Stone and Campbell congregations there united, the Stone group refused to allow the celebration of the Lord's Supper because no ordained elder was present—a move which resulted in the separation of the groups there for about two more years.

The Campbells' understanding of elders differed somewhat from Stone's. They too had been Presbyterians, members of a faction of the Church of Scotland. Yet even before coming to America, they had been influenced by reformers who had broken with the Scottish church and created independent congregations. One group, called Glasites after the Presbyterian minister John Glas, especially influenced the Campbells. Glas insisted that individual congregations must rule themselves to be biblical. Like main-stream Presbyterians, the Glasites had elders in each church, but their authority was restricted to their own congregation.

Partly as a result of Glasite influence, those in the Campbell Movement came to see elders as spiritual guardians only of the local congregation of which they were members. If an elder left a congregation, he would no longer hold that office. Within any congregation, the elders ordained its officers; and the elders were responsible for teaching, presiding over, and executing the laws of Christ in all the congregation's meetings. Yet Alexander Campbell maintained in the *Christian System* that any Christian could preach, baptize, dispense the Supper, and pray for others when circumstances demanded it.

Alexander Campbell's *The Christian System, In Reference to the Union of Christians, and a Restoration of Primitive Christianity, as Plead* [sic] *in the Current Reformation* (usually abbreviated *Christian System*) was first published in 1839, and was Campbell's attempt to bring together in one place the basic principles he saw as key to his reform movement.

136

Both the Stone and Campbell movements looked to faithful leaders to guide the church on its journey. They both rejected bodies with coercive power, like synods and presbyteries, because they believed such bodies were unscriptural. More importantly, they objected to such organizations because, in their attempts to control and remain in power, these bodies treated the church as an established city rather than a journeying people. Stone and Campbell differed, though, on the amount of control and authority elders should wield within individual congregations. Campbell's understanding of elders, rather than Stone's, became the dominant view in Churches of Christ as we moved into the 20th century. Although we soon learned that even congregational elders can sometimes lose sight of the church's role as a people in exile and come to view their position as one of power, many elders—perhaps most—cared deeply about God's mission and faihfully guided the transformation of peoples' lives.

The Stone-Campbell Movement and Churches of Christ have striven to be faithful to the story by turning to the same guides the church has always used, but they emphasized those most appropriate for their time and circumstance. In order to fight division, which they knew was contrary to the will of Christ, Stone, Campbell, and their followers turned primarily to a renewed emphasis on Scripture, a fresh examination of worship, and a reevaluation of leadership.

The Temptations of Churches of Christ

Like the generations before us, the needs of our specific time and place determined our focus. In emphasizing Scripture, worship, and leadership, we did not completely abandon other elements of the story such as holy living or a focus on the risen Lord. Yet in any time or place when individuals or movements focus intensely on things they believe most need correction, they run the risk of neglecting other parts of the story.

In 1885, F. G. Allen observed in "The Principles and Objects of the Current Reformation"

F. G. Allen (1836–1887) was founder and editor of the *Old Path Guide*, an influential 19th-century paper published in Kentucky.

we have had little or no controversy with our religious neighbors over the divinity of Christ, prayer,
repentance, godliness and the like. Not because we
do not value these things as highly as it is possible to
value anything else, but because they have not been
assailed. Let one of them be attacked, and the trumpet
will sound, the forces will rally, and the clash of arms
over that hitherto quiet point will awaken the sleeping
energies of Zion!

Was Allen right? In the attempt to correct the distortions they
saw, could Churches of Christ have neglected other important teachings and produced their own distortions? We've
seen in the previous chapter that every individual or group
faces the danger of neglecting important truths when focusing intensely on others. Throughout its 2000-year history, the
church has been tempted to do just that—and many times it
succumbed. Although the early leaders of Churches of Christ
were willing to take heroic stands because of their dedication
to Christ, no one is immune from the temptation to distort
the story, thereby becoming sidetracked on the journey.

Temptations in Our Anti-Denominationalism

One of the greatest strengths of Churches of Christ has
been their stand against anything that destroyed the visible
unity of Christ's church. Refusal to be complacent about the
divisions inherent in denominationalism is not wrong—it
is faithful to God and to the story. Yet our opposition to
the denominational system did not immunize us from the
social forces that all other human beings experience.

One leader in Churches of Christ who grappled with
how we could be undenominational Christians was G. C.
Brewer. He described the dilemma in the 1917 speech "Are We a
Denomination":

G. C. Brewer (1884–1956) was a widely-
known preacher, debater, and writer in
20th-century Churches of Christ. Much
of his work centered on controversies in
Churches of Christ such as the non-institutional issue.

138

we must admit that we are a distinct group. But it is
not our fault. We are forced to it. We are forced to be

> denominational by reason of the fact that we are unde-
> nominational. I can illustrate that this way: Let us suppose
> that we have on this desk a great heap of cards. Some of
> the cards are stamped with figures, 2, 4, 6, 8, etc., and there
> is a great number of them that are unstamped—have no
> figures on them. I am set to the task of separating these
> cards and classifying them. I place the "twos" in one stack,
> the "fours" in another, the "sixes" in still another stack
> and so on until I have stacked all the different numbers
> in separate stacks; and then I have a stack of cards that
> we would call nondescript—unstamped cards. They are a
> stack of cards just as much as the others are.

Although Brewer strongly resisted denominationalism and sought ways for the Churches of Christ to avoid it, he had to admit that individuals or groups can't exist in some kind of void that exempts them from human realities.

We are connected—biologically, socially, culturally, and theologically—to those who have gone before and those who are here now. Each congregation has a heritage and connections that have shaped it, whether it was established a hundred years ago or last week, because it is made of people who have come to that place from somewhere. In our very desire to be Christians only and to use only words of Scripture for our name, too often "we have, in spite of ourselves, become a sect whose special purpose is to contend against sectarianism" (G. C. Brewer, 1952 Harding College Lectures).

The temptation to sectarian exclusivism is not new, as Paul made clear in his rebuke to the Christians at Corinth (1 Corinthians 1:12). In our quest for the visible unity of Christ's church, in our rejection of the divisions embodied in the denominational system, we in Churches of Christ have too often believed that our anti-denominational position made us immune to human reality. We have frequently succumbed to pride, detaching our anti-denominational conviction from the larger story and believing that we were exempt from the sociological inevitability of denominating ourselves that all other groups face. By thinking we were standing, we risked a serious fall.

Churches of Christ must continue to resist the divisions inherent in the denominational system. However, we need to leave behind the burden of claiming we aren't vulnerable to the same kind of human grouping and attitudes that everyone else is; letting go of this prideful position frees us to continue our emphasis on the oneness of the church in a way that also welcomes the contributions of others outside our movement.

In their book *Coming Together in Christ*, Barry Callen and James North discuss the natural sociological process of people forming themselves into groups with names and characteristics that identify them. This is simply what always happens—it is unavoidable. The problem arises when one group looks down on and condemns others. They quote James Massey, who claims that "diversity is not division when the spirit of relating to those beyond the group is kept alive.... Diversity is one thing, while a spirit of division is quite another." Ironically, Churches of Christ have sometimes allowed the spirit of division to creep in even as we contended against division! In the words of Barton Stone and G. C. Brewer, some of us became anti-sectarian sectarians. Christians must eliminate the spirit of division wherever it raises its head—even, ironically, in our anti-division stance.

Temptations in Our Emphasis on Scripture

While other groups in the early 19th century also called for a return to Scripture, this call was a centerpiece of the Stone-Campbell Movement. Only through a return to the authority and clear teachings of Scripture could the visible unity of the church be realized. Because of this conviction, careful Bible study comprised a crucial part of our religious reform.

Yet on this subject, too, the prevailing ideas of American culture had a major impact on the church. The individualism and anti-intellectualism of the time tremendously influenced every part of American society, including the churches. One result was the belief that through simple common sense, every individual could read the Bible and understand it without any outside influences. Most people assumed that the Bible was essentially a book of facts, and that individual understandings were more important than understandings reached in communities of faith. Campbell and many others believed that the goal of reading the Bible is to use our intellects to dissect and scrutinize it, extracting the principles that are relevant to us today. A grave danger of this model is that it has us mastering the Scripture rather than allowing Scripture to master us.

Kentucky church leader Moses E. Lard (1818–1880) expressed this attitude in an 1864 article in his journal *Lard's Quarterly*. If the churches of the Stone-Campbell Movement had missed anything at all, or if they had added anything not taught in the Bible, he insisted, no one had been able to point it out. Forty years of sound criticism, enlightened reason, and honest judgment had proven that the "church of Christ" had gotten the facts right, unlike other groups. Statements like "we accept as the matter of our faith precisely and only what the Bible teaches, rejecting everything else…" indicate that Lard and others believed we were standing (1 Corinthians 10:12). As a result, they could not see or admit that we had been profoundly shaped by our American circumstances. Being shaped by culture is not wrong; in fact, it's an inevitable part of being faithful. However, by claiming to be immune to such influence, we succumbed to the temptation of pride and arrogance. We felt superior to others, forgetting that "all who exalt themselves will be humbled, and all who humble themselves will be exalted" (Matthew 23:12).

> **American Individualism & Anti-Intellectualism**
>
> The American belief that every individual had the ability to do anything he or she wanted to do was in part a reaction to the restrictive elitist society of Europe that assigned people to rigid positions in life based on their social class, not their abilities. There was a strong opposition among many Americans to formal education because that also gave certain access to position and opportunities that ought to be open to everyone. See Nathan O. Hatch, *The Democratization of American Christianity* (1989).

Paradoxically, despite the climate of anti-intellectualism, frontier America's almost unlimited optimism regarding human ability and reason created a powerful temptation to see intellectual mastery of the Bible as the key to true Christianity. Christian debaters who could devastate opponents

141

with a barrage of rational arguments became models of true religion for many, and Barton Stone's emphasis on sacrificial Christian love often gave way to Campbell's focus on knowledge. Of course, intimate knowledge of Scripture is central to Christianity. Scripture explains and models the church's identity and mission, and our emphasis on them has been one of our movement's great strengths. But whenever Churches of Christ detached that crucial emphasis from the larger story and made it a badge of pride that we had mastered Scripture, we succumbed to a destructive and divisive temptation.

Not everyone in the Stone-Campbell Movement focused on intellectual mastery of Scripture, though. There were always some, like T. B. Larimore and K. C. Moser, who saw the Bible primarily as the living, active, sword of God's Spirit (Ephesians 6:17; Hebrews 4:12). That understanding can lead the church to approach the study of Scripture with profound humility, anticipating the power of God's word to change us more into the likeness of Christ. Bible study becomes not simply an intellectual effort to "get the facts straight" but a transformative enterprise.

Some in Churches of Christ exhibited the desire to control Scripture by espousing the so-called "word only" doctrine. They taught that the Holy Spirit has worked solely through the written word since the close of the first century. This doctrine emerged partly as a reaction to two widely-held ideas in the 19th century. First, Calvinists taught that no one could respond to the gospel until the Holy Spirit acted on him or her in some mysterious way. Second, revivalists of the day claimed that the Holy Spirit caused uncontrollable physical displays during which people would fall unconscious and later recount ecstatic salvation experiences.

Alexander Campbell, Walter Scott, and many others in the Stone-Campbell Movement rejected such claims. No one had to wait for some capricious action of the Spirit to hear and accept the gospel, they said. The facts of the gospel were accessible to all, given by the Holy Spirit and embodied in the words of Scripture. Furthermore, since the Spirit of God was not one of confusion, it could not produce the

142

chaotic revival exercises. In the late 19th and early 20th century, when the Holiness and Pentecostal Movements made claims about the work of the Holy Spirit similar to those of earlier revivalists, the "word only" doctrine that rejected the idea of the Holy Spirit living in Christians other than through the words of the Bible became a majority position among Churches of Christ. Z. T. Sweeney's book *The Spirit and the Word* (1919) provides a classic example of this view. Nothing, he insisted, can be added to the revelation we have already received in Scripture nor to the reasons or motives we already have to follow Christ. "Of what use, then," he wrote, "would a direct indwelling Spirit be?"

Not everyone in Churches of Christ embraced the "word only" view, of course. Yet its usefulness in opposing the excesses of the Holiness and Pentecostal movements made it a powerful position. By the mid-1960s, increasing tension over the teachings of the Charismatic movement made the issue especially heated. Scores of articles appeared in 1966 and 1967 as "word only" advocates argued against those in Churches of Christ who taught a direct indwelling of the Spirit.

Calvinism, named after the 16th century reformer John Calvin, emphasized the absolute sovereignty of God. God had chosen those who were to be saved—humans could not manipulate God or initiate any action toward God. The revivalists of Stone and Campbell's day often reflected Calvinist ideas about the Holy Spirit's dramatic role in conversion, but began to abandon the idea that only a select few could be saved. They urged all to pray for the Spirit to come on them and convert them. In the 19th century a movement especially among Methodists began to teach that Christians could achieve instantaneous "holiness" by a miraculous gift of the Holy Spirit. In the early 20th century some Holiness advocates began teaching that the evidence of having received the Spirit was speaking in tongues like those on the Day of Pentecost. New Holiness and Pentecostal denominations like the Church of the Nazarene and the Assemblies of God formed based on these teachings. In the mid-20th century, some Pentecostals actively promoted their theology among non-Pentecostals, many of whom stayed in their original churches rather than joining Pentecostal bodies. This development is known as the Charismatic Movement.

The "word only" doctrine, its opponents declared, surrenders one of the Christian's greatest sources of strength and hope, replacing it with the assumption that the strength for living the Christian life must come primarily through our own intellectual efforts. Such a belief implies that the Holy Spirit works in our lives only through our mastery of biblical fact.

The tension between these two views of Scripture still persists in Churches of Christ today. How should we view the Bible and our relationship to it? The word of God is the sword of the Spirit (Ephesians 6:17), but is Scripture the Spirit's only means of interacting with us? Scripture itself answers this question. "God's love has been poured into our hearts through the Holy Spirit which has been given to us," says Paul (Romans 5:5). The Spirit dwells in us, bears witness with our spirit that we are children of God, and intercedes for us before God in ways we could never otherwise achieve (Romans 8). Christians are God's temple, and God's Spirit dwells in us (1 Corinthians 3:16). God sent the Spirit of Christ into our hearts because we are God's children (Galatians 4:6), and we are strengthened in our inner being with power through God's Spirit (Ephesians 3:16). Although part of our heritage has resisted any emphasis on the current activity of the Holy Spirit except in the written word, such a view denies the truth of Scripture itself.

Churches of Christ must not abandon an unwavering faithfulness to Scripture as the authoritative word of God, but we need to repent of the attitude that we alone, of all who try to follow Christ, are free from the influences and limitations of our particular experiences and circumstances. American independence and individualism have shaped how we view all areas of life, including Scripture. Being aware of this cultural influence enables us to resist the temptation to see the Bible as a book we must master rather than the living, active sword of the Spirit that masters us.

Temptations in Our Understandings of Worship

Since the church began, worshipping God has been essential to the Christian story. It directs our hearts toward that lasting city we have not yet reached. The priority Churches of Christ have always placed on true worship is a powerful asset. Our insistence that worship should be simple and participatory, should reflect what we see in the New Testament, and should be done "decently and in order" has been an integral part of our identity.

Though descriptions of the elements of worship like Alexander Campbell's appeared frequently, there was never a fixed list of the required "acts of worship" in the first generations of the Stone-Campbell Movement. Sometime in the early 20th century, Churches of Christ began using a list of "five acts of worship," though with some variations. The list usually included reading of Scripture (sometimes expressed as teaching or preaching the word), prayer, singing, the Lord's Supper, and the collection. Though the "invitation" (included in Campbell's list under "exhorting") was never included as a separate act in this more recent catalog, it became an essential piece of the services nevertheless. Baptism as an act of worship normally did not appear in these lists either, probably because it was not a necessary part of every public assembly.

> **The Items of Worship According to New Testament Plan**
>
> 1 Lord's Supper on first day; 2 Singing. This is the only music provided in the New Testament plan; 3 Prayer; 4 Fellowship, laying by in store according to prosperity; 5 Preaching and teaching the word of God.... A corruption of this plan of worship by changing the day, spirit, or item of worship furnished by Scripture, means the destruction of the Church as the Church of God. The consequence of doing so is the loss of divine recognition (2 John 9). "He that goeth onward and abideth not in the teachings of Christ hath not God."
>
> *Roy E. Cogdill*
> The New Testament Church, *1939*

This desire in Churches of Christ to develop rigid lists further reflects the attitude that the Bible is a book of facts we intellectually dissect and rearrange in precise catalogs and registers. In the eyes of many, the "five acts of worship" became a divine law, and any deviation from it completely disqualified that church and its worship as acceptable to God. The danger of this attitude was that worship could become primarily an obligation rather than a time of

145

joy; services could become less about glorifying God and building up the body and more about keeping the rules.

Jesus had something to say about this in his conversation with the Samaritan woman in John 4:23–24. There he describes the right kind of worship as being "in spirit and in truth" "spirit and truth." These terms are rich and demand much study and meditation. Yet both of these terms seem to point to a single certainty—that those who worship God must do it with the right kind of attitude, out of a profound relationship with him. Our worship cannot be pleasing to God if it is merely "going through the motions," even if the motions are technically "correct." This is nothing new in God's message to his people. A spirit of humility, love, and submission is foundational for any worship to be acceptable to God. Without a right heart, we cannot worship rightly. Although we in Churches of Christ have known and taught this all along, our desire to obey God's commands for worship has sometimes led us toward a legalistic focus on "getting the words and actions right."

The first Christians' worship practices reflected the forms of their times and background. Early descriptions of Christian worship indicate extensive reading of Scripture, first the Hebrew writings

> The most extensive description of an early Christian worship service is in Justin Martyr's *Apology*, written around 150 CE.

and eventually the new Christian writings. Whoever was presiding commented on the texts, urging the hearers to good deeds. One description of ancient worship reveals that it sometimes involved taking a solemn oath never to commit fraud, theft, adultery or other wicked deeds. They took the Lord's Supper, in the earliest times as part of a fellowship meal called the *agape*. They prayed, sang, gave thanks, collected funds for needy saints, and arranged for the Supper to be carried to the sick.

146   In every case, early Christian worship reflected their own culture and times, their own language and circumstances. Here Christians told the story and acted it out, praising God and receiving strength and encouragement. In worship, disciples were drawn closer to God and transformed into

the likeness of Christ, becoming stronger in their resolve to press on to the lasting city. These are the goals of Christian worship in every culture, past and present.

Clearly, though, the worship needs of a small, persecuted house church in the first-century Roman Empire would differ from our needs today. For example, in a society without printing presses, when the average Christian would not have owned a Bible, they would perhaps have devoted more time to the public reading of Scripture than we do in our services. These differences aren't wrong; in fact, they reflect a diversity that allows the church to remain relevant despite differences in time and culture.

Unfortunately, though, Churches of Christ, like others through the centuries, have been tempted to believe that our worship practices should apply "for all times." Largely unaware that those worship checklists were themselves significantly formed by the western and American context that shaped our thinking, we became imprisoned by our own limited perspective. We sang in four-part harmony, stopped using wine in the Lord's Supper after Prohibition, offered the invitation like it had been done in the frontier camp meetings, and, like other Protestants, elevated the sermon to a chief position in the service, all partly in response to American cultural influences. Engaging our culture is inevitable and necessary for the church's mission. But when we fail to acknowledge culture's influence and believe we have found the "right" combination of worship factors, we detach them from the story, perverting the very story we wish to protect. We risk becoming complacent and self-satisfied, feeling that our journey is completed and the city we've built here on earth is the lasting one.

Temptations in Our Understandings of Faithful Leaders
Toward the end of the 19th century, American society went through a period that historian Alan Trachtenberg has called "the incorporation of America." Partly as a result of the Civil War, society as a whole accepted the ideals of centralized control of government and business, of organization and efficiency, obedience and loyalty. This move toward central-

147

ization and power in government and business changed the way people thought about all of life, including religion.

Most American denominations developed centralized headquarters with strong bureaucracies and increasing numbers of agencies. In the larger Stone-Campbell Movement among the Christian Churches and Disciples, centralized control grew until eventually all the missionary and benevolent societies were consolidated into one umbrella agency in 1919—the United Christian Missionary Society. Although Churches of Christ maintained the tradition of autonomous congregations, they too were affected by the new spirit of incorporation. Elderships in many congregations were often reconceived to operate like boards of directors over business operations, with authority to make all decisions for the church. Not surprisingly, the "authority" of elders became a prominent issue at this time.

> A division took place in the Stone-Campbell Movement in the late 19th and early 20th centuries. Focused on visible issues like missionary societies and instrumental music in worship, it also reflected differences in response to modern thought as well as the sectionalism that had fueled the Civil War. When that division had run its course, the largely Southern churches that rejected societies and instruments identified themselves as Churches of Christ, while the other part of the Movement continued to use both the names Christian Churches and Disciples of Christ. A second division in that body occurred in the mid-20th century resulting in two groups known as the Christian Church (Disciples of Christ) and the Christian Churches (sometimes identified as independent Christian Churches).

Some like David Lipscomb and E. G. Sewell resisted this new corporate model of church leadership, insisting that the notion of "office" in the church did not mean a position that conferred power as it did in the world. Although in the American Standard Version (widely used at the time) 1 Timothy 3:1 declares: "If a man seeketh the office of a bishop, he desireth a good work," Lipscomb argued that "office" referred to a position of service and shepherding rather than control and privilege.

As for the authority of elders, Lipscomb wrote in July 1867 that "all the authority [elders] possess in any matter

148

is the moral weight their wisdom and devotion carry with them, gained through obedience to the will of God, and the express declaration that they and all of God's servants must be respected in doing the works assigned them by the Holy Spirit."

The biblical notion of "office," Lipscomb insisted, simply meant "duty"—the obligation to do a certain work. One became an elder by doing the work of an elder. Although at some point the congregation would officially acknowledge such a man's work by calling him "elder," he had already been appointed by the Holy Spirit. Some leaders, like J. W. McGarvey of Lexington, Kentucky opposed Lipscomb, insisting that "elder" was an official position in the church, that elders had authority from God to rule the church, and that they, in their capacity as teachers, functioned as judges of the law.

Despite Lipscomb's and Sewell's strong resistance, the corporate business model became the norm in most congregations, where elders were viewed as officers with power to make decisions, handle finances, perpetuate the eldership, and demand loyalty and obedience from the congregation. This controversy over the role of elders has continued to the present day. Among those in Churches of Christ in the 20th century who rejected the notion of a legal authority for elders were Reuel Lemmons, editor of the *Firm Foundation*, Jack Lewis, teacher at

...all the Greek terms when considered from the viewpoint of how the elder should conceive of himself stress images of sacrifice and service rather than images of authority.... If one may state what appears a paradox, the elder should conceive of himself, not in terms of authority, but in terms of "doing a good work"; while the congregation should relate to him as God's steward.

Jack P. Lewis
Leadership Questions Confronting the
Church, *1985*

Let us be exceedingly careful that we do not find ourselves in the unenviable position of rebellion against God and his servants. Elders, when functioning properly, are engaged in a work divinely authorized, and to oppose them is to oppose God.

Guy N. Woods
Questions & Answers Open Forum, *1976*

149

Harding Graduate School of Religion, and J. W. Roberts of Abilene Christian University. Others, like B. C. Goodpasture, Guy N. Woods of the *Gospel Advocate*, and preachers like Roy Lanier, Sr. advocated an autocratic model of eldership.

This western business model of eldership is not inherently evil—it is a cultural model that has served well in many congregations where the leaders are godly servants who give themselves to loving and guiding the flock. Yet this view has sometimes tended to make elders "lords" over the congregation, their primary function being that of unilateral decision making. True, elders make decisions and must do so in the best interest of the flock. Yet the nature of the elder's role depicted in Scripture seems to be more one of leading and feeding than authoritative decision-making. The role of the elder as shepherd is surely pictured in Matthew 18:12–14:

> If a man owns a hundred sheep, and one of them wanders away, will he not leave the ninety-nine on the hills and go to look for the one who wandered off? And if he finds it, I tell you the truth, he is happier about that one sheep than about the ninety-nine that did not wander off.

Conclusion

What makes a true church—one faithful to the story and to its journey toward God's lasting city? Beginning in 1824, in his "Search for the Ancient Order" series in the *Christian Baptist*, Alexander Campbell described what he felt were the marks of a true church, a list which included taking the Lord's Supper every Sunday, having bishops in every congregation, avoiding unscriptural terminology in songs and sermons, and so on. Later efforts among leaders in Churches of Christ to describe the marks of a true church produced similar lists. In *The Model Church* (1919), G. C. Brewer proposed that the ideal church "is one that measures to the New Testament pattern in organization, in work, and in worship." To Brewer, biblical organization involved autonomous congregations operating under elders to whom the members are subject. The congregation would be involved in evangelism and would set aside money each week to be put into the treasury for work that is planned in advance. Its worship would be focused, serious, and scriptural.

Brewer's book is testimony to what Churches of Christ have most often trusted to keep the story straight—system. He devotes five chapters to the role of elder, but the mission of the church and the Christian's life in the Spirit receive little attention. We have tracked two visions of the church in this chapter—visions that sometimes competed for loyalty in the story of Churches of Christ. Brewer's book provides evidence that Alexander Campbell's understanding of the church as a biblical system tended to prevail in our movement.

Still, the notion of the church as a holy community seen so strongly in Barton W. Stone was never completely eclipsed. In a striking paragraph near the end of the book Brewer turns to the criterion that Christ himself gave as the true mark of his followers—love (John 13:35).

> There will be no fault finding members in the model church, but each member will esteem others better than himself; they will in honor prefer one another; they will all be members one of another; they will bear one another's burdens; they will weep with those who weep and rejoice with those who rejoice. There will be no schism in the body, but love will be without hypocrisy among them. Thus working together, they will also be coworkers with God, and such a church will not be barren of good fruits—nay, it will be a city set on a hill, and no power can hide it from the world's view.

A church might have the system down "perfectly," but if those external categories and forms did not result in the kind of transformed body Brewer described at the end of the book, it could not be a true church. Even after focusing his entire study on the outward structural aspects, Brewer knew what the bottom line really was.

In recent years several books on the church written by members of Churches of Christ have focused on the church as a holy community. Renewing this strand of our understanding of the church is especially timely now. As we will see in the next chapter, the new cultural realities we are now

151

entering make recognizing our status as God's pilgrim people immensely important. We can be thankful that this view of the church has always been part of our spiritual DNA.

In the Old Testament, God made a solemn promise to Abraham; and although the people of God often needed correction—even suffering military defeat and exile because of their sins—nothing undid God's promise or obliterated their identity as his chosen people. In the same way, the New Testament church, the saints at Corinth, Galatia, and Laodicea, sometimes seemed marked more by wrong attitudes and actions than right ones—but they were still the church, the chosen people of God. They never lost their identity because Christ also made a solemn promise, a statement of eternal truth, that the church he established on the rock of His divine nature would never be defeated. Though the gates of hell itself assail it, Christ's church can never be overcome.

And throughout the church's history—our history— God has continued to work amidst our frailty and sin. God does not condone or make light of sin—it cost him everything. However, the church will never achieve perfection on this earth. Admitting our imperfection and understanding how we have been shaped both positively and negatively by our heritage and context reminds us of our need to remain humble. Such an understanding ought to energize us with a renewed commitment to continue our spiritual journey, because we humbly admit that, in some ways, we are no less susceptible to failings than any of God's people through the ages. We,

> No church is at any time wholly free from apostasy. The mystery of iniquity is continually working in all churches. That God does bear with evil doers and continue to recognize a church as a church of Christ after it has committed some very grave errors, the Bible clearly teaches. That such errors, if persisted in and increased, will carry the church beyond the limits of God's forbearance and cause him to cease to recognize it as a church of Christ, is also clearly taught. But the exact point where it ceases to be a church of Christ because of apostasy no man can tell.
>
> F. D. Srygley
> The New Testament Church, 1910

like they, are travelers—exiles in the world, called together by God to seek his will and not our own.

The church is always in need of reform because the human beings who make up the church are always in need of reform. Some in the Protestant Reformation used the Latin phrase *ecclesia reformata et semper reformanda*—"the church, reformed and always reforming." They understood the temptation of arrogance—of feeling that they had achieved perfection. So what now? Where does the church go from here? We've traced the story of God's people through the Old and New Testaments and the centuries that followed, seeing that they do God's will best when they see themselves as exiles, never feeling quite at home in the world. We've learned that the church is on a great journey and keeps to the road with the help of Scripture, worship, godly leaders, righteous living, and the Holy Spirit. By relying on these elements in ways appropriate to our own times and circumstances, we have continuity with the past as well as flexibility to meet the needs of our culture, but there is always the danger of corrupting our story if these elements become out of balance. Although our movement, like every movement made up of human beings, has made mistakes, Churches of Christ can learn from these errors and move forward, asking the crucial question: what will it mean for Churches of Christ to keep the story straight as we journey through the 21st century?

7

The Church Outside the Gates

> For the bodies of those animals whose blood is brought into the sanctuary by the high priest as a sacrifice for sin are burned outside the camp. Therefore Jesus also suffered outside the city gate in order to sanctify the people by his own blood. Let us then go to him outside the camp and bear the abuse he endured.
>
> *Hebrews 13:11–13*

Ivey visited our congregation for the first time the Sunday before Christmas. She came late and attempted to leave early. Before she got to the door, however, I stopped her, introduced myself and asked her if she had any place to spend Christmas. She burst into tears and pushed through the doors. I thought we had seen the last of Ivey.

But she was back the next week, and the next, and even the next. Each time she came late and left early. One week, I stopped her on her way out the door and asked if she'd like to meet and discuss what she was experiencing with our church. She agreed and we began meeting weekly, something we did for nearly a year.

Ivey had moved to Portland for romance. Recently divorced and alone in the world, she'd hoped a new relationship would give meaning to her life. When she arrived in Portland, however, she found the romantic doors closed. She came to church grasping for something, anything to give her life some meaning....

In our meetings we talked about the gospel and studied Scripture. Ivey had very little background in the faith, so everything we discussed was virtually brand new to

*her. I threw everything I had at her, went deep into my
evangelistic toolbox, but she remained unmoved.*

*In the meantime, however, she was becoming a regu-
lar part of our faith community. Though she didn't yet
believe, she became an active part of our congregation.
Ginny befriended her. Bill worked on her Jeep with her.
She accompanied the youth group downtown to feed the
homeless. She came to church workdays in her coveralls
and helped us care for the grounds.*

*At our last meeting together, I confessed to Ivey that
I had run out of things to say. Not knowing what else
to discuss, I asked her if there was anything she wanted
to talk about. She told me that it was hard for her to
believe in God because she was so unhappy. "I thought
Portland would be the promised land," she said. "But it
hasn't been. It's been a desert, and I don't think God is
present in the desert."*

*"Wait a minute!" I thought. "I know a story of God's
presence in the desert." And I began to recount to her
the story of the Exodus and God's provision in a barren
land. Tears immediately filled her eyes. God had not
abandoned his people. Manna, quail, water from a rock,
cloud by day, pillar of fire by night. We began to wonder
together about God's provision for Ivey in the wilderness
of her life. She agreed that her experience with the church
had indeed been God's manna. He had been present with
her all along. She asked me if she could be baptized.*

*I relate this story for two reasons. First, Ivey came
to faith when the story of God intersected her own
in a dramatic fashion. Coming to faith is a narrative
enterprise for many. Second, stories like hers may be
more and more common in an age when experience
often outweighs rationality. My brilliant Bible studies
had only limited appeal. Instead, she came to believe
in God only after a long sojourn with his people and an
investment in their story.*

—Mark

156

The movie version of the classic book series *The Lord of the
Rings* has introduced new generations to the harrowing
tale of a world in which the powers of darkness threaten
to overwhelm the realm of light. It's a story that resonates

with many people. And while our world is not filled with Tolkien's monsters, to many, the threats of the dark powers are very real. Those of us who have known the secure walls of a Christian America feel this threat especially sharply. Now it seems that the barbarians are at the gates.

Consider the state of our world. People starve by the thousands and die of easily treatable diseases while governments pursue their own wanton ways. In North America, more and more children live in poverty while we blindly chase the excesses of a consumer society, and even children from privileged families are often raised by minimum-wage childcare workers as their parents seek the elusive dream of ever-increasing prosperity. Respected business leaders use their power unethically to make millions while investors and workers lose everything.

Today resources for family and personal therapy seem almost unlimited, yet we don't seem to be able to hold the family together. More people in our society are single than ever before as maintaining relationships seems increasingly impossible. People feel alienated and alone, unable to connect with others in a meaningful way, so they turn to substitutes: TV, videogames, and a host of virtual substitutions meant to ease the ache they feel.

Unwanted babies are a throw-away commodity, and the elderly in our culture are similarly discarded. Many people walk through their lives in a chemically-induced haze, unable or unwilling to face the pressures of life. The abuse of drugs and alcohol reveals our unsuccessful attempt to insulate ourselves from the loss of human life and dignity that we see all around us.

Politics is a blood sport, and civility in American life is dying. Rudeness is defended as honesty. Lying is widely accepted in public and private life. Ethical behavior is seen as a quaint throwback, a sign of personal weakness or naïveté. Simple politeness is an endangered species. Indecency and lewdness attract increasingly large media audiences. The barbarians are at the gates.

How can it have happened? The last two hundred years have produced more technological advances than the previous two thousand, yet we are still left with a world in chaos. Wordsworth's 18th-century sentiments represent well those of many today: "Whither is fled the visionary gleam, where is it now, the glory and the dream?"

There is, of course, a great urge to see the church's primary mission in these dark days as defensive—a shelter in the midst of a terrible storm. Some who have seen the looming clouds grow dark and threatening argue that those in our churches are the only ones who can defend our city against the torrent of barbarians that waits just outside. The world may be in tumult, but we will not let it overwhelm us. As God's chosen people, we will remain in his protective embrace, untouched by the social and moral collapse around us. We will name the barbarians for what they are. We are determined that they won't enter the gates.

Yet even as God has called us to be a holy people, one set apart, we've seen how he's also called his people throughout history to transform the world through suffering and service. Perhaps God is once again calling the church to another way. Consider this strange passage from Hebrews.

> For the bodies of those animals whose blood is brought into the sanctuary by the high priest as a sacrifice for sin are burned outside the camp. Therefore, Jesus also suffered outside the city gate in order to sanctify the people by his own blood. Let us, then, go to him outside the camp and bear the abuse he endured. For here we have no lasting city, but we are looking for the city that is to come. (Hebrews 13:11–14)

The writer of Hebrews offers these Christians a different perspective on their place in the world by calling them to live out the story of the death of Jesus. In the midst of all of the first century's turmoil—persecution, idolatry, immorality of all sorts—he calls them not to the security of the city, but to the place of sacrifice and sanctification, that place outside the camp where Jesus redeemed the lost.

158

What does it mean to go to Jesus outside the city gates, rejecting all earthly cities to look for one that endures? What does it mean to leave the place of power and sanctuary in order to be offered up in a place of abuse and shame?

What does it mean to follow our Lord outside of the gates into the place of exile?

These are important questions for the church to answer if we are to continue finding our place in God's ongoing story. They're also painful questions—even threatening ones. As with God's people throughout history, we may find ourselves resistant, wishing to remain in the safety of the city, putting our trust in signs of power like king and temple. The uncertainty of our times—all that's wrong with our world—makes this temptation even more potent. Yet God is calling us to the wilderness, asking us to rely exclusively on him for help and sustenance on our journey. He is calling us once again in faith to leave the land we know.

The wilderness in which the church finds itself today is no safe or tame place; it's perilous, a place of seemingly inhospitable desolation. Yet it is nonetheless the place to which we are being called as we live out God's story, and his presence can make even the valley of the shadow of death a place without fear. Although the world today is characterized by three features—three "posts"—that can make it seem alien to people of faith, these features also present us with new opportunities to serve God and the people around us as we tread the paths of exile toward the city that is to come. How would we characterize today's world? It is post-Christian, postmodern, and postdenominational.

The Post-Christian Reality

Hebrews 13 paints a picture of a people who are called to live intentionally on the margins. Offering true sanctification in the new temple of his body, Jesus shows his people that they must leave the security of Jerusalem (and of the traditional practices of Judaism) to live in the wilderness for the sake of others. As the spiritual descendents of the sojourners to whom Hebrews was written, God's people today are still called to follow Jesus out of their places of established comfort, including those places where we often find our security—social, cultural, political, and even religious systems. We cannot live faithfully unless we set out for the city that is to come.

What does this call to live out the kingdom of God on the margins mean? It means that God's people are called to be Christians in a post-Christian Western world. There is no longer a safe haven for us here. We are exiles.

Over the past two thousand years, the church has experienced periods of both powerlessness and power. In the earliest days of the church, Christians were largely powerless and marginalized. However, after Constantine's Edict of Milan in 313 CE made Christianity a legitimate religion of the Empire, the church became a serious power broker. It held this position for over a millennium. During this time, Western culture and Christian culture were virtually synonymous, and the church was greatly intertwined with political power. This relationship of church and dominant culture is what we refer to as "Constantinian Christianity," or "Christendom."

Despite the constitutional separation of church and state in the United States, the experience of most American Christians has largely been that of Christendom, although with some exceptions (one of which would be black churches in the era of slavery and segregation). American culture and Christian culture have been so synonymous, in fact, that for much of the history of the United States, the question was generally not whether one's neighbors were Christians, but what brand of Christian they were. But this has been changing—and rapidly. In the past fifty years, the Christian consensus upon which American society has been traditionally based has largely broken down. Christianity can no longer be assumed to be the dominant force shaping people's lives and beliefs in the culture at large. It's not that our neighbors have never heard about Jesus; it's just that they seem to have moved on. Having witnessed a Christianity that they perceive as merely another tool of power, they have rejected it.

160 Many in our churches lament this "post-Christian" turn as one of the great tragedies of our time, but the position in which the church finds itself is definitely not new. While we may be tempted to grieve the loss of our secure city, we increasingly find ourselves in the intended place for

the people of God: outside the gates in the place of exile. Rather than enjoying the seat of power and authority, we may be returning to a time like that of the first three centuries when the church worked from a position of marginal status. It would be hard to overestimate the importance of this shift for the life and mission of the church. For some, however, the transition seems too much.

A number of responses to the current situation of the church are possible. One approach involves pulling out of culture entirely—retreating into a Christian "fortress" where we insulate ourselves from being influenced by the world. As a consequence, however, we would also have no influence on it. Like other movements discussed earlier, we would pervert the church's primary story in the very effort to preserve it. Withdrawing into a Christian stronghold for the sake of protecting ourselves is clearly not a godly option.

Two other approaches involve trying to resuscitate Christendom either by striving to regain political power (attempting to win in the legislature and the courts what has already been lost in the streets) or by marketing the church to the sensibilities of the

> Several recent books have addressed both the relevance of the gospel and the identity of the church in an emerging post-Christian North America. As examples, see Darrell L. Guder, *The Missional Church* (1998) and James V. Brownson, et al., *Stormfront* (2003).

dominant culture (effectively marrying the values of the dominant culture to those of the Christian faith so that they become inseparable). Both of these approaches also have serious problems. If the church ties itself to political power as it did during much of its history in western Europe, it risks losing the story of Christ, exchanging its spiritual heritage of grace and service for the earthly treasure of judgment and power. Such a move would be unlikely to have a positive affect on a world that has already rejected Christendom. It would simply be more of the same.

If the church tries to regain its hold on society by marketing itself to the culture, it faces similar problems, though they might not seem so obvious at first. It's clear, for example, that savvy demographic analysis and mar-

161

keting may cause churches to grow. However, when the church becomes a vendor of goods and services, competing for its market share, it's likely to give up some of the uncomfortable and challenging truths of God's story. And skillful marketing is no less a tool of power than political or legal maneuvering. Such an approach is just a more subtle expression of Christendom. Whether Christendom is carried by consumerism or imperial command, its need to control God's story is no less insidious. The threat of Christendom (in any guise) is that the church could gain the whole world and lose its own soul.

Keeping the Story Straight in a Post-Christian World

Rather than fighting to establish Christian dominance, the church needs to follow the approach Hebrews 13 suggests, accepting marginal status and becoming again the church "outside the camp." To take this approach would be to see North America as a mission field and to start thinking of ourselves as missionaries. Our identity would echo that of the Old Testament Jews in exile—or that of those first century Christians in Asia Minor identified as "resident aliens" (1 Peter 2:11). We would start to ask how we live out the story faithfully in exilic times.

"Post-Christian" refers to Christianity after it has ceased to be the only dominant power in its culture. It does not refer to the end of Christianity but the end of "Christendom."

One of the chief ways to practice Christianity outside the camp is to take an outsider's stance toward all expressions of worldly power and status. The church outside the camp not only refuses to pursue power, but it rejects it when power is proffered. This church recognizes that what appears to be a place of shame in the eyes of the world is the place of God's honor, according to Hebrews 13. This church will not try to influence the world through legislation or tirades of judgment; it will enact the simple charities of service and sacrifice—serving food to the poor and hungry, caring for neighborhood children who have few future prospects, helping those who have nothing to offer in return. As James writes, "Religion that God our Father accepts as pure and faultless is this: to look after orphans and widows in their distress and to keep oneself from being polluted by the world" (1:27). To deny the place of power and embrace the place of suffering service is to follow in the story of Christ, who, "having disarmed the powers and authorities... made a public spectacle of them, triumphing over them by the cross" (Colossians 2:15).

This church outside the camp is the voice for all outsiders, just as the Old Testament prophets and Jesus were. In a world dominated by consumerism where more wealth is the sole sign of success, this church embraces and speaks for the poor. Refusing to become a part of the structure of acquiring wealth, it does not judge its success by worldly standards like size, budget, and clout but by its faithfulness to the story of one who went outside of the gates to sanctify the lost.

Freed from Christendom's linking of Christian identity with national or ethnic identity, the church outside the camp is also "anti-tribal." It speaks for the racially marginalized and refuses to be a tool of the dominant ethnic culture, calling all people to the cross. While almost everyone else seeks security in ethnic or national identity, the church outside of the camp does not, for we do not have an enduring city here. In Christ there is neither Jew nor Greek.

The church outside the camp refuses to recognize or honor national borderlines in the kingdom of God. In a world at war, this is always an enormous challenge. Christendom often sees the interests of the kingdom and the interests of the nation as the same. It believes that the earthly kingdom directly mirrors the heavenly one. But the church outside the camp refuses any such identity. "Seek first his kingdom and his righteousness," Jesus said (Matthew 6:33), and he reminded his people, "In this world you will have trouble. But take heart! I have overcome the world" (John 16:33). This church defines its allegiances not by human boundaries but by God's vision of the new humanity. Ephesians shows that God's ultimate purpose was not simply to save individuals but to call those who are being saved into a new community where the walls of human division are torn down (Ephesians 2:11–3:21).

The church outside the camp also values diversity. Christendom always tries to bring everything in line with the dominant culture for the sake of peace. This peace, however, is achieved only through force. A church that is outside of this dominant culture's obsession with power will value diversity. It will allow and accept differences both within and outside of its fellowship. Perhaps one of the best scriptural examples of this is the debate over the necessity of Gentile circumcision. The question essentially came down to whether a Gentile had to become a good Jew in order to be a Christian. Of course, the resounding answer was "no," and the early church learned to embrace the diversity of its members. Christendom, on the other hand, has a hard time distinguishing between the interests of the gospel and the interests of the dominant culture when making converts. It converts them not just to *the* Way, but to *its* way, corrupting the story of God by insisting that its own perspective is the only one. The church that is looking for the city to come, on the other hand, remains open to the voices of others. This church plants the seed of the gospel in radically different soils and then watches to see what the plant will become rather than trying to control it and make it look just like itself.

Diversity & the Church on the Margins

The church outside the camp may look very different from many of our churches today. And to be honest, this is going to be a much harder way to do church. The easiest way to handle diversity is to extinguish it. Almost all church growth theory presupposes that homogenous groups are more likely to grow rapidly than heterogeneous ones. But the church outside the camp rejects this worldly view. Instead, it does the excruciatingly hard work of forging identity and unity in the midst of people from

164

wildly different ethnic, social, and economic backgrounds and with diverse worldviews. It embraces diversity from congregation to congregation, and most astonishingly, it plants churches that are not exact replicas of itself. In the post-Christian world, church planting is an act of humility rather than an affirmation of power or authority.

Such a church may seem totally revolutionary from the North American point of view.

> **The Church Refuses the Place of Honor**
>
> "Humble yourselves in the sight of the Lord, and he will lift you up" (James 4:10). "Blessed are the poor in spirit for theirs is the kingdom of heaven" (Matthew 5:3).

Even in mission efforts to foreign countries, Christendom has often tended to plant not just a church, but a culture. Mission work involved not just exporting the gospel but Western "civilization" as well. This is sometimes thought of as "the ugly American" syndrome. But missionaries gradually came to understand the importance of planting indigenous churches—congregations that reflect the culture in which they are embedded. Now missionaries make a great effort *not* to impose a certain culture on people as they come to faith in Jesus. This is a crucial and healthy development. Few of us would expect a congregation in Ghana, West Africa, to look exactly like a congregation in Abilene, Texas.

However, this development also has profound local implications in a post-Christian world. Viewing North America as a mission field means embracing the fact that a congregation in Oshkosh, Wisconsin should not be expected to look the same as a congregation in Montgomery, Alabama. Or that when a church plants another congregation in the same city, it will not so privilege its own perspective as to expect the new congregation to be a mere replica of itself.

The future of our churches in the ongoing story of God will largely be determined by our ability to accept the post-Christian situation in which we find ourselves. The imperial church of Christendom is passing away. Efforts to prop it up with power will fail. It must die to make room for God's people's ongoing work: following Christ outside of the gates to the place of sacrifice and redemption as they

165

forsake power, wealth, racial divisions, cultural elitism and domination. We do not despair outside the city gates because we know this is where we belong, the place where we join Christ. Outside the gates, we work among and minister to the marginalized as if we are ministering to Jesus himself (Matthew 25). And finally, from outside the gates we embark on our continuing journey in God's story. We are looking for a lasting city.

The Postmodern Shift

Not only is our culture post-Christian, but it is also postmodern, and this seriously impacts the church and its role in the world. Much has been made of the cultural shift from modernity to postmodernity, though a good deal of this discussion has been reactionary and silly. Many, indeed, have heard the term "postmodern" bandied about—and may have a generally negative impression about it—without having much notion of what it is. So before we begin talking about the impact of postmodernity on how we do church, we ought to try to define the term and provide a bit of context.

In order to understand postmodernity, we first have to understand the period it follows. The modern period had its origins in the *Renaissance* and the Enlightenment that followed (often called the "Age of Reason").

> Even in science it is now widely conceded that the observer impacts what he or she observes. "There is no theory-free data." We always bring something to the table.

During that time, the notion of scientific certainty was born. People began to believe that the universe behaved in predictable ways that could be traced and categorized by human reason. Prior to this point, theology had supplied all the answers, and religion had been the final arbiter of all truth. But with modernism, the church was supplanted by science; scientific truth became *the Truth* for most of Western culture. Science would supply the answers to life's difficult questions and would solve life's problems.

However, around the end of World War II, many began to doubt the ability of science to live up to its promises.

166

For example, the social and moral problems listed at the beginning of this chapter have not been helped by modernism; in fact, the scientific and materialistic emphases of modernism seem to have made some of them worse. Many people began to realize that modernism represented only one perspective, and so its claim to reveal *the Truth* was revised. Science was no longer seen as the final arbiter of Truth but rather as merely one important (and imperfect) way of knowing something about reality, a view to be placed alongside other ways of knowing—including religion. Postmodernity believes that multiple perspectives—multiple paths to truth—are possible and points out that the perspective from which we approach an issue may affect our understanding of its reality. This poses both benefits and challenges for Christianity. On the one hand, the time for religious people to be intimidated by all-knowing science is passing; on the other, the time for the church arrogantly to claim to have direct access to all Truth is also over.

Postmodernity calls all knowledge—theological, scientific, historical, psychological, sociological and philosophical—into question. Having

> Postmodernity isn't alone in calling human reason and institutions into question. Many Christians have been similarly skeptical:
>
> Human government originated in the rebellion of man against his Maker, and was the organized effort of man to govern himself and to promote his own good and to conduct the affairs of the world independently of the government of God. It was the organized rebellion of man against God and his government.
>
> *David Lipscomb*
> *Civil Government, 1913*

dethroned science, postmodernity threatens to leave us in a world of relativism, uncertainty, and even perhaps truthlessness. How does the church function in this radical new environment?

The church's approach to the world certainly must change. How do you talk about truth in a world that sees truth as elusive, partial, and perhaps even irrelevant? Yet in the postmodern world where Truth has been called into question, people have to believe in something, and they

167

do. What has been shaken is the ability to ground truth in the authority of human reason. This may be especially challenging to Churches of Christ, given our heritage of Alexander Campbell's belief that reason is the key to understanding God's will. Regardless, for many people the primary criterion for truth today isn't reason but experience. What is true is what one *experiences* to be true.

What this cultural shift from modernity to postmodernity means for how the church does its work might best be illustrated by thinking about evangelism. In modernist evangelism, the primary appeal was to reason, and the primary tool was argument. The Bible was presented as the authority, and the emphasis involved showing the logical contradictions in the other person's position, proving by reason the Bible's truth and using passages from it to show that the other person's belief or practice was faulty.

In postmodern evangelism, however, the appeal is to "come walk with me"—an appeal to experience. Rather than reading the Bible as an "objective" outsider and using its points to prove a logical contention, the evangelist invites a person to experience the truth of the story in the community of faith and then examine the Bible's claims. People are not argued into the kingdom; they are invited to walk in and check it out for themselves. In the story that opened this chapter, Ivey was not moved by facts and arguments but by relating her own *experience* to God's word. Ivey's attitude isn't unusual today; in a postmodern world, people look inward rather than outward to find truth.

For the church on the margins, the shift from modern argument to postmodern experience is a mixed bag. On the one hand, it tears down the strategies Christians have used for 500 years and asks us to find new ways of living, understanding, and sharing our faith. In other words, it asks us to give up the power and safety of our established city and go outside the gates, finding our meaning through our experience of God's guidance in the wilderness. Postmodernism's emphasis on multiple perspectives and experience makes many of us uncomfortable, to say the least. It's difficult to leave the city of modernism that we've known for so long. Yet as comfortable as it has become, modernism is not our native land. It's just a land where the church has been exiled for a time.

But postmodernism is no homeland either. Its problems are obvious. If people make judgments about truth based narrowly on their perspectives or experience, distortions are bound to occur. For example, a person might walk into a church and hear off-key music with obscure words; hear a long, incomprehensible lecture which, while baffling, is largely venomous in tone; see a ritual she doesn't fully comprehend; experience rude, unfriendly treatment before and after the service; and note the stunning absence of women doing anything but sitting in the pews. Our visitor might decide from this one narrow slice of experience that the Christian story has nothing relevant, important, or truthful for her.

Another visitor might have deep commitments to social justice. Thinking that allies would surely be found among the followers of Jesus, he attends a church only to find that there are *no* poor people attending and only a couple of members of a race other than the majority one. He finds this congregation has little interest in addressing the deep problems that afflict our local neighborhoods and larger society and quickly decides there is no significant truth here for him.

> If a people pleading for the union of all Christians cannot maintain the unity of the Spirit in the bond of peace in their own limited communion, and peaceably dispose of all questions…then is this plea for union as ridiculous a farce as was ever played before the public. The Apostolic churches had much graver errors in doctrine and practice to dispose of than any that are troubling us; and many had a strong propensity to file off into parties. The lessons of Christian liberty, of tolerance and forbearance, of patience and gentleness taught by the apostles, need to be carefully attended to.
>
> *Isaac Errett*
> Christian Standard, *1869*

169

Again, a visitor might walk into a church in search of a genuine and transcendent experience. Living a frantic, driven, successful-but-superficial existence, she longs to find something deeper than glitz. Feeling the tug of her childhood religion, she wonders if Christians might help her in her quest. What she finds is that church is nothing like the simple services she remembers. Instead, she witnesses a great show: magnificent music led by professionals, drama that looks like it's been in rehearsal for months, a technologically supported pithy little lesson, and warm greeters at every door with gifts for the visitor—and all this happens in precisely an hour. Predictably, our visitor might come away thinking the service was so professional that it's merely a variation of the superficial glitz that already dominates her life. She decides that Christianity is just another version of creative marketing.

But imagine that the woman's neighbor attends the same service. This man is exhilarated by the musical performance, loves the attention he receives, finds the short sermon relevant to his life, and becomes a member of the church that very day. Exasperatingly, one person's meaningless waste of time might be another's profound religious experience! Finding meaning through experience can indeed be a perilous business because it's influenced by so many factors.

Yet while the postmodern shift is not an unalloyed blessing, it's certainly not the unmitigated curse some have made it out to be. There's another side to the postmodern emphasis on experience, one that the church shouldn't discount out of hand. For many like Ivey in the story at the beginning of this chapter, the entry into Christian faith comes from an encounter with those who are authentically living out the story. Those who could never be argued into the kingdom might willingly follow a friend in. The best personal evangelist I've ever known claims never to have asked anyone for a Bible study. His life is such salt and light in the world and his living of the gospel story so radical that others ask him for the meaning of his life.

One successful evangelistic church summarizes the differences between evangelism in modern and postmodern worlds like this: in a modern world, people first believe, then affiliate, and finally participate in the life of the church. In postmodern evangelism, the sequence is often reversed. First, they experience the practice of an actual congregation, and on the basis of that experience choose to affiliate themselves with the church. What they believe may not be settled until long after they've become part of a practicing community of Christians.

In fact, if we're honest, we have to admit that the invitation to *experience* the truth of the gospel through community has always played a significant role in the life of the church. That's why the idea of a church that lives out the story is so important not just in our day but throughout history. In the living of the story within an actual community, reason and experience come together in authentic and profound ways. This emphasis on experience isn't new; it's just that it's especially productive in a postmodern setting.

To postmoderns who might reject the notion of any ultimate, transcendent truth, the church says that there is indeed one such truth in our story—that expressed in God's relentless love, a love that culminated in the cross and resurrection of Jesus. To moderns, the church says that it is not enough merely to understand the story correctly—it must be lived out in concrete, experiential ways.

Ultimately, the church can complain that postmoderns aren't reasonable enough, but this isn't the position of a church outside of the gates. It's the position of a protected church making itself safe behind the city walls, a church of Christendom. Alternatively, a church in exile will meet the needs of its time by living out the story in a way that gives people good reasons to take the story seriously. Rather than forcing people to conform to its needs and preferences, this latter kind of pilgrim church is willing to give itself up for others, to tread the paths of exile because it is seeking something beyond modernity or postmodernity: it is seeking a home that truly lasts.

171

The Postdenominational World

Even as it's becoming post-Christian and postmodern, our world is also rapidly becoming postdenominational. You may have noticed how radically the church landscape has changed in the past few years. As little as a generation ago, most people made their religious choices from among long-established and recognizable denominations. Yet the last three decades have witnessed the proliferation of community and Bible churches which are not clearly affiliated with any recognizable group (though they may have roots in one of several traditions). For these churches, their primary identity has nothing to do with a denominational affiliation.

But that isn't the whole story. Even within church bodies, there is an increasing diversity of congregations *within* a tradition. So you might find yourself in an Anglican Church with a rock band or a Baptist Church with elder leadership or a Church of Christ with a healing service. A congregation of one heritage may look more like the congregation of another denomination than like other churches of its own tradition.

But even that doesn't tell the whole story. Another blossoming movement has emerged that features single, reproducing house churches. These house churches never really move toward the kind of institutional structures that would clearly identify them as part of any particular denomination. They simply involve a dozen Christians meeting together—who in turn may give rise to another house church that in turn plants another. These simple churches have become a crucial piece of the postdenominational picture.

But even this fails to take in a wider world picture. Throughout the world, indigenous Christian movements are springing up with no denominational affiliation. There are literally millions of underground Christians in China, for instance, who have no clear association with any denomination. Indeed, there are probably more Christians in China than in North America, and few of them would understand the denominational issues and conflicts that have dominated Western Christianity.

The final piece of this post-denomination puzzle is that many Christians who are members of mainline denomina-

172

tions are members of a particular congregation for reasons that have nothing to do with its denominational roots. They may, in fact, be totally unaware of what the church's name signifies, and upon relocating will not necessarily be led in their search for a church home by the name on the sign. They are postdenominational Christians.

So what does it mean to be a church in a postdenominational setting? In a real way, the whole history of the American church has been one of denominational competition. If there was ever a time for such an approach, it's clearly over. Such an approach is a luxury of Christendom, not the stance for a church on the margins. Christians shouldn't necessarily forsake their particular traditions, but they need to understand how tradition shapes them, preserve what's good and transform what's not, and recognize that God has worked in countless traditions through the centuries. We are able to embrace God's people from other traditions openly because we do not find our *primary* identity in our particular heritage in Churches of Christ.

Our primary identity comes from our role as the bearers of God's story in the world. And in a hostile world, we gladly join hands with all others when they faithfully proclaim and live out aspects of that story. This approach leads to relatively open borders and a refusal to be obsessed with who's in and who's out. It means accepting those with whom we may disagree when God's kingdom work is being done. Building a Habitat house for the poor of the city together, walking through and praying for a neighborhood with a variety of believers, working in concert to oppose racial discrimination—these are acts that can unite us all as we travel toward a lasting city.

Such a call for community may seem radical—even dangerous. If so, it might be helpful to remember that the church serves the kingdom of God. When the church is the main point, overcoming such differences is difficult; when the kingdom is the main point, it's easier. Many of our readers most likely have experienced living in a culture so hostile to Christianity that all those who claimed Jesus as Lord were allies. Those situations are prevalent

173

around the world but rarer in North America. Still, the end of Christendom is rapidly becoming the new reality here, too, and its impact on denominationalism seems clear.

For those of us from the Stone-Campbell heritage, such a development shouldn't be threatening; it's a return to some of the very values that energized our forebears, an opportunity for realizing their dream of Christian unity. Our history has uniquely prepared us for the postdenominational world. The early pioneers of the Stone-Campbell Restoration Movement were determined to move across denominational boundaries. They welcomed all believers into their churches, striving to be "Christians only, not the only Christians." When we embrace a postdenominational world, we not only honor Jesus' call for unity (John 17); we continue in our heritage as a church outside of the camp, denying the comfort of the walls of denominationalism.

Our more recent history, however, has taught us the debilitating effects of sectarianism. We have worked to prove that others are in error, but what have these battles accomplished for God's kingdom? How have they affected our part in God's story? How has the bitter wrangling over what must surely appear to outsiders as arcane trivia affected our credibility in delivering Christ's message? The realities of the post-denominational world may be just the invitation we need to recover our original sensibilities.

The American religious scene that Barton W. Stone and Thomas and Alexander Campbell knew was one of open conflict between denominations. The literature of conflict is immense. For a couple of perspectives on this, see Walter Brownlow Posey, *Religious Strife on the Southern Frontier* (1965) and Robert Neelly Bellow, *Uncivil Religion: Interreligious Hostility in America* (1987).

And really, aren't the "weightier matters" of joining together in humble service to the kingdom closer to the center of God's story for his people? For example, why wouldn't we applaud those who willingly follow God's leading in choosing a church because of its ministry to the community rather than because of the name on its sign? The young people we work with are already there—they are primarily concerned with living out the story of Jesus

174

in a radical way within a community of faith. They want to impact the world with the gospel—not with what name is on a building.

We know that all religious heritages—and all particular congregations—have problems integrating doctrine and life. But in the postdenominational world, the proper stance is laid out in Jesus' parable of the wheat and weeds.

> He put before them another parable: "The kingdom of heaven may be compared to someone who sowed good seed in his field; but while everybody was asleep, an enemy came and sowed weeds among the wheat, and then went away. So when the plants came up and bore grain, then the weeds appeared as well. And the slaves of the householder came and said to him, 'Master, did you not sow good seed in your field? Where, then, did these weeds come from?' He answered, 'An enemy has done this.' The slaves said to him, 'Then do you want us to go and gather them?' But he replied, 'No; for in gathering the weeds you would uproot the wheat along with them. Let both of them grow together until the harvest; and at harvest time I will tell the reapers, "Collect the weeds first and bind them in bundles to be burned, but gather the wheat into my barn.""" Matthew 13:24-30

We are not called to cull out the weeds here but to treat everything in the field like wheat and leave it to God to make the final separation. This is not to say there is no such thing as a weed—but most of those judgments are in the future and in God's hands. So the time has come to join with all Christians in every way we can as we stand within a hostile world. Our borders must be open to other Christians because this is not our home. We are traveling together to a land of promise.

Conclusion

The church in a post-Christian, postmodern, postdenominational world is the exilic church, the missional church, the prophetic church, the marginalized church, the church of the cross that stands outside the city gates. These themes are not particularly new to the church's life. They are all embedded in our story. While their specific confluence in

175

our time and place may be unique, that's true of the church in every time and place. No church is exactly like any other.

This reflects the wisdom of God and the genius of the Gospel; its story is always the same story, its good news the same good news, its church the one and only church. Yet within this framework, God is constantly creating us anew for the sake of his kingdom work in the world. The church doesn't accommodate to culture in order to grow. It grows because it follows Christ to the place of service and sacrifice outside of the city gates. In this, it is radically counter-cultural, affirming that this is not our home.

But the church can only have a counter-cultural message if it is deeply engaged in culture. The church subverts the worldly values of culture while it is *in* the world, actively and genuinely serving the lost. What we often take for a counter-cultural stance is simply irrelevance. When the church is irrelevant, it does not subvert the darkness of culture; it simply stands aloof from it.

The picture of the world presented in this chapter and our suggestions about the stance the church ought to take may leave Christians feeling ambivalent—maybe even scared. That's not surprising. In many ways these are dark days and they call for extreme action. But since these are the days of God working out his story, they are also full of promise. What specific role will our churches play in telling that story in their various contexts? It is, of course, difficult to generalize. It's impossible to create a one-size-fits-all picture of the church for our time—that's the point of much of this book. Still, we'd like to offer some practical advice for being the church in a post-Christian, postmodern, post-denominational world, advice based on principles that will continue to guide the church as it seeks a lasting city.

8 How Should We Then Live?

We would say that the church of Christ is never an experiment, but wherever that church is true to its mission it will be experimenting, pioneering, blazing new paths, seeking how to speak the reconciling Word of God to its own age. It cannot do this if it is held captive by the structures of another day or is slave to its own structures.

—*Elizabeth O'Connor,* Call to Commitment, *1975*

It didn't happen at a building or even a particular congregation. But it was an extraordinary experience of church. It started with the baptism in the swimming pool. The 17-year-old boy was deadly serious about a commitment that most of his peers had made years before. The celebration was spontaneous and unrestrained as young people unprompted and uninhibited jumped into the pool to join their new brother. What a celebration of new life.

But as moving as it was, there was a more profound moment hours later. It was two o'clock in the morning as five teenage boys, including the new Christian, discussed intently what it means to live the new life of a baptized believer and how they could help one another.

They had all grown up "in church." But there was something about a peer coming to conviction after great struggle that caused them all to rethink what this baptismal commitment really meant to each one of them. The Christian camp setting encouraged the kind of candid interaction, not just about how to become a Christian,

*but what it really means to be one—interaction that too
often we never get to in our Sunday church experiences.
I said nothing but listened with a heart bursting with joy
as my boys discussed the burning question: how should
we then live?*

—Randy

It's one of the most famous movie moments. The man
in the white lab coat, his hair frazzled by his Herculean
effort to turn theory into reality, waits expectantly over his
experiment. Yet all seems lost. Nothing is happening. He
has studied and labored, experimented, built complicated
machines, sacrificed his personal life and his career to his
efforts, done everything he could, but now ... nothing. He's
heartbroken. And then it happens: a finger twitches. Dr.
Frankenstein cries out to the heavens, "It's alive! Alive!"

This may seem like a strange way to open a chapter on
how the church lives its story, but we think we can draw
some important lessons from our mad-scientist friend.
First, it's clear that people aren't typically satisfied with
theories; they want honest-to-goodness, real-world results.
Second, it's equally clear that effort and labor—and even
good intentions—aren't enough. People can end up making
a terrible mess of things when they try to cobble together
a bunch of fragments that don't belong together. Both of
these lessons are crucial for a discussion of the church.

The purpose of this book is to spark dialogue within
and among our churches, but it's wrong to think that this
book could give a single, easy answer that would solve all
of the difficulties the church faces today. This chapter will
offer some specific pictures of the way congregations are
following God as he leads them in the paths of exile, and
we hope they'll be inspirational and constructive. But it
would be a mistake to take these examples as the only
ways—or even as the very best ways—that the church can
live in our time. It would also be a mistake for any congregation to feel bound to try to implement all of the different
ways of living out the story that are described here. The last
thing this book seeks is to create an army of Frankenstein

monsters with parts from various bodies grafted together unnaturally. What we do hope is that the examples presented here will spark congregations to think creatively and faithfully about the way they are being called to leave the comfort and security of their own protective walls to join Christ outside the city gates.

Unity & Diversity

If there's anything we've learned from the history of Christianity, it's that each church must live its own part of the story in its own place and time. That means that a church in Uganda will look very different from a church in Ohio, and a church comprised largely of urban youth may worship differently from its rural counterpart. Yet for the church in exile, the church outside the gates, this diversity shouldn't be frightening. Keeping our eyes on the master, we may tread different paths, but our destination is the same—God's lasting city. And though each of us may have stressed different aspects as we've sought to live the story in our time and context, each of us has been nourished by worship, Scripture, faithful leaders, the Holy Spirit, and the living of distinctive lives as we've traveled through the wilderness of exile.

Of course, we've also seen that New Testament and other early churches chose different emphases as they sought to keep the story straight. Some trusted leadership more, while others trusted the guidance of the Spirit more. Different challenges and cultures have called for some of these to come to the fore and others to fade more into the background, though each of them has remained vital throughout the church's history. In the face of the challenges of heresy, for example, early Christians turned primarily to stronger leaders. Later, when the church became overly institutional, the reformers called the church to trust more in Scripture. So what does today's context of post-Christian, postmodern, postdenominational exile require?

179

In exile the pressures to conform to the conquering empire are tremendous. Letting the victors dictate the shape of our lives may seem almost inevitable, yet just as he did for his people generations ago in Babylon, God continues to call us to live distinctively. He calls us to bear witness and remain faithful to the one who relinquished everything to die on a cross. He calls us to live counter-cultural lives amid a culture that worships power and accumulation. He calls us to bear witness to sacrifice and surrender in a culture that celebrates individualism and worships the self as the highest good. He calls us to tell his story to a people uncertain about the possibility of tran-scendent meaning and suspicious of authority. He calls us to lives of faith among a people whose beliefs center on what they have seen and touched—on their experiences.

For this time and place—for meeting the needs of this particular culture and set of sensibilities—we believe that the church is being summoned especially to live ethically distinct lives. For this chapter of God's great story, the church must continue to offer clear leadership, to call people to Scripture, to celebrate in worship, and to nurture and care through the agency of the Holy Spirit. But in living lives of honesty, humility, sacrifice,

> Let us astound them by our way of life. For this is the main battle, the unanswerable argument, the argument from actions. For though we give ten thousand precepts of philosophy in words, if we do not exhibit a better life than theirs, the gain is nothing. For it is not what is said that draws their attention, but their inquiry is what we do.... Let us win them therefore by our life.
>
> —*John Chrysostom*
> Homily on 1 Corinthians, 4th century CE

love, and peace, we provide the most visible signpost for our age that points to the city that is to come.

One result of keeping the story straight through ethical living is that the faithful witness of the church becomes sharply visible and distinct. It's easier to tell how the church differs from the world around it when people can see it living life from a completely different set of values. Of course, the danger of this move is that if the church isn't careful to maintain the other ways of keeping the story straight, the distance between the church and the world that God loves can increase. In its distinctiveness, the church can become aloof, smug, and superior. In exile, distinctiveness can also be mistaken for permission to circle the wagons and take shots at the outside world. What is needed is a way for the church to live distinctively while being led into deeper engagement with the world. This is why the story of the cross outside the gates is so important: it marks the way for the church. By living the way of the cross, we will be distinctive. By living the way of the cross, we follow Jesus deeper into the broken places of the world. By living the cross, we help the church live for the sake of those who are lost.

Ethical Living: Enacting Exilic Values

In exile, God's people distinguished themselves from the values of the empire. Remember the image of the Servant in the book of Isaiah. Israel learned to view their exile as the place where God had brought them for the benefit of the nations. And they learned to place their trust not in worldly power and authorities, not in Cyrus, but in a suffering servant who sacrificed himself for others. In a similar way, New Testament writers encouraged their readers to view their lives on the margins of society as companionship with Jesus. Just as he had gone "outside the city gate in order to sanctify the people by his own blood" (Hebrews 13:12), the church is called outside the safety of the city, welcoming others through lives of sacrifice and sanctification. Like Israel and the early church, God asks us today to live apart from power as our culture defines it. Our lives of sacrifice—relinquishing power, privilege, and wealth—and our lives of sanctification—treating others with dignity, humanity, and grace—will color everything we do, affecting how we understand and interact with Scripture, the Holy Spirit, worship, and leadership. Our distinctive living provides the outline for this chapter of God's story. 181

In *Life on the Vine*, Phillip Kenneson suggests several ways the church can live distinctively in relation to the dominant culture today. For instance, in a culture of aggression, the church lives a life of gentleness. In a culture of manufactured desire, the church lives a life of joy. In a culture of self-sufficiency, the church lives a life of kindness. In a culture of addiction, the church lives a life of self-control. In a culture of impermanence, the church lives a life of faithfulness. In these ways and others, the Christian community uses the power of living distinctively to tell the world the continuing story of God.

The story of Jesus is strange in a culture that values power, success, and consumerism. After all, the story of Jesus is one of "downward mobility."

> Let the same mind be in you that was in Christ Jesus, who though he was in the form of God, did not regard equality with God as something to be exploited; but emptied himself, taking the form of a slave, being born in human likeness and being found in human form, he humbled himself and became obedient to the point of death, even death on a cross (Philippians 2:6–8).

For the sake of the church's mission, Christians must show that in this world our city doesn't exist. In both our individual lives and in the life of the church, we must embrace our marginal status, knowing that the one guiding us through the paths of exile relinquished everything to save and sanctify us. This means that we'll renounce all of the trappings of power, living differently than the spirit of our age dictates.

The thorniest issue for the church that resists the spirit of the age is wealth. This means addressing issues of possessions and money head-on. Material simplicity will be one of the marks of the church that is living out the story. The call to material simplicity applies not only to individuals hoping to follow Jesus into the world, but to churches as well. The materialism and consumerism that obsess 21st century Americans is played out not simply in the individual homes and possessions of Christians; it is equally played out in our church life. In too many cases, churches carry the burden of an extravagant life that demands constant attention. As a result, these congregations make little difference in the world around them. The

182

authors imagine a church that divests itself of all property and wealth to be set free in and for the world. Unfortunately, we're compromised in this area as well—we simply don't have the credibility to call for churches to embrace such material simplicity. So instead, let's listen to Jesus again in his conversation with the rich young ruler. Imagine this story played out in the context of a church rather than an individual:

> A certain church asked him, "Good teacher, what must we do to inherit eternal life?" Jesus said to them, "Why do you call me good? No one is good but God alone. You know the commandments: 'you shall not commit adultery; you shall not murder; you shall not steal; you shall not bear false witness; honor your father and mother.'" They replied, "We have kept all these since our youth." When Jesus heard this he said to them, "There is still one thing lacking. Sell all that you own and distribute the money to the poor, and you will have treasure in heaven; then come, follow me." But when they heard this, they became sad; for they were very rich. Jesus looked at them and said, "How hard it is for those who have wealth to enter the kingdom of God!" Indeed, it is easier for a camel to go through the eye of a needle than for those who are rich to enter the kingdom of God." Those who heard it said, "Then who can be saved?" He replied, "What is impossible for mortals is possible for God."

Is it so unimaginable that this is the conversation Jesus might have with some churches today? Is it possible for the church to do all the right things and still lack the one thing it needs? Is it possible for the church to be so consumed with its own life that it fails to care for the world around it? Is it possible for the church to retreat so deeply into its own righteousness that it no longer hears the cries of a lost world? To the extent that any of this is possible, the church needs to hear this text again as a word not just to individuals, but churches as well. In an age when churches, like the foolish man in Luke 12, are building bigger barns, it might be good to hear again that the call to follow Jesus into the world requires a relinquishing of our life. The church's call is not to gather a life, but to spend a life in the

183

name of Jesus for the sake of the world. It's time for the church to take a radical prophetic stance against a culture where wealth is the primary means of assessing success and worth. Will Christians follow Jesus down the ladder?

This downward mobility can take a variety of forms. Here are a few pictures that might offer guidance for churches seeking to live lives of sacrifice and sanctification in their own circumstances.

Church planters committed to the concept of "simple churches" are making remarkable strides in North America. These groups typically value simplicity, relationality, and mobility. They have a sense of being sent into the world. One group takes as a maxim the macabre saying, "If you see a foot buried in the sand, you assume there is a body attached to it." What they mean is that a new convert is where a new church starts; it's the place where a new body can be discovered. Instead of extracting new Christians from their environment and teaching them the complexities of church life, church planters following this model assume that a new congregation is waiting to be uncovered in the very concrete circumstances of the lives of new converts. These congregations meet in coffee shops and apartment complexes and living rooms. They own no property and have no committees. They have few programs to maintain. But they care for each other, teach each other to be disciples, and serve those around them.

Another group, Mission Arlington, began as an inner city benevolence ministry in Arlington, Texas. While this church's ministry helped many in the name of Jesus, few of those helped were able to transition into being active members of this large congregation. So those involved in Mission Arlington began to take seriously the notion that the church is a sent people. Leaving behind an "if we build it they will come" mentality, they let God send them into the worlds of those they were serving. They began worshipping in small groups in the apartment complexes where those they served lived. Real life worshipping communities began to form. Some involved in this mission began to move into the complexes where those new con-

184

gregations were taking shape. As word spread about the dramatic changes that were taking place in people's lives, apartment managers began requesting that churches be started in their complexes as well. What began in a few apartments in Arlington has now spread throughout the Dallas/Ft. Worth area.

These movements are not perfect. They are learning that mobility and fluidity bring unique challenges as well. Still, they are remarkable examples of how churches might look when they hear Jesus' call to sell what they have, give it to the poor, and follow him into the world. In these congregations, kingdom ways of living, like simplicity and sharing possessions, give the church identity as heavenly exiles in a culture of consumption.

In another church we know, Christ's call to live lives of sacrifice and sanctification looks very different. This large church has made itself a servant of its community, using its gifts and facilities to serve the impoverished neighborhood in which it's situated. Rather than hoarding its life or seeking to make itself an island fortress, this church has opened its doors to all who need it. Every day of the week, this congregation is using its wealth to serve its community—inviting society's outsiders to join God's great feast. A Boys and Girls Club meets daily in the church's large gym, and various twelve-step groups use its classrooms throughout the week to help people find lives of dignity and sobriety. Some of these activities are sponsored by the church, but many are community efforts that use the church's facilities at no cost. Not through its power and wealth but through its open life of sacrifice, this congregation has become a haven for people desperate for peace and refuge in a world gone wrong.

Church members have also "adopted" at-risk children in local housing projects, renting apartments there where they help the kids find comfort, safety, healthy food, and help with homework. Each year they buy school supplies, food, and clothing for hundreds of families, and their giving has become a vital part not just of their ministry, but of their worship. This congregation does all of this

185

with no hope of reward and no strings attached. Giving freely of its wealth and the gifts of its members, this congregation has found the rich blessings that come from true charity, giving all to sanctify others and help them find dignity. Although they recently undertook a large building expansion project, they did so not to have more for themselves, but to have more to offer others.

How do churches begin the process of downward mobility? They have to get out of the business of building bigger barns and strengthening city walls. Rather than trusting in their own sufficiency and status, they have to find their lives by losing them. The church that gives itself for the sanctification of others will stand out against a culture that cherishes power and wealth, and its distinct life will be a manifestation of its message. This church will value simplicity, knowing that the accumulation of wealth and power has a way of constantly demanding our attention. Instead, it lives purely and wholly for the sake of others. This church embraces movement, treading the paths of exile as it calls those around it to join it in its journey toward a lasting city.

Sadly, this image of the pilgrim church has been rare in the 2000 years since Christ's great commission. Our message has ceased to be credible to large numbers of people who know that much of Christian history has focused on the assertion of power and the amassing of wealth. And of course, these critics have plenty of evidence to make their case. The church has indeed been a wealthy power broker for centuries. But the days of Christendom are ending, and the church on the margins is being called to take a radical prophetic stance toward a culture where wealth is the primary means of assessing success and worth. After all, the one we call Lord and Master was born poor, lived poor, and died poor for the sake of others.

186 Yet while living a distinct life seems to be the primary way the church is being called to tell God's story to the world today, it's not the only way. The church also finds its path through Scripture, the work of the Holy Spirit, worship, and leadership.

Scripture: The Script We Enact

The exilic community is also a textual community. Living within another's story requires careful attention to our own. We remember that in exile much of Israel's Scripture came into being. Also, the synagogue was founded, at least in part as a place to remember Israel's story through the public reading of Scripture. In response to the threat of losing one's identity in exile, God's people turn to Scripture.

Today, two unhealthy responses to Scripture and scriptural knowledge are weakening our churches and threatening our identity. On the one hand, the increasing biblical illiteracy in our churches stands out as a serious problem that needs to be addressed. In our desire to make the Christian story approachable, we've sometimes de-emphasized knowledge and placed a greater premium on engaging, uplifting classes and services. Meeting the needs of today's audiences is, of course, important, but to do so at the expense of a humble willingness to study and learn God's word and to teach it to others is a grave mistake. Such an approach reveals a kind of willfulness, a belief that right intentions can replace knowledge and hard work. As any married person, parent, or friend knows, relationships require effort and knowledge of the other person to remain healthy. In our relationship with God, one way we gain deep knowledge of him is through Scripture, and so these times call us to a strong commitment to engage in ongoing biblical education.

On the other hand, while some are tempted to abandon serious biblical study, others succumb to the trap of feel-

> It was during the time of exile that Israel became a textual community. Living as strangers in a strange land, Israel's very identity as a people was threatened, so they read and they listened to stories to remind them of who they were and where their true home was…. It is now becoming clearer that the scriptural story is our home in exile. Now that the world no longer provides a home for the scriptural community, Scripture has become our home.
>
> —*Martin Copenhaver, Anthony Robinson, and William Willimon*
> Good News in Exile: Three Pastors Offer a Hopeful Vision for the Church, *1999*

187

ing self-sufficient regarding Scripture, denying the need for trained instruction and the communal experience of reading God's story. In many ways, the single most telling feature of contemporary American life is the availability of information. The seventh grader with a computer has more information available than the world's most knowledge-able people throughout history—and this includes biblical information. This has led to church controversies as individuals become more and more accustomed to researching issues and reaching conclusions on their own. While the ability to access instant information is a great asset, it can also be a liability, because knowledge, when separated from community and holiness, is of limited use. The focus of scriptural education must not be simply on the mastery of information but on transformational response.

How do church ministers and teachers respond to these challenges of the 21st century? No longer are they the guardians of esoteric biblical knowledge to be dispensed as they please. In fact, our role as educators has changed drastically. What people need today is encouragement and guidance, help in interpreting and applying what they read, which is why the educator's role is now primarily a *mentoring* one. Here again, holy living is the key. Beyond simply interpreting Scripture, we walk alongside to show how Scripture is lived. As people encounter Scripture, what is really happening is that they are learning a new story to live by—and that requires ongoing modeling and guidance.

All of us have had the experience, either in our own lives or in the lives of those close to us, where a child was given a certain story or identity by psychological or physical abuse. When a child learns early that he or she is stupid, ugly, or bad, that identity is ingrained so deeply that it is incredibly difficult to learn a new story—a new identity—to live out. Telling that person that he or she is worthy and good won't change anything. But showing it through loving action will. As one enters the world of Scripture, the same dynamic is at work. We all bear the scars of our worldly story, and we need to learn our new identity in Christ. However, this new story will never

188

become ours by lecture or study of Scripture alone, but by seeing how it is embodied in life. That's why our current Bible class systems are largely inadequate. They provide information that is already available without requiring the really hard work of ongoing embodiment. In our day, Jesus' way must become our way. In a time ruled by experience, mentoring must replace lecturing as the focal point of imparting Scripture.

How does this translate into practical application? Each congregation's needs will be different depending on the background of its members, but a basic, general principle for the church of the 21st century may be to "stay small." Of course, nothing is wrong with big or growing churches. It's natural for a healthy organism to grow, and there's no particular virtue in a small and dying congregation. However, there are huge churches that have made little impact on their piece of the world and small churches whose impact has been enormous. Furthermore, we have largely become a low-commitment group of people. Someone has wryly observed that the requirements for membership in most civic clubs greatly exceed those of churches.

At least in part, the solution to this is to see that the basic units of discipleship and mentoring are small, regardless of the size of the congregation. One church we know assigns every young person an adult mentor other than the parents. Another has its life blood in "house churches" as the basic unit of fellowship and mission. Creating groups that take absolute responsibility for "making disciples" of one another is the key. Since these relationships are primarily based not on dispersal of information but on the day-by-day living out of the story of Scripture, such groups must be small. Because of this, the basic structure for maintaining faithfulness to Scripture in our day (for adults) should not be the Bible school class but the mentoring group. And in this we go back to the approach of Jesus himself.

189

This would be a radical change in most churches, reflecting the radically new world in which we find ourselves. It is an excellent example of the truth that to be faithful to the story, the church must adapt. Our approach to Scripture today must capture this insight: the Bible is not merely a book to be intellectually grasped, but it is a call to action. So we attempt to enact Scripture and guide others to do the same.

The Holy Spirit: Power for the Ethically Enacted Life

In exilic times we live in a hostile culture. That is why it is crucial to be in step with God's spirit rather than with the spirit of our times. Being attuned to the Holy Spirit today calls for a strong commitment to prayer and the spiritual disciplines. In the language of the Church of the Savior in Washington DC, we must attend both to the "inward journey" and the "outward journey." While Churches of Christ have traditionally de-emphasized the inward journey of spiritual disciplines, tending to dwell more on doctrine instead, we must also immerse ourselves in practices that will help us discern the leading of the Spirit.

Although it has had many negative consequences, the dawning of the postmodern world has certainly revealed a deep spiritual yearning in surprising numbers of people. Yet better theology—better ways of expressing our doctrines—while important, will not bring about the renewal we need to remain true to our calling as God's chosen people in exile. Only through a transformative experience of the indwelling Spirit will we find the path to relevance and holiness.

As Churches of Christ were emerging on the 19th-century American frontier, the worst excesses of revivalism—from manifestations of mysterious laughter to falling down in fits—created a religious landscape in which an intellectual backlash was almost inevitable. In an understandable attempt to avoid such extremes, Churches of Christ followed a more intellectual path and looked with suspicion on supposed manifestations of the Spirit. However, in a proper desire for balance we overcorrected, virtually denying the existence of the Spirit's work outside the bounds of Scripture.

But given the move from modernity to postmodernity, our culture, which once tested everything by the "truth" of science, is now open to other paths. Even within our congregations, many Christians are no longer willing to look to Scripture alone for guidance and comfort and are now recognizing the need for a deeper, more personal relationship with the living Spirit of God. In a world more and more driven by experience, we long not only for intellectual knowledge but also for a direct encounter with God. This explains the remarkable success of the book *Experiencing God* in Churches of Christ.

However, lacking the necessary tools or guidance, we often pursue this longing for spiritual reality in very narrow ways. Many seek it primarily in enthusiastic and emotive worship (and there is certainly nothing wrong with that!) or an ecstatic experience of some sort. But the Christian tradition gives us another approach—the quieter and more prolonged transformation of our lives through the spiritual disciplines of meditation, prayer, silence, and fasting (among others), which are basically ways to attend to and be present before God.

> These three books provide a nice introduction to spiritual disciplines:
> Richard Foster's *Celebration of Discipline* (1978);
> Marjorie Thompson's *Soul Feast: An Invitation to the Spiritual Life* (1995); and
> Dallas Willard's *The Spirit of the Disciplines: Understanding How God Changes Lives* (1988).

We might compare 1 Kings 18 and Habakkuk 2, which contrast idol worship and the worship of the living God.

> So they took the bull that was given them, prepared it, and called on the name of Baal from morning until noon, crying, "O Baal, answer us!" But there was no voice, and no answer. They limped about the altar that they had made. At noon Elijah mocked them, saying, "Cry aloud! Surely he is a god; either he is meditating, or he has wandered away, or he is on a journey, or perhaps he is asleep and must be awakened." Then they cried aloud and, as was their custom, they cut themselves with swords and lances until the blood gushed out over them. As midday passed, they raved on until the time of the offering of the oblation, but there was no voice, no answer, and no response. (1 Kings 18:26–29)

191

> What use is an idol once its maker has shaped it—a
> cast image, a teacher of lies? For its maker trusts in
> what has been made, though the product is only an
> idol that cannot speak! Alas for you who say to the
> wood, "Wake up!" to silent stone, "Rouse yourself!"
> Can it teach? See, it is gold and silver plated, and
> there is no breath in it at all. But the Lord is in his
> holy temple; let all the earth keep silence before him!
> (Habakkuk 2:18–20)

When worshipping an idol, noise and frantic activity are the order of the day, for the idol does nothing—all the activity must be human-generated. But when one comes before the living God, one becomes silent because God *is* at home and might well have something to say. The spiritual disciplines are ways of attending to this living God and avoiding idolatry.

Too often in our churches, people assume that the only alternative to our intellectual tradition is a charismatic or neo-charismatic one. Christians longing for deeper spirituality leave Churches of Christ to search for a personal experience of God in some such group, but this need not be.

In the past, when people wanted to know how to become a Christian, we in the Churches of Christ knew just what to tell them. But when they wanted to know how to have a deeper, richer spiritual life, we didn't know what to say. So we told them to go do the "big two"—read the Bible and pray.

But this question about deeper spiritual life is exactly what increasing numbers of people are asking today. They are less and less concerned with doctrinal issues that have been our primary focus, but they have a keen interest in how they can have the spiritual life they desire but that seems to have eluded them.

In our effort to find connection with the Holy Spirit, we must be careful not to over-correct. It would be a terrible mistake to back away from our strong intellectual moorings of rigorous Bible study as a way of knowing God. However, we do believe there is room alongside the intellectual for the tradition of spiritual disciplines as a way of experiencing God more deeply in our daily lives.

Given people's profound longings for just such a life, if we ignore this spiritual desire, they will surely look elsewhere, and they should.

What could seeking contact with the Holy Spirit look like in Churches of Christ? How can we find ways that avoid wild excesses while still meeting the spirit of the risen Lord in our daily walk with God and with each other? Each congregation's approach will be creatively different, but the following are a few examples of how it can be done.

We know of a congregation that holds prayer vigils; when a special situation arises, such as a natural disaster, a crisis in the life of the church family, or even a special collection for missions, members sign up to pray in half-hour increments around the clock. These Christians not only pray, but they represent the entire body in prayer, so that at every moment the congregation is calling upon the Holy Spirit to bless and intercede. This same church appoints volunteers to pray for the high school students of the congregation, so that each student knows that someone is lifting him or her up to God in prayer each day. These methods do not involve establishing special programs, spending money, or having organizational meetings. They simply require time, love, and a desire to meet and commune with the spirit of God.

We know a congregation that practices communal discernment not just on community decisions, but on members' personal decisions too! No one in this church would think about a job change or location change without everyone seeking the Spirit's guidance. No one experiences this as an invasion of privacy, for God leads us to peace.

We know of a congregation that doesn't officially plan many of its ancillary programs but leaves their instigation to the Holy Spirit. When a member or group of members feels called by the spirit to begin a good work in the church, the elders don't vote on whether or not the congregation should add this new program to its budget, nor do they appoint a committee to oversee it. They meet with those who have felt the calling, pray over them, and commission them to do the will of God with the blessing of the church. In this way, the

193

Holy Spirit has acted in this church to implement a hospitality house so that the families of hospitalized people can have a free place to stay; a job training program to help the unemployed and undereducated learn basic skills necessary to find work; a free car maintenance clinic one Saturday a month in the church parking lot for the poor, widows, and anyone else unable to pay for automotive service; a "prayer walk" in which members of the church walk the neighborhood once a week, knocking on doors and asking people if they have something they need prayers for, and many other spiritual activities as well. Most of these programs are staffed by volunteers from the congregation and require minimal funding, but the impact on the surrounding community is enormous. It's exciting to see the Spirit working so powerfully through ordinary Christians.

These are not by any means prescriptions for how the Spirit should and will work in every congregation. Rather, they are examples of how the Holy Spirit can move in and through Christians who are open to his voice. By practicing such spiritual disciplines as constant prayer, meditation, and fasting, we find ourselves increasingly able to hear and follow what the Spirit has to say, whatever that may be. Unlike some of the charismatic groups' more demonstrative manifestations, which mainly provide edification for the individual or perhaps the congregation, this kind of disciplined and studied commitment to listening to the Spirit's voice inevitably turns outward to the community. In this way, ethical and holy living manifest themselves as the primary emphasis of the church in our time as the Holy Spirit guides us toward ways we can live out the gospel in the face of a post-Christian world.

Worship: The Story Reenacted

194 The culture in which exiled Christians find themselves tries constantly to convince them that their story is not true. One of the primary ways we keep our story straight is by rehearsing it in worship. Worship has been one of the most controversial and contentious issues in the church

over the last twenty-five years. Here again, ethics provide the lens through which to view the vital role of worship in the 21st century.

How does worship help us keep our story straight today? Some feel that there is serious work to be done here. The worship renewal movement that swept through most denominations has largely been driven by the notion that worship has somehow become disconnected from and is irrelevant to the life of the worshippers. The plea for more contemporary worship is generally one for more relevant worship.

It certainly is true that worship images can be so old-fashioned that the worshippers simply don't understand them. Agricultural, shepherding or sea-faring symbols can be very distant to urban and suburban Christians. For example, when asked about the song "Let the Lower Lights be Burning," which depends on some knowledge of light houses and shorelines, few people know what they're singing about. The lyrics might as well be in a foreign language.

In other instances, scholars such as Marva Dawn have complained about the "dumbing down" of worship. She argues that in the attempt to "connect," we have become superficial and lost the depth and the dignity and the majesty and awe of coming before God. Since much worship renewal is driven by youth culture, the content of the songs reflects the experiential, emotive, and energetic qualities of young Christians. Understandably, though, older Christians may relate better to other types of music, prayer, and so on.

How do we negotiate between these two impulses? On the one hand, for worship to be transforming it must be relevant and connect with the congregation. On the other hand, we must guard against allowing our worship to become anemic, overly-focused on the exciting to the neglect of other important aspects of worship, such as expressing awe, grieving for loss, and rebuking sin.

Again, we believe that ethical living provides the key to healthy worship today. In particular, the attribute of authenticity, as opposed to hypocrisy, must be the primary characteristic of all worship, no matter what its style. Yet this emphasis on authenticity is not anything new. It is the lack of authenticity, after all, that outrages Amos:

> I hate, I despise your festivals, and I take no delight in your solemn assemblies. Even though you offer me your burnt offerings and grain offerings, I will not accept them; and the offerings of well-being of your fatted animals I will not look upon. Take away from me the noise of your songs; I will not listen to the melody of your harps. But let justice roll down like waters, and righteousness like an ever-flowing stream. (Amos 5:21–24)

How can one praise God and then practice injustice? Such worship is an affront to God. If our chief concern with worship is whether or not we're singing the right kind of songs, perhaps we need to reexamine our priorities. How does the concept of authenticity work in a narrative context?

Profound and transformative worship happens when God's story meets and transforms our story. All of us bring our own stories to church with us—the story of our lives, in our woundedness, hurt, confusion, joy, and triumph. And our stories are deeply embedded in our personal cultural experiences—in languages, images and histories.

But we don't just bring a story—we also meet a story. The story of God's relentless love and ultimate triumph is expressed in its finality in the death and resurrection of Jesus Christ. Authenticity happens in worship as this story—*the Story*—encounters ours and makes it meaningful even as it redeems and transforms it.

Authentic worship can be thwarted in two ways. First, if the story of God is never encountered, worship can't happen. We have all probably had these unfortunate "non-worship" experiences. Second, if God's story gets presented but never engages our own story, authenticity is not achieved. When this happens, we find ourselves unable to figure out why what we're doing matters.

So worship finds its anchor in the story of Jesus, and we keep the story straight by rehearsing that story Sunday after Sunday. This is one of the reasons why weekly Lord's

196

Supper is so important—it is a rehearsal of and participation in the story of Jesus. No amount of human enthusiasm or energy will create authentic worship where the story is not present. So the presentation of God's story is the constant in worship in all times and all places. Since it is the reason for our presence at all, this is a non-negotiable.

But the stories we bring to worship are unique, so authentic worship experiences at different times and places will have their own distinct characteristics. The story of God redeems our story; it does not obliterate it. A slave who responded to the gospel in the 19th-century American South was a Christian slave, and we could expect to get a Christian slave worship experience, as indeed we did. The moving spirituals borne from this culture are a powerful testimony to the suffering, steadfastness, and hope of a people in exile. When a poverty-ridden unemployed person in the Great Depression encountered the gospel, he did not cease to be in those circumstances though he was a Christian. Thus as his story met God's story, the Stamps-Baxter music of the day, with its focus on heavenly reward and the temporary nature of earthly troubles, bore witness to this authentic worship experience. In the same way, a hiphop artist who responds to the gospel today is now a Christian hiphop artist, and we can expect to get Christian hiphop worship.

Therefore, when we worship, our main priority must be to show how the story of Jesus redeems all other stories. If we do this, the worship that grows out of this focus will be an authentic pouring out of our wonder and gratitude at the riches and wisdom of God. It is both folly and unfaithfulness to claim that the worship that grows out of the encounter of God's story and mine is the only valid one. Rather than judging all others by our story, we should say in awe as we see the diverse ways worship breaks forth, "So that's what happens when God's story breaks out in that kind of setting! Blessed be the name of the Lord!"

However, questions of practical application still remain. How do we resolve the tensions we often feel between the newer and more traditional styles of worship? What is the

197

key to authenticity in these situations? If the hiphopper described earlier worships in the same congregation with an elderly widow who finds comfort in the older songs and worship patterns, how does the church conduct itself while still remaining true to the story of Christ?

A few guiding principles can help. Once again, ethics, or holy living, provides the key. A congregation that spends its time wrangling over which style of worship to use has missed the point. Mature leaders in the faith must guide the congregation toward the godly ethic of mutual submission. Those who prefer a more traditional worship need to rejoice that, by surrendering their will, they are helping their younger brothers and sisters in Christ have a more meaningful worship experience. Likewise, when the older, less demonstrative songs are sung, those who find that style dull and lifeless should willingly and whole-heartedly participate, knowing that in so doing they are blessing fellow Christians.

This principle has powerful implications for how we do church. For example, many larger congregations have attempted to solve these problems by moving to segregated services to meet the needs of everyone. They conduct one traditional and one contemporary service at different times in the same building, and that way everyone's preferences are met. The problem with this approach is that it is based on the premise that the individual member's personal likes and dislikes are paramount. Such an assumption runs counter to the Christian ethic of exile and cannot be allowed to prevail. Self-sacrifice and generosity to others are virtues that cannot be gained without practice and effort. Rather than taking the easy way out, our congregations need to do the hard work of growing in the faith.

A final word regarding worship: we sometimes hear debates regarding whether worship is for God's sake or for the benefit of the worshippers. But there is a third party in the worship equation—the world we live in and serve. We have all heard the well-meaning closing prayer that asks God to bless us as we leave worship and go into the "real" world. But in fact worship *is the reality* that we enact on

198

behalf of a world beset by illusions and cut off from the reality of the glory of God. Just as Moses represented the Israelites before God, and just as the nation of Israel was sent as a servant to the nations, so we worship for the sake of the world.

In fact, in this time of exile, our worship should also prepare us to live distinctively and ethically for the world's sake. Let's take the language of wor-

> In worship, we see and sense who it is we are to be and how it is we are to move in order to become. Worship is an enactment of the core dynamics of the Christian life.... To grow morally means, for Christians, to have one's whole life increasingly be conformed to the pattern of worship. To grow morally means to turn one's life into worship.
>
> —*Craig Dykstra*
> Vision and Character: A Christian
> Educator's Alternative to Kohlberg, *1981*

ship—praise and blessing—as an example of how worship teaches us to live distinctively. We live in a world where speech is used to belittle and diminish others; we find this everywhere, from gossip magazines in the checkout line to the bantering of radio political pundits. In worship, Christians learn a different way of using their tongues. Just as God created the world through the spoken word, so Christians join his work of new creation through life-giving speech. In particular, the practice of blessing carries the promise of God's re-creative purposes for the world.

We know a church where blessing has not only enriched the worshipping life of the congregation, but it has also spilled over into their life for the world. Often, their worship is occupied with blessing babies or mission teams or new leaders or those who are ill. Now, baby showers are times of extended blessing. Each room in a new home provides the setting for words of life. In these settings, non-members are often present, and they sometimes ask these Christians to bless their babies and homes as well. Beyond these formal times of blessing, though, the church is learning patterns of speaking that carry over into all their relationships. In a speech-debased world, the language of worship creates a distinctive people living for the sake of others.

199

Other worship practices also teach the church to live distinctively for the sake of the world. In chapter three, we noticed how the church learned to welcome others around the Lord's table. The welcome of God experienced by Christians around the Lord's Supper table is also the welcome they carry into the world. Christians learn practices of hospitality in worship. One congregation we know begins every Lord's Supper meditation with the words, "Welcome to the table of the Lord." This practice has changed more than just their worship services. The focus on welcome and fellowship has affected the way they live and treat others. They now use a home they own to welcome the homeless. And they've turned some of their property into a community garden. In worship, they're learning to live distinctly for the sake of the world.

Leadership: Modeling the Ethically Enacted Life

What will leadership for an exilic people look like? It is one of the marks of our postmodern age to distrust *positional* power. Leaders can no longer expect to get respect simply because they hold a certain office or position, as has sometimes been the case in the past. The time for authoritarian leadership is passing away. Elders who could once count on everyone to be compliant simply because they were elders now attempt to assert the power of their position at their own peril.

For the last couple of decades, old-style authoritarian "because-I-said-so" leadership has been on the wane. But what has replaced it is a corporate model that, while less authoritarian, is still positional. This new breed of leader is a careful decision-maker who seeks to be sensitive to the needs and desires of a constituency—the church. Such leaders make decisions based on studied conclusions about what is in the overall best interest of the church, as any good corporate board member would.

Even though this approach to leadership is people-centered and people-sensitive, it still presumes that the primary task of church leaders is to make good decisions and that they have the positional power to do that. The primary quality for eldering in this scenario is the ability to think through complex problems, gather input, and formulate sound policy. This approach is a profoundly modern idea of spiritual leadership. Elders have moved from church boss to corporate executive, but neither is a sufficient view of church leadership for the postmodern world.

> The rule-driven approach to church structure has proved to be unsuitable for a new generation. Alas, too many church leaders, who were put into power through this structure, have proved unwilling to modify the organizational structures by which they got power.... An openness to the leading of the Holy Spirit requires a structure that is flexible, adaptable, lean, and trusting in the surprising intrusions of the Spirit among us.
>
> —*William Willimon*
> Pastor: The Theology and Practice of Ordained Ministry, *2002*

This is also an information age where there is more help for church leaders and elders than ever before. In terms of leadership techniques, our elders have never been better trained. In areas as diverse as conflict resolution, team building, staff relations, legal regulations, consensus building, decision making processes, and employee compensation, church leaderships have become better informed and much more sophisticated. But still, this simply leads to better *positional* leadership. We call for a different way.

In his book *Spiritual Preparation for Christian Leadership*, E. Glenn Hinson argues that what the church needs most are saints—those who have been truly transformed by the gospel. In the same way, we believe our great need is not for better techniques in leadership but for genuinely spiritual people leading. Leadership must be re-envisioned not primarily as an opportunity for decision-making but as an opportunity for spiritual guidance. Spiritual leadership means walking alongside people for the purpose of helping them discern God's will and mission for their lives.

The primary criteria for spiritual leadership are prayer and an awareness of God's presence at each moment. The

201

spiritual leader is the one who pays attention to what God is doing. Spiritual leadership is spiritual guidance.

Spiritual guidance is more than just telling people what the Bible says, though Bible knowledge is indispensable to the task. Spiritual guidance works through deep relationships with God and with other people, helping them discern what God is doing and might desire to do in their lives. Yet such guidance only comes about in constant prayer and spiritual attentiveness. A person will only accept spiritual guidance from one whose own life is clearly spirit-guided. The leadership in such a situation is completely relational, not positional. Position does not and cannot make one a spiritual leader.

So now the question about potential leaders is not about the quality of their strategic thinking ability, but about the quality of their prayer lives and attentiveness to God. People long for this kind of leadership. Today most people can make their own decisions and generally want to do so—congregations can learn to self-govern—but we all desire the relationship with that person who can guide us into the depths of the heart of God. We all need that spiritual friend and guide.

How will this need for spiritual leadership affect the way we select elders and other leaders of the church? What are the practical implications of such a shift in point of view? We know a congregation where the elders are willing to relinquish power. Rather than insisting on making all the major decisions themselves, they appoint groups of members of the church to select new elders, make financial decisions, and more. While they offer guidance when necessary, these elders do not see themselves as executives but as servants and mentors. They lay hands on the sick, meet with and pray for those in crisis, know the names of the children and spend time with them. They aren't divorced from the administrative needs of the church, but they don't see them as their primary function, either.

202

This is what spiritual leadership in the new world will be. The time for a board of directors approach has passed. The key to leadership in our churches today is ethical, holy living; what we desperately need now are spiritual guides. Will our leaders hear the call?

Conclusion

As has been true throughout the history of the people of God, we have an obligation to find ways to live out our purpose in authentic ways that are true to our culture and heritage while never forgetting our place of exile. In the past, the church has responded to the demands of its time by emphasizing certain elements of the faith over others—elements like leadership, the Holy Spirit, worship, and Scripture. While all these are vital to healthy churches, given the particular challenges of our time, we believe that ethical, holy living is the key today to living out the story of the people of God.

Whether we like it or not, we live in a world dominated by experience; people are no longer willing to accept ideas based on empirical evidence or rational argument alone. In a world fraught with uncertainty, paradox, and dizzying change, people need more. They must feel in their hearts the truth of something before they believe. How do we help them experience the truth of the gospel? They cannot unless they experience it in us. Now more than ever our willingness to live out the story will determine whether or not the world will meet God. Our worship, leadership, use of Scripture, and relationship with the Holy Spirit all will be viewed through the lens of our attitudes and behavior.

Because of this, our churches must resist the spirit of our age, which is driven by power, success and consumerism, and instead live out the "downward mobility" of Jesus, expressed in submission, self-sacrifice, and the willingness to spend what we have on behalf of others. As we embrace the living out of Scripture, we need to enter joyfully into the intimacy of discipling and mentoring to teach and learn what it means to practice a biblical worldview. The spiritual disciplines of prayer, fasting, and meditation, among others, when practiced faithfully, will aid us in living and telling the story of God through the

203

Holy Spirit, an essential element to experiencing God in our age. Through authentic worship, God's eternal story will connect with and transform our own. Finally, we must live out our faith in submission to leaders whose task is primarily to offer spiritual guidance, helping others to discern the work of God in their lives and the mission to which they are being called.

When all is said and done, all church is "local church" and there is no one-size-fits-all formula to implement these important elements. But do you hear the call to a new experience of the deep spiritual reality we call church? Can we declare our determination that it will not just be business as usual? We don't want to be like the Kentucky farmer who won the lotto. When asked what he was going to do with his millions, he said, "keep farming until it's gone." We can keep doing what we're doing and call it faithfulness until it's all gone. Or we can declare boldly that we will not sit here as if this were our lasting city; rather, we will let God call us into his good future.

Living the Story

The authors hope that this book serves as an invitation to consider the life of the church as a great adventure. The church, we have argued, is a story-formed, story-living people. The best way to understand the church, therefore, is to give attention to its story. When we do that, we define the church not so much by its structures as by its way of life. The question, "what story are we living?" keeps the church's life vital and missional. Moreover, constant attention to this question keeps the practices and structures of the church vibrant and full of meaning, safeguarding them from a dry formalism. In fact, the ongoing story of God calls the church away from the temptation toward self-preserving maintenance to a life of self-emptying mission.

Both the promise and peril of understanding the church as a story-living community revolve around the open-ended nature of stories. Stories are always going somewhere, which means they are always leaving someplace as well. The call to seek a lasting city is always accompanied by the call to leave the land we know. While this is a summons to adventure, it can also be an occasion for anxiety.

These are indeed anxious times. The anxiety produced by a world in conflict is joined by the anxiety produced by a church in flux. In a chaotic world, we're tempted toward a false security generated by church life that is static and unchanging. We ask, "can't things just stay the same?"

Nonetheless, the authors carry great hope for our congregations in this time of transition. Yet we have no easy security to offer. These are dangerous times in our world and challenging times to live out the mission of God. Being the church that bears out God's story does not lend itself to stress-free church life. True—too often these days stress and conflict are generated by the wrong things—what style of songs we sing rather than how to share our lives with a hurting world, but we want to close with a word of reassurance by emphasizing a few themes central to this book.

First, the church is at its best when on the move and most prone to unfaithfulness when it loses its movement. When the church finds itself in the anxiety of change, it should at least find comfort that this is precisely the condition in which it regains movement. From this perspective, it is possible to see our current transition as birth pangs, not death throes. With regard to the church, changelessness is a sign of death, not faithfulness.

This is true in part because we worship a relational God. Think for a moment about how the Greek philosopher Aristotle describes his god. He is so transcendent, so above and beyond the world that he has nothing to do with his creation (for it is beneath him), and he sits in the heavens contemplating himself because there is nothing else worthy of his contemplation. Not so with the Judeo-Christian God who enters into relationship with his creatures and calls them into ever deeper relationship with himself. But relationships are messy, and, therefore, so is the history of the church.

The church constantly tries to move deeper into the heart and mission of God. These efforts are not always successful, but that is the jeopardy of all relationships—there is no alternative. To answer God's call in the world is to be on the move—we are a wayfaring community. Jesus' summons to "come follow me" involves the risk of constantly pulling up familiar and secure stakes and sometimes losing our way. But Jesus keeps calling and the church always finds his voice again, for God is a gracious God. *Not* moving certainly can make us less anxious as we face the future, but at what price? We may gain security, but we lose the very mission that is the point of our existence.

Second, the primary temptation of the church is to become the end in itself. Reinhold Niebuhr, the great 20th century theologian, pointed out years ago that the strongest tendency of any institution is to ensure its own continued existence and well being. Like any other organization, the church is prone to see its own welfare as the ultimate end. We have seen this in the fiasco of the Catholic Church's attempt to deal with the scandal of widespread child abuse among priests. All too often, apparently, there has been more concern for the reputation of the church than for the wounded victims. But there's no need just to point the finger there. Virtually every congregation of every stripe spends an inordinate amount of time securing its future—even at the expense of the very people that need it.

This self-preoccupation betrays an excessively institutional view of the church and a misunderstanding of our story. The church serves the mission of God, not itself as an institution. It is as wrong for the church to be self-centered as it would be for any particular individual. But the church follows a savior who lays down his life, and as far as we are his disciples, that is what we do—as individuals and as the church.

The church need not worry about its future because it is in God's hands. The desire to "protect the church" or worse yet "save the church" is almost always wrongheaded. No particular manifestation of the church is the final goal but only serves God's goal of bringing all things under his sway. Congregations and traditions may come and go, but the kingdom of God remains.

Once we come to understand and believe this, we are greatly liberated, and the anxiety we talked about earlier recedes. The kingdom of God will endure even if our effort comes to nothing. The kingdom is not dependent on the success of our particular incarnation of church.

It is crucial at this point that we remember our story— the death and resurrection of Jesus. It is precisely in our weakness and failure that the resurrection power of God is revealed. If we try to secure the church by our power and make it the focus of all our efforts, we are no longer avail-

207

able to God's power to raise us up when we lay our lives down. The church is healthiest when it takes up its cross and dies daily on behalf of a mission greater than itself.

Third, the church loses its way when one aspect of its identity dominates all others and becomes the sole reason for existence. We pointed out a number of ways that the church attempts to keep its story straight, but whenever any aspect of the church's life becomes the sole reason for it to exist, a distortion in the life of the church occurs. Let's look at a couple of examples.

The mainline denominations became increasingly involved in addressing the great social upheavals of our day throughout the later half of the 20th century. Especially on the issues of race, poverty, and social justice they made enormous contributions. Yet, unfortunately, in too many cases this became their only identity. A person's stance on a particular political issue might determine his or her stance with that religious group. And as important as those issues are (and they're crucial, according to Matthew 25) they're not the full story of the church's mission or identity.

But perhaps we should look closer to home. Within Churches of Christ much of our identity came to be tied up in a few distinctive doctrinal positions and the system of interpretation that gave rise to them. For many congregations, the protection of these positions came to be the only real identity they had. The exclusive use of *a cappella* music in worship (and condemnation of all other practices), leadership by men at the local congregational level, no organization greater than the local church, weekly participation in the Lord's Supper as the only acceptable pattern, and baptism as the essential threshold step in the process of salvation, became *the* identifying marks of these churches. To be correct on these issues defined what it meant for a church to be faithful.

208   All of the above issues have importance—but their importance is measured by asking the question, "What is the story we are living?" Some things are more important than others because of their direct connection to the story. For example, baptism and the Lord's Supper show Chris-

tians what story we are living more than a commitment to *a cappella* music does. Failure to recognize the connection between story and practice can lead to two possible kinds of distortion. The most obvious is that some aspect of the church's life that is not very important assumes a more significant role than it deserves. But a second and more subtle problem is that some aspect which really is very significant becomes so prominent that it virtually obliterates all the other important aspects of the church's identity and mission. In both cases the church loses its way.

Fourth, the church finds its faithfulness in the tension between continuity and discontinuity. Its continuity is found in its changeless story—the death and resurrection of Jesus Christ. With all of this talk about change, it is fair to be concerned that the church might lose its way. It is worth emphasizing one more time that the story cannot be just anything we want it to be. It is not as if we can just make things up. The church really does become unfaithful to God and his mission when disengaged from the death and resurrection of Jesus Christ. We are the church of the cross and empty tomb.

It is interesting that in the book of Philippians, Paul, among his other reasons for writing, is trying to solve a common and mundane problem: that two sisters (Euodia and Syntyche) can't get along. His approach? He anchors himself in the story of Jesus' death and resurrection. The solution to this problem—and others—is to return to our story. This is, in fact, the way we address all problems and the way we constantly re-orient ourselves—our compass points squarely to the cross and resurrection of Jesus.

This is why baptism is central to the ongoing nature of the story. In 1 Corinthians 1:13, as Paul is trying to get the Corinthians to understand their true Christian identity, he asks "was Paul crucified for you? Or were you baptized in the name of Paul?" Here he brings together the story (the cross) and our participation in it (baptism). To be faithful to the story means to participate fully in its reality.

Discontinuity is experienced in the reality that this is an ongoing living story. The story must constantly be

209

re-experienced in different times, different places and different ways. We constantly seek to know, "What does the story require of us in this situation?" This continuing participation in the ongoing story means it is never a static monument but a living reality. So the church cannot and must not look exactly the same from place to place and time to time. It harkens to the same story but lives it out in constantly new, fresh and creative ways. The God of Scripture is the God of new things—we participate in a new creation! The church functions best as it lives in the tension of the continuity of the story and the discontinuity of living it out in new ways.

And finally, the church is an eschatological community, always defined by the future into which God is leading it. Nowhere is this more eloquently described than in Romans 8:18–25, which is indeed a fit ending for this book.

> I consider that the sufferings of this present time are not worth comparing with the glory about to be revealed to us. For the creation waits with eager long-ing for the revealing of the children of God; for the creation was subjected to futility, not of its own will but by the will of the one who subjected it, in hope that the creation itself will be set free from its bondage to decay and will obtain the freedom of the glory of the children of God. We know that the whole creation has been groaning in labor pains until now; and not only the creation, but we ourselves, who have the first fruits of the Spirit, groan inwardly while we wait for adoption, the redemption of our bodies. For in hope we were saved. Now hope that is seen is not hope. For who hopes for what is seen? But if we hope for what we do not see, we wait for it with patience.

It is true that we groan in travail awaiting the full real-ity of what God is bringing to birth. Today we are often anxious about the future of Christ's church and our own congregations. But we do not believe these birth pangs are worth comparing to the glory to come.

These are in many ways troubled times in the church— but then the faithful church is always in trouble. As William Russel Malty says in E. Glenn Hinson's *Spiritual*

Preparation for Christian Leadership, Jesus promised his followers that they would be "absurdly happy, entirely fearless, and always in trouble" (184).

We are absurdly happy and entirely fearless because we know the end of the story. Knowing this, we are always in trouble because we always reach beyond our own resources to the point where we must depend on God above.

We are attacked and besieged but not in despair. Though everything may fall apart around us, we rejoice because we have a lasting city beyond. "The kingdoms of earth pass away one by one, but the kingdom of Heaven remains." We are sustained in hope—the story God has started he will finish in glorious victory, regardless of how things may look today. Amen. Come, Lord Jesus.

Study Guide

This study guide has three sections: a section of chapter discussion questions, a section of scenarios, and a section including a case study.

Discussion questions for each chapter are designed to assist readers in processing the material in the book and also to challenge them to deeper reflection and prayer. These questions can be used by individuals to enhance personal insight or by groups in various settings to improve sharing and discussion.

Following this section, four scenarios offer readers an opportunity to explore and apply the concepts presented in *Seeking a Lasting City* in true-to-life situations. After each scenario, discussion questions are included to assist readers in probing the issues presented. The scenarios provide models for individuals or congregations to use in examining their own unique situations and in exploring how the material from this book might be used to address them.

Finally, the last section offers a case study that provides readers with more comprehensive opportunities to enter real circumstances and discuss issues vital to living within the community of faith. Teaching notes are included with the case to aid readers in processing it. For further information about case teaching, the Association for Case Teaching offers a useful website at <www.caseteaching.org>.

213

—*Jeanene*

Chapter Discussion Questions

Chapter 1 · In the Beginning...

For Study & Analysis

1 Why are stories so important in the life of the church? What stories have helped give your congregation its identity? In what sense does the Bible function primarily as narrative—as a story? Why do you think the Bible contains so many stories? How do all these stories connect to God's story? To your story?

2 What difference does it make for Christians to look primarily at the church's story rather than its structure? What happens when the church's focus on its structure is disconnected from understanding the story that gave the church its life?

3 What do the authors mean when they say that "story and mission go together" (p. 7)? How does the plot of God's story clarify our mission? How do we find our proper place in relation to the coming of Jesus?

4 In what ways does the church's story reveal both continuity and change? Why are both crucial to God's story? To the health of the church?

5 Describe the difference between seeing church as "a set of propositions to be believed," "a set of forms to be erected," or experiencing church as "a call to action in the world" (p. 12). What kind of church would each of these create? What kind of Christians would they make? What do you think is the relationship between God's story and the organization or structure of the church?

For Reflection & Prayer

1 Imagine that the story of your congregation is to be told as a witness to others of God's faithful activity and his people's loving response—that your story is a continuation of the larger biblical story. What anecdotes do you think would need to be included? What

214

people must be included in the telling of this story and why? How does thinking of your congregation narratively help you better understand it?

2 What does your congregation need for you and others to pray about?

3 Spend time in prayer praising God for the many ways your congregation has been blessed, thanking him for the events and people that have shaped it, and asking for his help in growing into greater Christlikeness.

Chapter 2 · The Old Testament & the People of God

For Study & Analysis

1 The story of the Exodus serves as the fundamental story of the Old Testament. What are the crucial parts of this story? Who is God in the story? How are the people of Israel portrayed? Why do you think this is the foundational story for the people of Israel? Is this story important for the church as well? Why? How?

2 In what ways did the people of Israel "live by a different script than the nations surrounding them" (p. 20)? What role do the words of God play in Israel's self-understanding? What is the relationship between God's commandments and his unfolding story in relation to his people?

3 In what ways was Israel "a priest to the nations" (p. 22)? How do you think that the church serves such a role? How would such a perspective affect our worship? In what ways have Christians in North America substituted worship for the church's role as "priest"?

4 How do the stories of the creation and the Exodus explain God's plan for redeeming his creation? How does he accomplish this plan?

215

5 In what way did the temple and the king serve as symbols of security for Israel? What roles do they play in the story of God in the Old Testament?

6 In what way did the prophets play a vital role in Israel's history? What was their basic message to the people of God? How did they stand in relation to the household of God as memory and conscience? Are these roles important today? Who should be playing them?

7 What vision of Israel did the prophets have during the exile? What was their vision of the future? How do these visions contribute to the unfolding story of God?

For Reflection & Prayer

1 Share your favorite Bible story from childhood. Why do you think it was special to you in your youth? How has your perspective on this story changed as you've aged? How has your perspective been affected by reading this chapter?

2 Reflect on why the story of the Old Testament is so important for the church, how it shapes us as Christians, and what it calls us to be.

3 Pray about the insights you've gained and pray for God to continue to reveal himself and his purposes to your congregation through all of Scripture.

Chapter 3 · The People of God & the End of the Age

For Study & Analysis

1 In what way was the coming of Jesus a decisive "turn of the ages" (p. 45)? How does this turn reflect the story of God in the Old Testament? What new elements does it introduce to the story?

2 What is the significance of Jesus' connection of Messiah with Suffering Servant? How does this reflect God's ongoing story? How does this understanding of Jesus as Messiah and Suffering Servant shape the church's story?

3 Why is living out the implications of the kingdom hardest for those with the most to lose? How does this reality play into the church's story?

4 What kind of church did the Holy Spirit launch at Pentecost? What were the implications for the earliest Christians? What are the implications for your congregation?

5 In what ways did the early church have to negotiate the new social and cultural realities of God's reign? How well did they do it? What do they have to teach us about living in our world?

6 What role does baptism play in the church's story? What does it signify? Seeing baptism as a key part of Christ's story and the church's story is very different from viewing it as merely a Christian requirement. How would you characterize this difference?

7 How is the Lord's Supper a family event for the church? What does it mean to say that the church is family for those who live without social standing or privilege? What role does the Supper play in the church's story?

8 Why is it important not to separate the mission of the church from issues like worship or church governance? In what way is the mission of the church at the heart of its identity rather than being merely one of its activities? What are the implications of this for your congregation?

9 How should Christians living in the "new age" view ethnic and social divisions? How does the church's story inform our judgment in this matter? How would a transformation from an individualistic to a communal understanding of salvation affect our view of race, gender, and other issues of social boundaries?

For Reflection & Prayer

1 Reflect on the implications of seeing baptism as an event of the Christian community and not just as an individual action. How would this change the way your congregation practices baptism? In what ways does baptism mediate "Spirit-inspired virtues?" What

evidence do you see of these virtues growing in yourself and others?

2 Consider one of your favorite family gatherings. What made it special? Why do you remember this specific gathering with such fondness? What could the church learn from this gathering that would help its celebration of the Lord's Supper be more special or memorable?

3 Meditate on what it means for Christians to live in a "new age." Where in your congregational life is this perspective most needed and why?

4 Spend time in prayer about the insights you've gained.

Chapter 4 · Keeping the Story Straight

For Study & Analysis

1 The question at the heart of this chapter is: "can a narrative approach to understanding the church adequately account for the rich set of practices we find in earliest Christianity?" (p. 72). What are some potential advantages of the narrative approach? Disadvantages?

2 Other approaches tend to understand the church primarily by categories such as acts of worship, structure, name, mission, etc. What are some inherent problems with these approaches? Advantages? Why do you think these other approaches are more popular than a narrative approach?

3 The authors describe two extremes related to the diversity of church practices. One could be characterized as "we've never done it that way before" and the other as "out with the old, in with the new." How does a commitment to connecting church practices to the story of Jesus challenge both extremes?

4 How did the early Christians "keep the story straight?" In what ways did their worship contribute to it? Scripture? Faithful leaders? What about the role of ethical

living and the work of the Holy Spirit? How did each of these tie early Christians to God's story? How did these help Christians authenticate their role in God's story? What might contemporary Christians learn from the early church's reliance on these elements?

5 If early Christians manifested a measure of diversity in their practices, how did they keep the story straight? What are the implications—to them and us—of their diversity? Are there limits to Christian diversity? How does the story of Christ both encourage and limit Christian diversity?

6 What do the authors mean when they say "while the practices of the church are necessary for the people of God to keep the story straight, they are never to be thought of as ends in themselves" (p. 92)? What does it mean for us today to live as "New Testament Christians?"

7 Review the following statements from the end of Chapter 4 and, on a scale of 1 to 10 (1 is low, 10 is high), rate your congregation's ability to live at this time as part of God's story. Be prepared to explain your response: a·finding your place in the world by constantly reenacting the story of deliverance; b·living as a distinct community for the sake of the world; c·daily trusting in the mercies of God; d·avoiding the idolatry of making the church's life—or any aspect of it—an end in itself; e·fulfilling the mission of God in the world by fixing your eyes on God's in-breaking future; f·adapting and responding to each new cultural context you encounter in an effort to bring the blessing of God to all people.

For Reflection & Prayer

219

1 Reflect on what the word "remember" means in Scripture. How is this meaning the same as or different from our modern use of the word? What are the implications for our worship? Our mission? Our identity?

2 The authors show how the church has always "trusted" each of the following to help them keep the story straight: a · worship; b · leaders; c · Scripture; d · a distinct life; e · the risen Lord. How well does your congregation trust each of these? Why is the idea of trust so difficult for Christians today? What things are necessary to our ability to trust? What part do you specifically play in contributing to trust or mistrust in the church?

3 Spend time in prayer for your congregation. Praise God for the ways in which your community has and is faithfully living out God's story today. Intercede for your congregation in areas where you think it's most vulnerable.

Chapter 5 · The Story Continues

For Study & Analysis

1 The authors assert, "knowing how and why the church of the past made specific choices provides crucial insight for discerning when the church kept the story straight ... and when it has failed to do so" (p. 99). Why is this understanding important for Christians today? How does it affect our desire to keep the story straight within our own congregations?

2 How are contemporary Christians tempted to be prideful in relation to people of the past? What kinds of challenges have past Christians had in keeping the story straight? How might these shed light on our own challenges and choices?

3 The authors suggest that "the doctrines about Christ are essential not simply because they are factually correct but because they make a difference in the way the church thinks and acts" (p. 101). What do you think they mean by this statement? How did doctrine affect early Christian practices? How does this understanding impact our view of church and how we live each day?

4 How did the early church respond to Gnosticism? Marcionism? Montanism? Early Jewish sects? What did Christians of the first few centuries do to keep the story straight in response to these threats? In what ways are these movements—and the churches' response to them—relevant to us today?

5 In what ways did some Christians in the early church neglect some truths of the gospel in order to emphasize other truths that they felt were threatened? How did these activities detach certain truths from the whole story? Why did the activities of these Christians come to be called "heresy?"

6 What was the impact of the shift in the church's identity from being at odds with the Roman culture to being at home with it? What was the impact of this shift on Christian leadership? How does this ancient shift still affect us? What can we learn from it?

7 How did 16th-century Anabaptists threaten the prominent churches of the day? In what ways did they embody a pilgrim identity? What were the consequences of their commitments? What part of the Christian story did they preserve? What can we learn from them?

For Reflection & Prayer

1 How can Christians today best balance freedom and diversity in the church with protection from the threat of heresy? How do both heresies and over-correction in response to those heresies threaten the church today?

2 Pray for your congregation to have the grace to handle diversity now and in the future while also shielding itself from the potential threat of heresy.

Chapter 6 · Churches of Christ: Being Faithful to the Story   221

For Study & Analysis

1 According to the authors, what two distinct visions, represented by Stone and Campbell, have been part

of Churches of Christ from the earliest days of this movement? How did these visions conflict? How did they complement each other? How have these visions affected churches over the last two centuries?

2 What was taking place in the early 19th century that caused so many to yearn for unity? In light of such an inclination, how did these individuals view denominational organizations and creeds? On what did they base their commitment to unity?

3 How did Campbell and Stone differ regarding their view of Scripture and the Holy Spirit? How did they differ regarding the meaning and practice of worship? Regarding elders? How did each view the task of getting the story straight? How do these differing views affect us today?

4 How did the needs of a specific time and place determine the focus of early 19th-century restorationists? How did a focus on certain elements lead to neglect of other parts of the story? What needs and concerns affect the church's focus today? What can today's congregations learn from seeing how particular social, cultural, and historical contexts affected the focus of churches in the past?

5 Why did Churches of Christ historically oppose denominationalism? What have been the consequences—both positive and negative—of this opposition? How have Churches of Christ also been vulnerable to the kinds of human grouping and attitudes toward grouping common in our world?

6 What are some of the differences between viewing Scripture as a book of data to be interpreted by individual common sense and viewing it as the shared story of a living, active community of faith? How do the influences and limitations of particular experiences and circumstances affect our view of Scripture?

7 In what ways did the worship of early churches reflect the culture and experiences of their times? How have 20th- and 21st-century worship services in Churches of

Christ reflected contemporary culture and experiences? What are the consequences of assuming that worship practices in one time should apply for all times?

8 According to the authors, Churches of Christ have exhibited two primary understandings of the task and authority of elders. How did these views originate? How have they affected the function of churches? How does each of these views connect with the story of God found in Scripture?

For Reflection & Prayer

1 Reflect on insights you've gained from this chapter's discussion of the history and heritage of Churches of Christ. What, if anything, has been useful to your understanding of our story? What areas have been or still are especially troubling to you? Spend time in prayer for your congregation and for others in the Stone-Campbell Movement.

2 How does your understanding of the history and heritage of Churches of Christ help or hinder your perception of God's story? How does it affect your perception of the church's role in that story? What's behind your response? Pray about how your congregation can see itself as participating in God's story now and in the future.

Chapter 7 · The Church Outside the Gates

For Study & Analysis

1 What pressures and temptations faced Christians in the early years of the 20th century? What caused these issues? What resources did the church use to address these issues? Which of these resources can Christians still use as they seek to live authentically?

2 What are the implications of living in a "post-Christian" Western world? What issues does the church face in such a world? In what sense does this help Christians function as exiles in this world?

223

3 What are the consequences of the church tying itself closely to political or cultural power? In what ways might the gospel be better served if the church had a marginal status in society? What do the authors mean when they write that "if the church ties itself to political power as it did during much of its history in western Europe, it risks losing the story of Christ" (p. 161)? Do you agree or disagree with this statement? Why?

4 If the church, working "outside the camp," does not judge itself by worldly standards such as size, budget, or power, how should it assess its effectiveness? What criteria will churches use to determine whether or not they are carrying out the mission of God effectively?

5 In what sense does a church "outside the camp" value diversity? Why would it do so? How does this emphasis on diversity allow the church to stay connected to God's story?

6 The authors suggest that "in the post-Christian world, church planting is an act of humility rather than an affirmation of power or authority" (pp. 164–5). What are the consequences of churches planting churches that are not exact replicas of themselves?

7 In what ways is North American culture not just post-Christian but also postmodern? What are the chief characteristics of postmodernity? Why have some churches and Christians reacted so negatively to it? What benefits might a postmodern view bring to the church "outside the camp"?

8 In what ways is North America becoming postdenominational? How might this emerging development both threaten and energize churches?

For Reflection & Prayer

224

1 Reflect on the obstacles and opportunities facing churches in a post-Christian, postmodern, and post-denominational era. How do these apply specifically to Churches of Christ? To your particular congregation?

2 How has the post-Christian, postmodern, postdenominational era affected your congregation's missional
identity? What would it take for your congregation
to become more missional? How does a missional
identity differ from identities based on power, authority, or superiority? Why is this missional identity so
important in the story of God?

3 Pray for your congregation to be wise and humble as
it navigates these difficult times.

Chapter 8 · How Should We Then Live?

For Study & Analysis

1 The authors assert that "in exile the pressures to conform to the conquering empire are tremendous" (p.
179). In what sense are we living under the power of
a "conquering empire?" What pressures is the church
currently facing? How does the story of Scripture call
us to live in these circumstances?

2 How does the church keep the story straight through
ethical living? What is the relationship between the
story of God and our lives of sacrifice and sanctification? What is the impact of this kind of life on the
surrounding world? What are the dangers for those
who live ethically but neglect other means of keeping
the story straight?

3 In what ways is the story of Jesus about "downward
mobility?" How is this message an affront to the prevailing culture? Why is it important for the church to
live distinctively within this culture? What does the
church's distinctive life say about God's story? About
our stories? About our mission? In what ways can
Christians embrace a marginal status?

4 What does it mean for an exilic community to be a
"textual community?" What two unhealthy responses
do the authors suggest have developed within churches
trying to be textual communities. Why are these

225

responses unhealthy? What suggestions would you make for overcoming them?

5 The authors suggest that many churches have become low-commitment groups. What do they mean by this? Do you agree? How would you assess your own congregation in light of this concern? Where has the impulse toward low commitment come from? In what ways does seeing faith as a participation in the story of God counteract low commitment?

6 Why did many Churches of Christ in the past become suspicious of churches that emphasized very public demonstrations of the Holy Spirit? How did these circumstances form (at least in part) our emphasis on the intellectual pursuit of God? In the current environment, how are churches tempted to overcorrect past emphases? How can spiritual and intellectual disciplines work together? How can the "inward journey" of spiritual discipline be encouraged within your congregation?

7 Many of the conflicts about worship reflect what individual worshippers like or what's familiar. What are the larger issues at stake in how we worship? How can our worship both reflect and critique our culture? In what sense is Christian worship the "real world?"

8 How can we worship on behalf of the world? Why is our worship so important for the sake of the world? For God? For ourselves?

9 What is "positional leadership?" How does it typically function? In what ways is such leadership inadequate for the spiritual guidance needed in our congregations and called for in Scripture? What do the authors mean when they claim that "our great need is not for better techniques in leadership but for genuinely spiritual people leading" (p. 201)? What would this sort of leadership look like—what commitments and practices would it involve? What impact would it have on your congregation? How would an emphasis on spiritual leadership connect the church to the story of God?

For Reflection & Prayer

1 Reflect on what you think it would mean for your congregation to consider itself in light of each of the following areas: **a**·living as a community in exile; **b**·practicing downward mobility; **c**·becoming more of a textual community; **d**·challenging low commitment; **e**·encouraging an inward journey. Which one is most significant for your congregation at this point? Why? In what area do you see substantial growth already taking place? Give specific examples.

2 Spend time in prayer praising God for the growth you've noted and asking his help in the ongoing transformation of your community of faith.

Chapter 9 · Living the Story

For Study & Analysis

1 What do the authors mean when they write that "with regard to the church, changelessness is a sign of death, not faithfulness" (p. 206)? Do you agree? In what way are we faithful to God's call when we are always on the move?

2 Discuss the relationship between the changelessness of the gospel and the changes and adaptations that take place within congregations. In this light, why is it so important to keep the story straight? Do you agree that the church is a "militant community?" Why or why not?

3 How are churches tempted to become ends in themselves? What are the symptoms of this sort of mindset? The authors warn of an "excessively institutional view of the church" (p. 207). What do they mean? Have you seen evidence of this? What is God's role in shaping our future? What specific steps can your congregation take to trust God more?

4 How do the various aspects of our identity as a church relate to the story of God? What happens when one

aspect of our identity dominates all others? Give some examples. What is the antidote to such a tendency? What can the church do to keep from losing its way in this regard?

5 In what sense is your congregation aligned with the story of the gospel? In what way is it divergent? In what sense is it true that "the church cannot and must not look exactly the same from place to place and time to time" (p. 210)? Do you agree? Give examples. How can the church live with such tension?

6 What do the authors mean that "the church is an eschatological community" (p. 210)? In what ways do we live now with the future in mind? How does this commitment affect our behavior in relation to the world? To other Christians? What difference does it make when we know how the story ends?

For Reflection & Prayer

1 How would you evaluate the current status of your congregation in relation to what the authors say in this chapter about how churches "live the story"? What specific examples would you give?

2 In what specific ways could your congregation more fully live out the gospel story? How could you help with that effort? Pray about your response.

Scenarios & Discussion Questions

Read the following scenarios (each is followed by a set of possible discussion questions). All of them are fictional, but they represent congregational issues that many will find familiar. These situations are not based on any one specific congregation but rather are composites of people and churches that have struggled in various ways. The purpose of each scenario is to draw learners into true-to-life situations that will assist in processing what they have read in *Seeking a Lasting City*. Remember that, while these

228

incidents have no single conclusion or "right" answer, they provide opportunities for individuals to decide what they would do in these situations and why they would make particular choices.

The main task of the teacher in using scenarios (as well as the case study in the following section) is to serve as a facilitator by fostering meaningful discussion, highlighting significant insights, and assisting in the examination of the ramifications of actions and attitudes. The teacher serves as a guide, leading the participants to discover their own insights rather than being one who supplies all the information or who coaches participants to arrive at predetermined conclusions. Preparation for teaching a scenario demands that the teacher assume a learning stance alongside the other participants. More—rather than less—study, analysis, and preparation are required to teach a scenario effectively.

The first step in preparing to teach a scenario is to read it thoroughly. The teacher may choose to list the central issues presented, the main characters portrayed, or the major events or dates indicated—any details that help "flesh out" the situation.

The second step involves exploring the various paths that a scenario or case might take. Given the make-up of the group and the teaching situation, the teacher should determine which issues posed by the scenario would be most useful to explore. The teacher then decides on a possible direction and selects teaching tools (role playing, voting, small groups, video clips or other visual aids, etc.) that will best facilitate the discussion. The teacher should develop questions that involve the participants in reviewing the basic details of the scenario, clarifying key issues, and formulating possible solutions.

Finally, the teacher should prepare a wrap-up of the discussion. This might include summarizing what participants have shared or asking them to list what they have learned. The leader might want to share personal insights about the scenario or case at this point but must be careful not to trump the learning process or invalidate the contribution of others.

229

Scenario 1: "What Are We Building?"

The Situation

The Mid-City Church was once the "mother church" of the city. First established just after the Second World War, it quickly became a congregation that was dedicated to foreign missions. Many of its founding members returned from the war with a new perspective, and they wanted to emulate the Acts 2 model and take the gospel "to the uttermost parts of the world."

For the past fifty years Mid-City has been visionary, tirelessly supporting foreign missions and sending many of the first teams into unreached areas of the world to make converts and establish churches. The congregation has been a vital presence in one Latin-American country for over thirty years and currently supports American missionaries who serve as the teachers at a preacher training school established by the Mid-City congregation.

The whole congregation has committed to missions, making this work a central focus. In fact, for the past ten years over half of the budget of Mid-City has gone to foreign missions. In the past five years, however, Mid-City has begun to experience a decline in membership and many of its facilities have started to fall into serious disrepair. The elders have begun to discuss how they can cut back their missions budget without completely debilitating the work abroad. They know that they must repair their facilities or launch a building campaign to build new ones.

For Discussion

Ask participants to gather in groups of 4 or 5 to answer the following questions, making sure each group is as diverse as possible. These smaller groups should be prepared to share the details of their discussion when they reconvene with the larger group.

1 On a scale of 1 to 5 (1 is extremely dissimilar, 5 is extremely similar), how does this situation compare

with situations at other congregations you know about today? Without giving away any names or identities, are there any examples you would like to share? How are these congregations dealing with their situations? What lessons might the people at the Mid-City Church glean from these examples?

2 What do you see as the key issue facing the Mid-City Church? What makes this issue so significant? What concerns are complicating or affecting this issue?

3 What factors are at stake for the identity of the Mid-City Church as it faces this situation and works to come up with options that address it? How do these factors tie in with the story of the church at Mid-City?

4 What options are available for the Mid-City Church in addressing the key issues you've identified? Do these options have more to do with the *story* of the church, or with its *structure*? What role might the distinctions between story and structure play in helping Mid-City evaluate these options?

5 If you had to advise the leadership of the Mid-City Church at this point, what action would you recommend that they take? What rationale is behind this recommendation?

6 How should the Mid-City Church go about making a decision concerning the direction they'll take? Why is it important for Mid-City to consider this process carefully?

After gathering the whole group back together and summarizing each small group's responses to the above questions, discuss the following questions:

7 What situations or decisions is your congregation facing that pose similar concerns? What is your congregation doing to address them? How do these issues tie in with the story of the church at your congregation?

8 How would distinguishing between story and structure affect these decisions or choices at your congregation?

Close by spending time together in prayer for your congregation as it makes decisions and seeks to live the story faithfully.

Scenario 2: "Politically Correct or Not?"

The Situation

Mike and Carla Evans just moved into a new community and placed membership at a local church that promotes family values and outreach to the neighborhood. They were surprised to read the following announcement in the church bulletin just a few weeks after their arrival:

SPECIAL ANNOUNCEMENT TO ALL COMMITTED CHRISTIANS:

Faithful believers from a number of churches in our city are forming a Christian Political Action Committee (CPAC) to study and promote issues that are of concern to people of faith. We plan to investigate thoroughly the religious beliefs and personal lives of every candidate for public office—on the city, state, and national levels. These facts will then be passed on to our communities of faith so that we make our voice better heard on critical issues.

We are particularly interested in presenting a united front to those who are not Christians. Our initial emphasis will be in working as a lobbying group to preserve traditional moral values, address family issues, lower taxes, and oppose the liberal agenda. We want each local congregation to encourage its members to join.

Many of the members of the Evans' Sunday school class seemed particularly enthusiastic about this new committee and were urging everyone to join. Mike and Carla weren't sure this was the kind of action they wanted to take in their new community, but they were uncertain about how to express their concerns and reservations.

232

For Discussion

Ask participants to gather in groups of 5 to 7 people to roleplay the situation. Prior to roleplaying, the groups should briefly discuss the following questions. One person in each group should serve as a facilitator and another should record the group's discussion.

1 If you had to sum up the central issue in this situation in one sentence, what would it be?

2 Why do you think Mike and Carla might be concerned about joining CPAC as new members in the community?

3 What do you think makes this new committee appealing to members of the Sunday School class?

4 What have the authors of *Seeking a Lasting City* said is at stake when the church ties itself to political power? What do you think Christians hope to gain in situations like this one? What is at risk? Why?

Now, roleplay the scenario. Two people in each group should take on the roles of the Evanses while the rest take on the roles of those who favor membership in the CPAC. The "Evanses" should try to articulate why they're hesitant to join while the "class" tries to persuade them.

Once the groups have worked through the scenario, bring everyone back together to summarize what happened. When each group has reported about its roleplaying, discuss the following questions:

5 What were the primary concerns of the characters you roleplayed? What rationales are behind these concerns? What common ground could the Evanses find with the members of their Sunday School class?

6 What were your own concerns as you observed and participated in the roleplaying? How would you respond in a situation similar to that faced by the Evanses? What aspects of the church and its story would influence your concerns and choices?

233

7 How can Christians exhibit servanthood, submission, and mutual respect when disagreeing on major issues? Why is it often so difficult for Christians to do this? What are the practical challenges of Christian diversity?

7 What from *Seeking a Lasting City* might offer guidance in these sorts of situations?

Following your discussion, spend time together in prayer for your congregation as it interacts with its culture.

Scenario 3: "From Homelessness to Hopefulness"

The Situation

Two years after a homeless person interrupted the worship committee meeting at Central Church, the local newspaper ran a feature article with the headline, "From Homelessness to Hopefulness: At Central Church, Caring Counts." It opened with an interview from Sarah who told how members at Central Church helped her escape the streets and set up a small, safe apartment of her own. She became a member of the church and soon helped form an outreach to other homeless individuals in the community. The emphasis of the program was on giving individuals a "hand up, not a hand-out."

Now the program is growing and has become a model for similar ministries in other communities. Central Church has never experienced such growth in spirit or numbers. Yet not everyone is happy; ironically, the congregation has also experienced some negative repercussions. Some of the members are frustrated at the "riffraff" that are now coming to their church. Several of the new additions are drug addicts and have criminal records, creating an atmosphere that some feel is not healthy for their children. They note that Sarah was the exception, not the rule....

Also, the neighborhood surrounding the church frequently complains that more and more "undesirable people" keep moving into the area. Even some of the local public agencies have expressed concern at the flood of people now seeking assistance as they've come into the community. Central Church wants to continue reaching out to the less fortunate but isn't sure exactly how to handle this increasingly complex situation.

For Discussion

Have the whole group answer the following questions, which will help you divide into smaller groups for further discussion.

1 Why do you think the opening incident in this scenario was considered newsworthy?

2 Make two columns on the board or on a notepad— one labeled "Common" and one "Uncommon." What elements in this scenario fit into each category (as compared to what happens in the life of most congregations)? Why do you think these elements are common or uncommon?

3 Identify all of the characters or constituencies from the scenario and record these on the board or notepad. Next, identify the issues of interest to each of the characters or constituencies. What is at stake for each? Why?

Next, "vote" by identifying with the character or constituency that you would most likely support if you were at this church. Once everyone has voted, form smaller groups of 6–8 comprised of at least one person representing each position. These new groups should briefly discuss the following questions. One person in each group should serve as a facilitator and another should record the group's discussion.

4 From your reading of *Seeking a Lasting City*, what do you think is most important to consider in this situation? Why?

5 Why and in what ways might the leaders of Central Church be tempted to pay more attention to the church's structure than to its story? What connections can you make from this scenario to the larger, ongoing story of God's people?

6 What situations do you find in your own congregation that resonate with those in the scenario? How has your church viewed or handled these similar situations?

7 What can you learn from the discussion of this scenario that's applicable to your own setting?

Following the discussion, come together and have each group briefly summarize its responses to questions 4–7. Close your time together with a prayer.

Scenario 4: "The Boundaries of Fellowship"

The Situation

George Edwards was a single man in his mid-forties who served as a teacher in the high school class at the Fifth and Main Church in your city. He'd been in the area working with young people in school, church, and community activities for the past fifteen years. Although both family and friends through the years introduced several marriageable women to George, he never showed any inclination towards marriage. No one had ever seriously questioned George's lack of interest until a Gay Rights Group began to "out" several well-known individuals; George was among them.

George's close friends staunchly denied the accusation, but others immediately began to gossip about him and wanted the situation to be investigated. Before things could get out of hand, George visited the elders of his congregation, the administration of his school, and family and friends to discuss the situation. He acknowledged that he had struggled with same-sex attraction as a young man, but he explained that above all, he has been a committed Christian who lives a celibate life and has no interest in the Gay Rights movement. He feels that his record of service and his relationship with the church and community should stand as evidence of his convictions.

George's situation has caused quite a stir at the Fifth and Main Church. Some are crying for George to be removed from his work with young people while others think he should continue in his ministry, fully supported by the congregation's love, care and trust.

236

For Discussion

To start, discuss the following, sharing your response with 1 or 2 people near you:

1 On a scale of 1 to 10 (1 is very uncomfortable, 10 is very comfortable), rate your comfort level in discussing this scenario. Why do you feel this way?

Have 3 or 4 volunteers share their rating and concerns about the scenario. Write the major issues that emerge from this discussion on the board or on a notepad. Next, ask participants to gather in groups of 4 or 5 to discuss how this situation challenges the Fifth and Main congregation. Each group should address the following questions:

2 What's at stake for the Fifth and Main Church in dealing with the potential ethical and social issues surrounding this controversial topic?

3 How are these stakes the same or different for your congregation as it faces similar issues?

4 How will the Fifth and Main congregation's perspective on this situation be affected as it strives to live out each of the following principles from *Seeking a Lasting City*: a·dealing with difficulties as a community and not just as individuals; b·keeping the story straight through ethical living; c·living distinctively within the prevailing culture; d·serving as a witness to the watching world; e·being an exile community committed to the biblical text; f·trusting the ongoing activity of the Holy Spirit?

5 What other principles do you feel are pertinent to this discussion? Why are these principles significant?

As the session concludes, come together and ask the groups to summarize what they think is most important 237
to remember in dealing with George, with his critics, with the larger community, and with the Gay Rights group. Close your time together with a prayer.

Case Study & Teaching Notes

The Case Study "Where Is the Real Disease?" reflects an urban church setting and many of the natural struggles experienced there. The characters and settings have been renamed to protect privacy, but the events described are taken from an actual, historical church situation.

Following the case, suggested teaching notes are provided to help in preparing the case for presentation. You may use these notes, or you may develop an approach of your own. You may also wish to reexamine the directions that precede the congregational scenario section for helpful suggestions on how to maximize teaching effectiveness.

Case Study: "Where Is the Real Disease?"

Wednesday, July 17, 1873 · The First Dilemma Unfolds

As I scanned through the bundle of mail, I was excited to see the latest edition of *The Gospel Advocate*, and I eagerly retired to the drawing room with my eyeglasses to read it. News had been scarce since the cholera outbreak in Nashville.

My wife, Edna, our three children and I, along with many of our friends and neighbors, had left the city at the first outbreak in May out of fear of infection. I had almost stayed behind to tend to my business, but Edna had pleaded with me to stay with the family, and I had acquiesced.

We were fortunate to have the means to leave Nashville and also to have family who owned a rather large farm just outside the city. Granted, the war had brought much destruction, but in the last few years, everyone had been eager to rebuild, and much progress had been made.

We were grateful to be safe from disease in a place where the children had plenty of room to play. Edna seemed to enjoy the stay greatly, helping her sister in the kitchen, catching up with family news, and visiting country cousins. On the other hand, I had to admit that I found the experience quite tedious. I had very little in common with my brother-in-law as I had grown up in the city and knew nothing of farming. Visiting family had never exactly been my ideal for the most productive or entertaining use of my time, yet being unable to attend to my business had been even more challenging than I had anticipated.

As I opened the paper, I realized how much I missed being at our congregation, where I served as deacon and where my wife was active in the women's Bible studies. I was eager for some sort of connection with our little community. So I began enthusiastically reading the front page article, "The Cholera and the Christian Religion," by the esteemed preacher and scholar, David Lipscomb. He wrote:

> The object of giving to man the Christian religion is to educate him up to the full observance of the will of God, as Christ observed it. Christ came to do his will even unto death that we might live according to the will of God. The great object of all God's dealings with man is to induce him to give himself up unreservedly to do the will of God, to submit to his laws. Christ's life was a perfect submission to the will of his Father in Heaven. The religion of Jesus Christ, then, proposes to reproduce in our lives the life of Christ, both in spirit and active labor. The reproduction in our lives of the life of Christ is the end before us, for our attainment. To this work, we pledge ourselves when we profess to become his followers. We say, we will, with the help of God, strive to live according to his precepts.

Reading these words, I was reminded of what an outstanding minister of the gospel Lipscomb is. "No wonder he's able to be such a charismatic leader even in these difficult times," I thought.

I read on with interest as Lipscomb spoke of how "each man is baptized out of himself, out of the world and its institutions, and is baptized into Christ that he may walk in him, obey him, enter into his spirit, and that Christ may be formed in him." "No wonder I've been missing Nashville and our church," I mused. "The countryside simply can't offer a preacher who writes with such clarity and conviction."

239

Lipscomb continued to emphasize how each of us, in reproducing the life of Christ, becomes his representative to the world. He wrote,

A man with talent and social position confesses Christ, puts him on in baptism. He pledges to God most sacredly, before the world, he will use that talent or ability as Christ would use it. A man with one, two, ten, or a hundred thousand dollars, is baptized out of himself into Christ; he pledges as a servant of Christ to try to act as Christ would, were he here on earth situated as this individual is, with his one, ten, or one hundred thousand dollars. That is the obligation, nothing less. (I have no utopian idea that Christ in such circumstances would divide his ten or one hundred thousand dollars among a set of lazy, thriftless vagrants or spendthrifts, that would be no better off with it, than without it. But he would so use it as to relieve the pressing necessities of the suffering and to help the helpless, and teach all the way of industry, righteousness, godliness, and thrift.)

I continued to agree wholeheartedly with brother Lipscomb until I reached the next paragraph. Suddenly he posed a couple of piercing questions about how we Christians act for Christ and how we represent him. I began to feel increasingly uneasy. This article wasn't just reminding Christians about how we were to live for Christ, nor was it merely reporting on the cholera outbreak. As I read, I realized that Brother Lipscomb was chastising those of us who had left Nashville to avoid contamination.

The article told some especially gruesome stories about the suffering among the poor—especially among the Negro population. Then Lipscomb wrote:

Now in view of these things and the wild panic that seized the population, what would Christ have done in the emergency? Had he been a resident of Nashville with ten, twenty or a hundred thousand dollars, what would he have done? What did he do in the person of his representatives here?

Would he have become panic-stricken with fear—fear of death, and have used his means to get himself and family, with their fashionable and luxurious appendages out of danger, to some fashionable resort and pleasure, and left his poor brethren and neighbors to suffer and perish from neglect and want?

My stomach felt queasy, and sweat broke out on my forehead. I continued to read but much of my enthusiasm for the news from Nashville was quelled.

Lipscomb continued his harsh accusations against those of us who had fled the crisis, though he did commend several groups of people who had remained in Nashville and had served the suffering with much grace and sacrifice—the Roman Catholic Sisters of Charity, the Robertson Association, and several young men from the Churches of Christ.

I put the article down with mixed feelings. Part of me felt guilty; maybe I should have sent Edna and the children out to the country and stayed in town to help out. Lipscomb's point about God saving Shadrach, Meshach, and Abednego from the fiery furnace and his being able to preserve the lives of those in service even under the harshest conditions still stuck in my mind. But I had to ask myself, "Who would manage my business if something happened to me? Who would care for my family or help support my aged mother and mother-in-law?"

Another part of me felt ashamed, almost like Lipscomb had written this article especially to me. Maybe I had let fear lead me instead of the Lord. Maybe I didn't trust him enough. "What will my fellow deacons think?" I wondered. "Will Edna and I lose our standing in the church? Will others consider me dishonorable?"

Yet such questions were rubbish. The more I thought about Lipscomb's article, the angrier I became. How dare he think he could address honest Christian men and women like that? Who did he think he was, after all? I believed in Christ, had given him my life, had served his church faithfully, and had always given generously to those in need. So what was this man's defense? Didn't the Bible say we should refrain from judging each other?"

241

By the time Edna insisted I come to dinner with the rest of the family, I had a response half written. But in spite of my ill mood, I had to admit...I still wasn't certain about my decision to leave Nashville.

Thursday, July 18, 1873

I didn't share my distress with anyone that night but finished the letter and put it in the post before I lost my courage. The rest of the day I vacillated between elation that I had responded to what I thought was an unwarranted and inexcusable attack on Lipscomb's part and frustration that I hadn't been more direct and forceful in my letter. Now I simply had to wait until the next *Gospel Advocate* was published....

Wednesday, August 21, 1873 · The Second Dilemma is Manifest

My hands trembled slightly as I opened the next *Advocate*. It was a bit shocking to see my own words in print. They were included in a column titled, "Consistency:"

> D. Lipscomb: Dear Bro.—Since Christ, had he been on earth during the recent sickness would have contributed any amount of money, & c., he may have had in supporting and relieving the sick and needy, and as you are so strenuously in favor of others doing so to imitate Him, claiming yourself to have reflected his likeness yourself, of course you spent all you had on hand, (glad we have one person in our city, who so glitteringly reflects the image of our adorable Redeemer) judging from your article, "Cholera and Religion," in last *Advocate*. Would it not be right for a contribution to be raised now for you, by those who left the city, to relieve your wants—since you must, according to your own argument be left without a "red." By doing so, could not those who "went fishing" partially restore their religious standing? Would you accept of this generous offering, which certainly would answer in place of what they should have done if they had been here? Let's hear from you in the *Advocate*.
>
> —*Admirer of Truth and Consistency.*
> *Nashville, Tennessee, July 18, 1873*

Brother Lipscomb's response was printed below:

Ah, my brother, you feel badly over your course. I
know you do. I am glad of it. I am in hopes you will
feel worse and worse until you determine you will
never do so again. —You will never again say, by
your actions, that Christ, whose representative you
profess to be, whose work you have pledged yourself
to perform, would flee from his home and neighbors
who were dying for want of food and attention. You
bore a false testimony concerning him as you do
concerning me in your bitter note, to which you were
ashamed to place your name. It would have been so
much more manly—so much more like a Christian,
and then you would have felt so much better, just to
have said, "I had not considered my duty and obligation in the premises, I became infected with panic,
acted unworthily, but by the help of God will try to
do so no more," and then like an honest and true
man, signed your name to it. It is so bad for a man,
especially a Christian man, to write or do a thing of
which he is ashamed! I know you feel worse since
you wrote it. I am sorry for you, but I can bear your
petty malice with perfect composure. But you take
the wrong course to get right. You again misrepre-
sent your master. You have said by your action as
his servant, Christ would do such a little, unworthy,
spiteful thing as this. You know he would not. You
say I have claimed to reflect the likeness of Christ
during our plague. You know I did no such thing.
You know no man could know from that article,
whether I was in the city or not, whether I had done
my duty or not. I live in the country; ten miles from
the city—had a sick family when and before the
cholera broke out, had cholera in my own neighborhood and might have been perfectly justifiable in
staying away from the city, while you were without
excuse in fleeing from it. Beside I do not write for
the *Advocate* to tell what I do, but what the scriptures
teach. I do not make the measure of my action, the
rule of interpreting or teaching the scriptures. I fail
often to do my duty; that does not prevent my seeing
the truth. Whether I was in the city or not, whether I
did my duty or not, would not change the truth of my
article, nor cause me the less to declare it. The article
is true, just and scriptural, and you betray your sense
of impenitent guilt by misrepresenting it and me.
But were I hungry and needy, I know too much of

243

the world to expect a man who ran from the cholera and then wrote such a letter as the above, would aid me. Such men are usually only generous in "offering." You may be an exception. I intend to test you. While then I am very scarce of "reds" as you call them, and my purse is in as perfect collapse as if it had had the cholera, I am no object of charity. Never expect to be while God blesses me with health and vigor. But to ease your conscience and relieve your overburdened purse, I will yet find victims of the cholera, sadly in need of Christian help, to which I will appropriate all your surplus cash.

Or, to guarantee that it will be faithfully applied, you can pay it to the church treasurer, Bro. Dortch, and under the direction of the Elders or deacons, it shall be appropriated. I will only present to them the cases of need. I have not seen the time for the last eight years that I could not find cases needing Christian help in your city. Now, dear sir, let us see you show that you love truth and consistency in yourself, as well as in others, by being "generous" not only in "offering" but in the doing. I know you will be ashamed to let any one know who wrote such a little spiteful piece, professedly in the name of Christ. So you can enclose your "generosity" in a letter signed as you did the above. A good generous gift to the poor, in the name of Christ, would relieve your soul of its bitter bile and you would feel better, much better.

—D. L.

I sat back in my chair, stunned. I hardly knew what to feel. The guilt, shame, remorse, frustration, and anger that had been my constant companions these past several weeks now gave way to an overwhelming numbness.

This man, David Lipscomb, whom I so respected and admired, had judged me and others like me. He clearly did not think I was fit for the Kingdom of God, and does not believe that Christ lives and works within me. "How," I asked myself, "did I get into such a mess? And what in the world should I do now?" My need for anonymity had clearly been taken as cowardice, so to make my financial contribution in a like manner now seemed unthinkable.

Sunday, September 28, 1873 · The Third Dilemma Emerges

I woke early this morning for my usual ritual of coffee and time in prayer before Edna and the children awakened. We had only been back in Nashville a few weeks, but things had not returned to normal as quickly as I had hoped. The children seemed to be getting along well at school; Edna seemed content to be back among her friends. But I continued to feel uneasy. It was at church that I was most keenly aware of the difference; my comfort there had not been restored.

Sometimes I'm tempted to think that the problem is all mine—that had I been more forthcoming with my wife, my friends, and my brothers and sisters in Christ, I wouldn't have this dull ache in my heart and this quandary over my actions and attitude.

Yet I am not the only one who was chastised. Many of us suffered whelps from the tongue lashings Lipscomb gave and continues to give in these weeks after the epidemic has subsided. He has called for repentance from those of us who left the city; he preaches constantly about our need to love and serve those less fortunate. Who can disagree with him? How can we sit down and reason with one another? What effects will all of these responses have on our congregation?

Last week's paper listed the death toll from the epidemic at 750, though many suspect it was much higher since numerous deaths among the poor and the Negro population have likely not been reported. As a leader in a predominately white, wealthy Nashville congregation, I feel I have a specific responsibility to help my brothers and sisters get past these difficult and troubling days and press on to being God's people, yet I am also profoundly aware of the thorn of guilt those of us who are well-off and who left the city continue to feel. For us, the divisions between rich and poor, privileged and unprivileged, righteous and unrighteous have rarely been clearer.

"How shall I proceed?" I wondered. "What will it take for us once again to see ourselves as God's people;

245

those who trust him, who live without fear, who know how to forgive one another?"

I rose from my chair to wake Edna and the children. It was time for us to prepare for Sunday worship....

Teaching Notes

Preparation

1 Before teaching this case, read it over and identify some of the key points from *Seeking a Lasting City* and from Scripture that you think would be important to help frame the discussion. What main issues are at stake in this case? How do Scripture and the material presented in this book help to deal with these issues?

2 Prepare a "mini-lecture" that introduces participants to the main historical context of Nashville's cholera epidemic. Though you'll read and work through the case together as a group, an introduction to some of the case's main details may make this activity more approachable and successful for participants. In preparing your "mini-lecture," you may find the following resources useful:

> Allen, C. Leonard. *Distant Voices: Discovering a Forgotten Past for a Changing Church* (Abilene, TX: ACU Press, 1993).
>
> Hooper, Robert E. *A Call to Remember: Chapters in Nashville Restoration History.* (Nashville: David Lipscomb College, 1977).
>
> West, Earl Irvin. *The Life and Times of David Lipscomb.* (Henderson, TN: Religious Book Service, 1954).

You may also want to consult the original sources:

> Lipscomb, David, "The Cholera and the Christian Religion," *The Gospel Advocate*, 15/28 (July 17, 1873): 649–53.
>
> Lipscomb, David and anonymous author, "Consistency," *The Gospel Advocate*, 15/33 (August 31, 1873): 774–6.

Goals

1 To discuss the dynamics of power, prestige, and position as we make decisions that affect our lives and the lives of others;

2 To examine the underlying values that form our understanding of what it means to be God's people;

3 To evaluate the role of communication in interpersonal and community relationships;

4 To explore a historical context in which Churches of Christ were challenged to live out the story of the gospel;

5 To determine how decisions made in the past and in the present shape our formation as the people of God;

6 To share theological reflection that shapes and challenges our ongoing practice of ministry.

Detailed Questions & Activities

Several possibilities exist for processing this case. The method presented here processes each of the case's dilemmas in order using both group discussion and small group models.

Introduction (7 minutes)

1 Begin by delivering your "mini-lecture," highlighting both the historical context and the key points from *Seeking a Lasting City* and from Scripture that you identified as important for processing this case.

2 Before you begin processing the case, ask participants what thoughts or feelings this situation initially invokes. What concerns would they have in this situation? Why? What difficulties or tensions can they imagine Christians living in the community would have faced at this time? Write the responses in a list for everyone to see.

247

The First Dilemma (15 minutes)

As a large group, read the information given for Wednesday, July 17, 1783 and Thursday, July 18, 1873. Someone should record responses to the following prompts on the board or on a notepad.

1 What do you know about the situation at this point? What are the central issues or factors?

2 Identify the main characters found in the case. Which issues would present the most concern for each character? Why?

Having examined the characters and issues, determine which one you most identify with. Once everyone has "voted," gather together into groups of 3 or 4 comprised of at least one person who relates to each character or issue. These new, smaller groups should briefly discuss the following prompts. One person in each group should serve as a facilitator and another should record the group's discussion.

3 What chief dilemma do you see in the situation to this point? What biblical texts might be useful in addressing this dilemma?

Reassemble the entire group and have each of the smaller groups share its conclusions about the dilemma and the scriptures that might affect responses to it. Record these on the board or notepad.

The Second Dilemma (10 minutes)

Divide back into the smaller groups and read the information given for Wednesday, August 21, 1873. Again, one person in each group should serve as a facilitator and another should record the group's discussion.

1 What new information is presented in this part of the case? Why is it significant? What effect would Lipscomb's response have had on you if you had been the letter writer?

2 How have the developments in this section of the case affected your perspective on the characters and issues involved in this situation? Would your vote on these have changed with this new information? If so why? If not, why not?

3 What chief dilemma do you see in this situation now? What biblical texts might be useful in addressing this dilemma?

Again, reassemble and ask for each smaller group to share its conclusions about the chief dilemma in the situation up to this point. Write these in another list on the board or on a notepad. Examining both lists, address the following:

4 How have the dilemmas changed or stayed the same up to this point? Why? Why is this important?

The Third Dilemma (20 minutes)

Again, divide back into small groups and read the information for Sunday, September 28, 1873. Again, each group should have a facilitator and a recorder.

1 What new information is presented in this part of the case? Why is it significant? How are the developments here related to the earlier events recorded in the case?

2 What chief dilemma do you see in this situation now? Is it the same as dilemmas from the first two sections of the case, or has it changed? Why? In what way is it similar or different?

Imagine yourselves as an advisory committee of members from local churches gathered to advise the larger Christian community on how to handle this situation. How would you address each of the following?

1 What do you imagine will be the impact of the events of these six months in Nashville in 1873 on the local congregations? On the church at large?

2 What unique opportunities does this situation present? What are the threats?

3 In what ways does this event connect with the larger biblical story—especially with the story of the Gospel?

4 How are the decisions made in this situation likely to affect the church? How do such decisions continue to affect the church in the future?

249

5 What insights have you gained from this discussion that apply to issues currently facing your congregation or the church at large?

Conclusion (7 minutes)

Reassemble and ask each smaller group to share one or two final thoughts or insights about the case. At the conclusion of your discussion, close with a prayer.

Postscript

One of the most astonishing features of the cholera epidemic of 1873 was its potential to break down social, economic, racial, and religious barriers. Though the case clearly shows that some barriers were actually strengthened during this time, the crisis offered powerful opportunities for people to connect with and serve one another. The groups commended by Lipscomb in his article offer an interesting insight into the way people pulled together, and the story of the crisis offers us an important example of God's people living out his story.

Lipscomb primarily commends other leaders in Churches of Christ (all but one preacher reportedly stayed in Nashville) with whom he worked in serving those suffering from cholera. The young men he mentions also received his greatest respect and admiration, particularly because they spent most of their time among the blacks in the Bethel Community in Wilson Bottom where the epidemic reportedly reached its terrible height. The situation in Nashville between whites and blacks after the Civil War was still tense, so the sacrifices made by these young men were especially noteworthy.

The Robertson Association, an organization created before the Civil War to aid in times of distress, was also praised by Lipscomb. At one point, this group reportedly did not want to treat some of the disreputable characters who had been struck with cholera, but after being challenged by Lipscomb to serve any in need first and preach to them later, they helped care for these people as well.

Perhaps the most surprising group to receive Lipscomb's praise is the Catholic Sisters of Charity. For Lipscomb to collaborate with Catholics and commend them publicly is

250

especially noteworthy considering the prevailing sectarian nature of Churches of Christ at this time. Several sources noted that Lipscomb not only expressed continual admiration and respect for the Sisters, but that he also frequently assisted them by using his buggy to transport them so they could care for the sick.

Lipscomb himself suffered from poor health at the time of the epidemic, and he was greatly needed by his family and in great demand from numerous individuals and churches in the area. Yet he persevered and continued to call people to serve one another; many viewed him as a hero for these efforts during the crisis.

Recommended Reading

General Church History

Frend, W. H. C. *The Rise of Christianity* (Minneapolis: Augsburg Fortress, 1986).

A comprehensive history of the church's first 600 years by one of the world's leading historians of early Christianity. Frend details the emergence and development of the church from its Jewish roots through the councils of the 6th century, focusing on people, doctrine, and events, including early heresies and divisions. In addition, the book's maps, photos, time lines, and bibliographies make this the best single source for information on this crucial period in the church's history.

Gonzalez, Justo L. *The Story of Christianity*, 2 vols. (San Francisco: HarperSanFrancisco, 1984).

Highly readable narrative history of the church through its two-thousand-year history. Though a solid scholarly work, Gonzalez brings to life the people and events of the church in a style that reads at times more like a novel than a text book. Gonzalez demonstrates at each point what new challenges and opportunities faced the church, and how Christians struggled with the various options open to them, thereby shaping the future direction of the church.

253

Jay, Eric George. *The Church: Its Changing Image Through Twenty Centuries* (Louisville: John Knox, 1980).

A survey of the ways the church has been understood in different eras of its history. Beginning with an examination of how the word "church" is used in the New Testament, Jay proceeds in five additional chapters to look at the major "ecclesiologies" in the early, medieval, and Reformation periods, as well as the 18th, 19th, and 20th centuries. The book's documentation and numerous quotes from documents make it a valuable reference work.

The Church & Mission

Barrett, Lois, et al., eds. *Treasure in Clay Jars: Patterns in Missional Faithfulness* (Grand Rapids, MI: Eerdmans, 2004).

Barrett and her co-authors report on their interactions with churches they see pursuing a missional purpose. After their interaction with nine congregations, the authors identify eight patterns of missional faithfulness: discerning missional vocation, biblical formation and discipleship, taking risks as a contrast community, practices that demonstrate God's intent for the world, the public witness of worship, dependence on the Holy Spirit, pointing toward the reign of God, and missional authority.

Guder, Darrell, and Lois Barrett, eds. *Missional Church: A Vision for the Sending of the Church in North America* (Grand Rapids, MI: Eerdmans, 1998).

Guder and his team of insightful coauthors give a compelling picture of the sending of the church in a post-Christian North America. Beyond many treatments of the church which view congregations primarily in pragmatic terms, *Missional Church* shows the impressive gains in one's understanding of the church when defined in relation to the mission of God. A must read for those interested in the missional church conversation.

Guder, Darrell. *The Continuing Conversion of the Church* (Grand Rapids, MI: Eerdmans, 2000).
The following quote sums up Guder's thesis well: "The New Testament is addressed to believers from beginning to end, and it evangelizes at every turning. Evangelizing churches are churches that are being evangelized. For the sake of its evangelistic vocation, the continuing conversion of the church is essential."

Clapp, Rodney. *A Peculiar People: The Church as Culture in a Post-Christian Society* (Downer's Grove, IL: InterVarsity Press, 1996).
Clapp calls the church away from its function within Christendom, namely to serve as sponsoring chaplains for the larger culture, so that it might embrace its role as a counter-cultural representative of the reign of God. Clapp's vision is integrated and compelling.

Stone-Campbell Movement & Churches of Christ

Cogdill, Roy E. *The New Testament Church*, 11th ed. (Lufkin, TX: Gospel Guardian, 1959).
First published in the late 1930s, Cogdill's collection of teaching outlines on the church went through numerous editions and was studied in countless Sunday School classes in Churches of Christ throughout the 20th century. Cogdill's purpose in publishing the book was "to make the distinctive position occupied by the Church of Christ outstanding and easily discernible. Members, both young and old, need to know the difference between the Church and denominations."

Foster, Douglas A., et al., eds. *The Encyclopedia of the Stone-Campbell Movement* (Grand Rapids, MI: Eerdmans, 2005). 255
The first comprehensive reference work ever compiled on the movement of which Churches of Christ are part. Though most readers wouldn't think of read-

ing an encyclopedia straight through like other kinds of books, this one actually lends itself to such a reading. The almost 700 articles and over 200 rare photos, as well as timelines and charts, will inform anyone interested in a broad understanding of the major people, ideas, and events that have shaped all parts the Stone-Campbell Movement. A thorough index makes even obscure information easily accessible. *The Encyclopedia of the Stone-Campbell Movement* is the standard reference work for libraries, churches, and individuals.

Holloway, Gary and Douglas A. Foster. *Renewing God's People: A Concise History of Churches of Christ* (Abilene TX: ACU Press, 2002).

Designed as a basic introduction to the history of the Stone-Campbell Movement and Churches of Christ for use by individuals or classes. The authors give a brief but comprehensive tour of the beginnings and development of Churches of Christ from the 19th through the 21st centuries. Each chapter includes discussion questions, photographs, and references for further reading.

Hughes, Richard T. *Reviving the Ancient Faith: The Story of Churches of Christ in America* (Grand Rapids, MI: Eerdmans, 1996).

An intimate look at how Churches of Christ have been shaped over the past two centuries. Filled with valuable insights, this sweeping history has no rivals among histories of Churches of Christ. Hughes sees Churches of Christ as embodying early an "apocalyptic" mentality that came especially from the Barton Stone movement. He contends, however, that this other-worldly attitude was lost in the controversies of the 20th century. The author includes information on minority movements in Churches of Christ, as well as women who have been especially important leaders.

Issues of Racial Reconciliation

Emerson, Michael O. and Christian Smith. *Divided by Faith: Evangelical Religion and the Problem of Race in America* (New York: Oxford University Press, 2001).

Using data collected from a nationwide survey, the authors found that conservative evangelical Christians seem to be preserving America's racial division. Most racial problems, the subjects told the authors, can be solved by the repentance and conversion of the sinful individuals. The authors contend, however, that this emphasis on individualism, free will, and personal relationships makes the injustice that perpetuates racial inequality invisible to whites.

DeYoung, Curtiss Paul, et al. *United by Faith: The Multiracial Congregation As an Answer to the Problem of Race* (New York: Oxford University Press, 2004).

Of all American institutions, the church is one of the few that remains largely segregated. In this book the multiracial team of writers argues that multiracial Christian congregations offer a key to opening the still-locked door between the races in the United States. They examine the question from biblical, historical, and theological perspectives to make their case. They also look in detail at the theological arguments in favor of racial separation, as voiced in the African-American, Latino, Asian-American, Native-American, and white contexts. The authors close with the beginnings of a theology upholding the central role that multiracial congregations must play in racial reconciliation in a divided America.

Looking for more? Check out the other books in the *Heart of the Restoration* series!